BEDE
GRIFFITHS

AN INTRODUCTION TO HIS
INTERSPIRITUAL THOUGHT

WAYNE TEASDALE
FOREWORD BY BEDE GRIFFITHS

Bede Griffiths:
An Introduction to His Interspiritual Thought

© 2003 by Wayne Teasdale

Library of Congress Cataloging-in-Publication Data
Teasdale, Wayne.
Bede Griffiths: an introduction to his interspiritual thought / Wayne Teasdale; foreword by Bede Griffiths—Rev. ed.
        p.   cm.
Includes bibliographical references (p.   ) and index.
ISBN 1–893361–77–2 (pbk)
ISBN 978-1-68162-988-9 (hc)
1. Griffiths, Bede, 1906–2. Christianity and other religions—Hinduism. I. Title.
BX4705.G6226T43 2003
261.2'45'092—dc21

                                                          2003001370

Manufactured in the United States of America
An earlier edition of this book was published in India in 1987 by Asian Trading

SkyLight Paths Publishing is creating a place where people of different spiritual traditions come together for challenge and inspiration, a place where we can help each other understand the mystery that lies at the heart of our existence.

SkyLight Paths sees both believers and seekers as a community that increasingly transcends traditional boundaries of religion and denomination—people wanting to learn from each other, *walking together, finding the way.*

Corporation as "Toward a Christian Vedanta: The Encounter of Hinduism and Christianity According to Bede Griffiths."

SkyLight Paths, "Walking Together, Finding the Way" and colophon are trademarks of LongHill Partners, Inc., registered in the U.S. Patent and Trademark Office.

Walking Together, Finding the Way
Published by SkyLight Paths Publishing
An Imprint of Turner Publishing Company
4507 Charlotte Avenue, Suite 100
Nashville, TN 37209
Tel: (615) 255-2665
www.skylightpaths.com

To the contemplatives around the world
in all traditions
who are slowly transforming
the consciousness of society.

Contents

Foreword

I T IS ONLY SLOWLY that we are beginning to realize how totally Western are the structures of the Catholic Church. Christianity began as a religion of the Middle East, Semitic in culture and Judaic in its forms of belief and worship. Jesus was a Jew who spoke Aramaic, attended the services in the synagogue, worshiped in the temple, and celebrated the Last Supper according to Jewish rites. His thinking, moreover, was molded by the traditions and customs of the Palestine in which he lived. But as Christianity came to break with Judaism, so this Jewish Christianity faded into the past. With Saint Paul, Christianity moved out into the "Gentile" world, that is, the Greco-Roman world of the Roman Empire. It passed from Jerusalem through Greece to Rome, and adopted the culture of the Greco-Roman world. The Gospels themselves were written in Greek, though a tradition that Matthew wrote his Gospel in Aramaic has survived. The New Testament itself is a translation of the original Christian message into the language of the West.

From this time onward, Christianity pursued its course in the West. Its liturgy, its theology, its canon law were all the products of the Greek genius. As it passed from eastern to western Europe, it began to speak Latin, and gradually a Latin Catholicism arose. The liturgy was celebrated in Latin; Plato and Aristotle were translated into Latin, and scholastic theology came to translate the Christian Gospel into terms of Western philosophy. Canon law was also developed as an instrument for organizing the Church around the center of the Papacy. Thus the great system of medieval Catholicism arose, expressing the Christian religion in the language and structures of western Europe.

There was, however, another movement of the Gospel toward the East. Early in the second century, Edessa on the borders of Syria and Mesopotamia became the center of a Syriac Christianity (Syriac being a form of Aramaic). This Syrian Christianity spread through Persia to India and China, and in the seventh and eighth centuries there were Christian churches spread throughout Asia. But the Mongol invasions swallowed them up, and they were eventually overwhelmed by Islam. A few churches survived, however, of which the most conspicuous is that of the Syrian Christians in Kerala. This was originally an authentic form of Eastern Christianity, but missionaries from Europe, first of all Latin Catholics and then Anglicans and Protestants, gradually changed it into another form of Western Christianity, only its Syrian liturgy being retained.

The Reformation attempted to break away from this traditional form of Latin Christianity, by a return to the Bible, but it was the Bible interpreted by the Western mind, and its structures remained as firmly Western as those of Roman Catholicism or Greek Orthodoxy. The Christianity that we have inherited today remains a totally Western form of religion. It has never been touched, except in the most superficial way, by the genius of India or China or the people of Asia as a whole. There was, however, a movement toward an Asian form of Christianity begun by two men of genius in the sixteenth century. Matteo Ricci in China and Roberto de Nobili in India attempted a genuine "indigenization" of Christianity. They became masters of Mandarin Chinese and of Sanskrit and Tamil, respectively, and lived entirely according to Chinese and Indian customs, thus providing a model for the inculturation of Christianity in Asia. But their experiment was short-lived, and the Church soon returned to its Western ways.

The movement toward inculturation was taken up in the twentieth century, first of all by the great brahmin convert Brahmabandhab Upadhyay. His attempt was frustrated by the Polish Papal Nuncio, who was unable to conceive of anything other than a Latin Catholicism. After him it was revived by two French fathers, Jules Monchanin and Henri Le Saux, who were both men of genius. They founded the ashram of Shantivanam in Tamil Nadu, giving it the name of Saccidananda Ashram, and there the movement toward inculturation finally took root. The present work of Dr. Wayne Teasdale is an attempt to make known the growth of this movement and to expound the principles on which it has been built up. The movement has now spread all over India, and many theologians are engaged in seeking to express the Christian Gospel in terms that are meaningful to the people of India.

The focus of theology in India today is, however, mainly centered on social justice and the "option for the poor." Considering the immensity of the poverty and suffering of the people of India this development is necessary and inevitable. But it should not allow us to forget that the need for change in church and society in India goes far beyond the need for economic and social change. The Christian message has to be rethought and restated in the language and thought forms of the people of India; it has to embrace the culture of India in all its richness and variety. But this means that it must go back to the roots of that culture in the Vedas, the Upaniṣads, and the Bhagavad Gita, and follow it through all its developments in the Epics, the Puranas, the Darśanas, and the Śastras down to its encounter with western science and democracy today. Christianity has to become as deeply rooted in the culture of India as it once was in the culture of Greece and Rome.

This is the real subject of this book. How can the Church in

India learn to shed its Western forms and structures and become, in the words of the founder of Shantivanam, "totally Indian and totally Christian"? Perhaps the key to the answer to this question was given in the words of the great French theologian Henri de Lubac addressed to his friend Jules Monchanin when he departed for India: "You have to rethink everything in terms of theology and rethink theology in terms of mysticism." It is this mystical dimension that is essential to any theology in India. The Greek genius was a genius for rational thought, for abstract, logical analytical thought; the Roman genius was for law and morality, but was no less essentially based on abstract rational thought, on universal ideas and propositions. It is this that has given to Western Christianity its strength but also its limitations. The West has never been at home in mysticism. It has had great mystics and its greatest theologians, like Saint Augustine and Saint Thomas Aquinas, have been touched by mystical experience, but the structure of its life and thought remains basically rational and logical.

Today, with the spread of Western science and technology, we are discovering the disastrous limitations of this mode of thinking. We are discovering that it comes from using one half of the brain; the other half of the brain, which is responsible for concrete, intuitive thought, has been neglected. Our civilization remains fundamentally unbalanced, so that it threatens the actual destruction of the world. We are realizing that our Western culture is a patriarchal culture and that it has developed the masculine mind, what the Chinese call the Yang, at the expense of the feminine mind, the Yin. If the world is to recover its balance, it has to rediscover the feminine mind. While the masculine mind is abstract, logical, analytical, scientific, and rational, the feminine mind is concrete, symbolic, synthetic, imaginative, and intuitive. These two minds are complementary, and human health and wholeness depend on the balance of these opposites.

It is at this point that the meeting of East and West has to take place. Although the Western mind is predominantly rational, the other faculties are, of course, never wholly lost; the Eastern mind is predominantly intuitive, and it is the intuitive wisdom of the East that the Western world and the Western Church have to learn. This work is only a small beginning in this direction, but it is hoped that it will inspire others to take up the challenge and release the Church from its bondage to the West.

Bede Griffiths
Shantivanam
December 1986

Preface

T HIS BOOK WAS originally my doctoral dissertation in the theology department at Fordham University in 1985, entitled "Toward a Christian Vedanta: The Encounter of Hinduism and Christianity According to Bede Griffiths"; it was subsequently published in India in 1987 by a press called Asian Trading Corporation, under the same title. It was the first actual study of the contemplative theology of Bede Griffiths, an English Benedictine monk who made his way to the subcontinent in 1955 and remained there until his death in 1993 at the age of eighty-six.

Father Bede, who was intensely interested in every aspect of the world, carried the entire humanity and all sentient beings into his personal prayer and that of his community of Shantivanam Ashram. He always emphasized solidarity with everyone and the whole planet itself. He did not feel his prayer was complete if the world or any segment of it was left out. He would certainly not be surprised by many of the changes that have happened since his death: a worsening ecological crisis, which is the greatest moral problem of our age; the emergence of global terrorism; corporate scandals that call into question the moral adequacy of capitalism; and a Catholic Church confronting a diminishing moral credibility. He predicted some of these problems and was always a critic of the abuse of power, whether by civil or ecclesial authority.

Passionately committed to a synthetic approach in understanding reality, Bede conceived of a collaboration among science, mysticism, and faith, and this was a synthesis he discerned from his contemplative awareness and his study of mysticism (particularly Hindu, Buddhist, Christian, and Sufi) in concert with his deep faith. He often spoke of this synthesis, which represented a common ground discovered in the convergence of insight of these three activities in the heart of the one reality and truth they share in consciousness. The fruit of his insight, reflection, and experience on this movement into synthesis and common ground among these powerful realms of knowing became his masterpiece, *A New Vision of Reality: Western Science, Eastern Mysticism, and Christian Faith*,[1] which did not appear until after the publication of my dissertation, though it represented an enduring theme of his thought. Bede's vision was essentially an approach based on an integrative insight: that reality is one, and so all forms of knowing must somehow converge on the one truth, the oneness of reality itself in consciousness.

He admired the work of Ken Wilber, the great integral thinker of our time, but his understanding of the integration of knowledge did not reach the same level of comprehensiveness and maturity that we see in Wilber's articulation, though Bede's depth certainly is equal. For instance, a more comprehensive view would include nature, art, music, and symbol. Of course, he did allocate a place for myth. Bede's understanding of mysticism was as profound as Ken Wilber's grasp of science, philosophy, psychology, economics, government, commerce, and ecology. Bede's enterprise of synthesis shared the spirit of Wilber's more ambitious task of formulating a unified view of knowledge that brings all ways of knowing together. This unified experience of knowing overcomes what I call epistemological schizophrenia, the problem of scientific thought dominating, or even excluding, other forms of knowing, such as intuition, mystical and religious knowledge, aesthetic experience, interpersonal love, and poetic imagination.

Bede's contribution exceeds his integral interest in the areas of culture, knowledge, creativity, and faith. He was one of the great pioneers in the twentieth century of what can be called *interspirituality*, which I have discussed in great detail in *The Mystic Heart*.[2] Interspirituality is the activity and process of exploring other traditions in more than an academic sense. It presupposes an intense personal interest in these other forms of faith and spirituality. Such a level of interest reflects a commitment that affects one's spiritual life itself. In the West, and other parts of the world, there is a growing movement of interspirituality. This movement in India, especially among Christians in relation to Hinduism, Buddhism, and even Sufism, is more than a casual interest or fascination; it is a substantial and mature commitment to a careful process of assimilation. Bede, and predecessors like Jules Monchanin, Abhishiktananda, and others, was a master of interspiritual wisdom, as this book demonstrates without introducing any notion of interspirituality in the original text. It is clear how profound this development is: the creation at Shantivanam of a new culture that is equally Christian and Hindu without sacrificing the inherent nature of each.

Another factor of this interspiritual experiment at Shantivanam is inculturation, that is, the emergence of a genuinely Indian Christianity that is thoroughly Indian, and thus Hindu in culture though Christian in faith. Inculturation involves a slow, careful process of assimilation, and Bede saw this assimilation as the great gift of the patristic period in Christian history. The Fathers of the Church spent the first five centuries absorbing the wisdom of Greece and Rome. This was not a haphazard process but a thoughtful development in which precious resources from these two ancient cultures were incorporated into the Christian tradition and made available to this culture in its theology, canon law, cosmology, and culture.

Father Bede realized that this same activity of assimilation with regard to Eastern wisdom needed to be a goal of the Church in our age. It was a constant theme in his public discourses, homilies, lectures, interviews, conversations, writings, and letters. He would make this point to every audience because he grasped so well its importance as the task of our age. He knew that interspirituality was the work we have to be about, the way that would advance the reconciliation of divided cultures, political systems, economic structures, and faiths. He pursued this vision within the Catholic Church and perceived the importance of the Church's contribution to this bridge-building effort. One reason he emphasized this activity as a leadership role the Church must assume is her history, and her genius for assimilation and experimentation. This vision has now become a dominant movement in the third millennium and is really here to stay, putting down roots in world culture. Bede was fond of saying, "We are entering a new age," and it can now be said that we *have* entered this new age, and it is the Interspiritual Age. In many ways, his works are all interspiritual, spanning two or more traditions, especially the Hindu and Buddhist, uniting them to the Christian, and so to the Jewish and Muslim as well.

It is not desirable to rewrite this book, for then it would cease to be the original work I had wrought. I wish rather to make the original available in a minimally revised edition that takes into account further development in Bede's thought in an epilogue on his significance and an expanded bibliography. In this way it is hoped this book will continue to contribute to making Father Bede better known and understood.

PART ONE

Background to
a Christian Vedanta

1

Bede's Quest for the Absolute

B ede Griffiths has been a well-known figure ever since the appearance of his autobiography in 1954, and yet there is very little written on him.[1] This fact is quite puzzling since he was a respected monastic theologian and transcultural thinker whose books are widely read and whose life and example remain fairly influential. He was an important spiritual leader with a significant following all around the world. It is thus difficult to understand why so little attention is given to him in the Western academy. He was, after all, a serious scholar and lecturer. I believe his contribution is significant and important for the future. This intuition has become clear to me with the passage of time, especially after reading an article on him published in a popular magazine.[2] After considerable thought, I decided to embark on a study of his life and thought, and so to break new ground, while trying to correct the deficiency in Bedean studies. This is the origin of my efforts here.

This book examines Bede Griffiths's thought as it evolved from his own experience of the living encounter between Christianity and Hinduism. It is an attempt to uncover his profound understanding of how they converge together in the depths of contemplative consciousness, or in the deepest dimension of both traditions. I want to inquire as to how this convergence or encounter is possible as he conceived it from his own rich experience and reflection, and to show what form it takes. He maintained that a convergence could result in the emergence of a Christian form of Vedanta—on the speculative, theological level—and a Christian kind of Tantra[3] on the level of spiritual life and practice. I will probe this project of his to determine whether it works and what it means. Bede attempted to formulate and express the Christian faith and mystery in the terms, categories, and symbols of the Vedanta. He further proposed to study, experience, meditate on, and assimilate the Vedanta in the light of Christ and the Trinity. My aim in this work will be to inquire into the validity of this approach, this commitment, and to adduce his reasons for pursuing it and advancing it in the Church. I will examine these reasons and arguments with care in order to determine whether or not they seem sound. I want to determine, as far as this is possible, whether he was in fact successful in developing an Indian Christian theology that is also a Christian form of the Vedanta.[4] Is this Christian theology authentically Indian and Vedantist? I would like to ask further: Just how genuinely Vedantic are the categories and terms he used in his new theological enterprise? Can there be a Christian Advaita? Also, how genuinely Tantric are the concepts he employed in his new vision of spirituality?

But in order to unfold an Indian Christian theology that strives toward the ideal of being "totally Indian and totally Christian,"[5] Bede claimed we have to adopt the Vedantic categories of Advaita[6] and Saccidānanda, and adapt them to the Christian experience and doctrine of the Trinity—the unity, or nonduality (advaita) of the Persons—and relate Saccidānanda, which is the mystical experience of absolute Being-Consciousness-Bliss, to the inner reality of the Trinity, a reality that we must first come to know through faith. Father Bede believed that in some essential way these two great traditions are united, and that this unity centers on the experiential awareness of Advaita, which flowers into the mystical realization of Saccidānanda and the trinitarian intuition. And so in this volume I will consider the Hindu experience of the Absolute—Advaita and Saccidānanda—as Bede conceived them, and I will examine his understanding of the Trinity, showing how we achieve a knowledge of it in Christ and in contemplative experience. How to relate and reconcile Advaita and Trinity was an important point of his life's work. A large part of the task is to see if this reconciliation is possible.

According to Father Bede, the trinitarian doctrinal intuition, insight, experience, or profound contemplative illumination in God is at once complementary to Advaita and Saccidānanda, and yet surpasses it by revealing a deeper dimension in the Godhead: communion or love. The Godhead as Trinity is personal. We must discover whether in fact these two approaches are complementary in the experiential depths of contemplation and, if they are, precisely what that would mean. An Indian Christian theology would have to relate these two traditions on this level of the Absolute, the level of greatest depth and penetration of the mystery. Is Saccidānanda an equivalent realization that lacks the personalist connotations? And is the personal dimension of the experience reached when one's consciousness of Saccidānanda is probed further and deeper? Or is the realization of the Trinity a more ultimate plane of mystical consciousness? These and other questions will be raised in this connection.

The personal aspect of the divine reality in Hinduism is expressed, among other ways, in the ancient notion of Puruṣa (or Purusha),[7] but it does not convey the essential note of dynamic communion found in the Christian experience and doctrine of the Trinity. Puruṣa is the crucial term in Hinduism that Bede thought could be used in the formulation of an Indian Christology. We will see how he conceived this term of Puruṣa as the key to a new Christology because it seems to have significant similarities with the way in which we understand Christ, especially as Lord of the creation and the Cosmic Man, the New Adam. We must inquire whether or not Puruṣa possesses these meanings as well. Does this term legitimately serve the needs of an Indian theology? I will indicate why and how Bede was convinced of the centrality of this Vedantic notion.

As we proceed in this book, it will become clear that the point of deepest encounter, according to Bede, the meeting place or convergence between Hinduism and Christianity, is in the "cave of the heart,"[8] in the deep abyss of mystical consciousness. It is only on this plane of interiority, as Bede viewed it, that we can actually experience how Saccidānanda and the Trinity are intimately connected in a relationship that can truly be described as a *continuum*, a continuum of the same absolute reality, the reality of the Ultimate Source of being and consciousness; it is an ontological continuum.

It is not enough, however, to relate and integrate the profoundest insights of both traditions on a conceptual level alone. For doing so fails to reveal the concrete unity from which both traditions spring, that unity which is the inner truth, the living reality of the divine actuality, a reality that, perhaps, expresses itself in both Saccidānanda and the Trinity, in the nonduality or Advaita of the Spirit. Nor does the conceptual approach "touch" this reality, though it may indeed suggest a "taste" for it. Bede Griffiths firmly maintained that the encounter or convergence of Hinduism and the Christian faith is finally a matter of mystical realization that shows us, in an experiential way, how and why they are essentially relatable and complementary, but without obliterating the distinction between them. Contemplation is thus the key method of their interaction, and a Christian Vedanta would be the creative fruit of such contemplative activity, according to Bede. We must discover how this can be so. Now, when this point is probed and understood sufficiently, it then becomes transparent that what Bede Griffiths was engaged in is what I would like to call an *existential convergence.*[9] It was "existential" in a far more subtle sense than any other type of dialogical activity that tries to bring persons of differing faiths together, since it originated in a deep commitment and openness to Hinduism, to the ultimate truth and experience of that tradition, but this commitment and openness of Bede Griffiths's were themselves the result of his very profound penetration of the Christian mystery and the Church's contemplative tradition, at once so vast, diverse, and rich, and an inner relating of them in a similar depth. To put the matter another way, Father Bede was not "experimenting" with dialogue, in a Hindu-Christian or any other context, but was *living* his dialogical commitment. And so I call this method of his an *existential convergence* between Hinduism and Christianity. Furthermore, it was never merely formal or academic in nature, though these are or can be factors as well. Here I am referring to that precise quality and depth of his dialogue that constituted a special type,[10] elements conducive to convergence.

The form that his life assumed in India is *sannyāsa,* the Hindu ideal of monkhood involving total renunciation and freedom from all attachments, ties, and responsibilities. Taking *sannyāsa* incarnated his ideal, and it made the meeting, and hence convergence, of Hinduism and Christianity possible, an encounter that occurs again on the level of contemplative awareness. It is important to keep in mind that *sannyāsa* is a state given exclusively to spiritual development, to the quest for the Absolute in the silence and solitude of meditation and contemplative consciousness. The *sannyāsi* and *sannyāsini* (the nun)—be they Christian or Hindu—are the real pioneers of that definitive encounter of Hinduism and Christianity in the mystical consciousness that reconciles Advaita, the fullest experience of which is Saccidānanda, and the Trinitarian realization, if indeed they can and should be reconciled.

The context of a possible encounter between these two traditions—at least in Bede's experience and that of his immediate predecessors, Jules Monchanin and Henri Le Saux (whose Indian name was Abhishiktananda)—was that of *sannyāsa* united with a form of Benedictine monastic life. Such an attempt, in their view, resulted in a type of Christian *sannyāsa* unique in the history of monasticism, and it opened a new chapter in this history, one that stressed *adaptation*. The point is that the convergence—which is actually an encounter in depth and a confluence of two streams of tradition in the Source—lies in a mystical realization that is perhaps best cultivated through the lifelong quest for union with Ultimate Reality to which the monk and the *sannyāsi* specifically commit themselves, and to which they owe their vocation. There will be more on this point in chapter 6, where I will consider its validity. In this introduction, at this point, I am highlighting certain essential principles for a proper understanding of this study, the foci that—like so many spokes of a wheel—bring it together into an intelligible whole. In the course of this book, the primary themes should become clearer, particularly the terms of the encounter, and indeed what is meant by "encounter" and "convergence."

SOURCES

For primary texts in this study I used a variety of available materials, including Bede's published works, some articles, unpublished talks, taped lectures, essays, and personal letters. These materials are introduced into the body of this work where appropriate, especially when they illuminate an obscure idea, insight, or intuition. The following chronological list of his books indicates the use to which I put them in this volume.

The Golden String: An Autobiography (Springfield, Ill.: Templegate, 1980)[11] takes us through Bede's early life and education, and his long and fruitful friendship with C. S. Lewis, which began at Oxford. More important, however, it describes the process of his conversion and subsequent entrance into a monastery in England. The updated version is written from the vantage point of his years in India. *The Golden String* is particularly relevant in the historical section on his life, in the last part of chapter 2, and for giving a good insight into his inner life, his struggles, and his intellectual activities, which served his deeper aspirations for truth, knowledge, and God.

Christ in India: Essays towards a Hindu-Christian Dialogue (New York: Scribner's, 1966)[12] presents a history of the movement to create an Indian Christian monasticism, and the broader theme of an Indian Catholicism. It makes suggestions about what India can contribute to the building of a truly nonviolent society and details some of the history of significant encounters between East and West. It also has a valuable chapter titled "The Unknown Christ of Hinduism" and one on the future of the Church, her mission, and the challenge to become more universal in all the cultures of the world by presenting herself in a form they can understand and accept, which manifests their genius and character.

Vedanta and Christian Faith (Los Angeles: Dawn Horse Press, 1973)[13] is one of Father Bede's earlier attempts at a substantive relating of the two traditions.

Return to the Centre (Springfield, Ill.: Templegate, 1977)[14] covers most of the points of his life's work and their focus: the bringing together of East and West, specifically the Christian faith and Hinduism.

The Marriage of East and West: A Sequel to "The Golden String" (Springfield, Ill.: Templegate, 1982)[15] is really Bede's masterpiece, systematically dealing with most if not all of the major ideas of his thought and experience.

The Cosmic Revelation: The Hindu Way to God (Springfield, Ill.: Templegate, 1983)[16] is an excellent little summa of his thought on Hinduism and its relationship to Christian Revelation.

The Bhagavad Gita: A Christian Reading (Warwick, N.Y.: Amity House, 1987).[17] Having obtained a copy of the manuscript before its publication, I drew on it only in a minimal way for the section on *sannyāsa* in chapter 6.

Furthermore, there were a number of taped lectures by Father Bede that had not yet been transcribed and published. I introduce this important material at different points, in particular where it provides details that are lacking elsewhere, explains obscurities, covers new ground, or just adds clarification by way of additional elaboration. The significance of this class of material cannot be underestimated.

STRUCTURE AND METHOD

The book is divided into two parts. Part one, with three chapters, includes the introduction, the historical context, and Bede's epistemology, with his critique of rationalism and the old science, his metaphysics, and his own method of contemplative theology, entailing as it does an *existential convergence.* Part two, the more essential part, has four chapters. Chapter 4 deals with his theological "system," with myth, the cosmic covenant, and the Vedic revelation; chapter 5 with Advaita, Saccidānanda, and the Trinity, or the doctrine of God. Chapter 5 is pivotal, since it relates the two traditions around the essential mystical realization of each: Saccidānanda and the Trinity. Chapter 6, more practical, ponders Bede's understanding of Christology, monasticism or Christian *sannyāsa* and Tantrism, and the Church. Chapter 7 presents a critical appraisal of Bedean theology, evaluating his attempt to develop a Christian Vedanta and so to unite the two traditions in an experiential synthesis. This final chapter has a conclusion of sorts, in which I also bring forward some of my own thoughts that have emerged from this challenging but fascinating study. These thoughts represent my creative reactions.

My method has unfolded quite naturally in an organic fashion from the available sources and the essential points or propositions to be studied in order to determine whether they can be harmonized in their goal: a possible Christian Vedanta. This Christian form of the Vedanta, if indeed it is possible, would be a spiritual theology[18] and metaphysics that are based on and evolve from the language and symbolism of the Vedanta. We must explore this development in order to discover the status of this attempt, to see whether it is a genuine evolution into a harmonious relationship or a forced synthesis. The question is: Can the Christian mystery be expressed in this Indian worldview, which at once unites theoria and spiritual praxis, that is, unites metaphysical reflection and meditation, or contemplation? Bede Griffiths was convinced that it could, and this book examines his reasons and presentation.

The general method followed here is textual. I study Bede's statements, arguments, claims, and insights; his way of presenting the relationship of these two great traditions; and his view of the elements in each taken alone and together. The point of this textual approach should be clear: to arrive at an understanding of the experience and thought that give a solid foundation to his main ideas. In the primary chapters, after I have established his position on a given issue or group of issues, I probe his reasons and arguments as to discern whether or not his positions are well grounded, and thus valid.

The textual study and analysis, furthermore, involves a phenomenological[19] method because I am studying precisely his own consciousness. I am trying to determine the nature and depth of his contemplative awareness. Needless to say, this requires a certain degree of empathy. To put the matter a little differently, I am studying Bede Griffiths's consciousness with the hope of making this consciousness accessible to our understanding, and I am doing so by a close examination of his important points, their interrelationships, and so forth. So this approach is in a sense phenomenological in the way described above. It is crucial to know his system and its points—to know them well—before attempting an evaluative criticism.

Now, the presuppositions of this comparative study of the Christian faith and Hinduism in the search for an interior convergence are three.[20] First, the whole enterprise requires or presupposes common ground. It is surely no use trying to relate these two religions if there is no common ground. And I think most—if not all—engaged in interreligious dialogue would accept the notion that there is in fact some common ground. The second presupposition flows directly from the first: that the common ground is in the spiritual experience and realization of their complementary relationship in the mystical core reality of Saccidānanda and Trinity. There is common ground perhaps because these two experiences at the heart of the Real are in a relationship of organic continuity: they are the same, but at different levels of depth. This of course has to be established and clarified, and I deal with it at length in chapter 5. Finally, the third presupposition of this study is the incomparable value to be gained for humanity in relating these two world religions in such a new and creative way. The world is so divided at this juncture of history, in such a state of chaos, that to find a real depth encounter between these two significant paths is, in some sense, to take a giant step toward reconciliation on a global scale. Few would question this value accruing to humankind. For then, such a harmonious relationship can become a living model of dialogue on all levels of reality. The value of dialogue, of existential convergence as a model, is discussed in chapter 7.

The overarching assumption—that a Christian Vedanta, or an Indian theology, is possible and indeed already exists—rests on a deep spiritual need of the Church to actualize her ideal nature as universal and fully present in each culture. This requires that she develop a Christian theology and spirituality, in the Indian context, drawn from the riches of that cultural configuration. For Western theology and spirituality are in general too much the product of the European mind, with its propensity for the abstract and the analytical. This is how Bede Griffiths would express this important principle: just as the early Church developed a Christian theology, spirituality and liturgy from Greek philosophy and pagan rites, and just as she patterned her canon law and ecclesial organization after the Roman Empire, she must now develop a Christian theology, spirituality, liturgy, canon law, and ecclesial organization from the categories and historical experience of Hinduism and Indian culture, especially from the Vedanta, the authentic ancient tradition of Indian civilization. In other words, the Church has to assimilate the cultural and spiritual heritage of India and make it her own, just as she once did with Greco-Roman philosophy and culture.[21] It is this assumption that really justifies Bede's efforts in theology and contemplative doctrine, something that I will examine in the unfolding of this volume.

The first part, with its three chapters, is mostly background material that sets the stage for the more important chapters of part two. At the same time, chapter 3 is not unimportant. Chapter 2 provides a sketch of the basic history of the movement to which Bede Griffiths belonged and was the successor. This should serve to give us an understanding of the context, which is primarily a monastic one. In this movement, it will be shown how the essential commitment is to the state of *sannyāsa* as a way to mystical contemplation, liberation, and the integration of Vedanta with the Gospel. Chapter 2 briefly touches upon the lives and contributions of Roberto de Nobili, who was a Christian *sannyāsi* but whose orientation was missionary; the Indian Carmelites of Mary Immaculate, and Brahmabandhab Upadhyay, a Christian convert who tried to synthesize Vedanta and the Christian faith and so is a significant link with the contemporary movement. We then look at Jules Monchanin's life and many contributions to this movement, followed by a consideration of Abhishiktananda (Henri Le Saux), who went all the way in his adoption of *sannyāsa* and who made extraordinary mystical and theological discoveries. Chapter 2 closes with a brief treatment of Father Bede's life, work, and writings, which are situated historically and in relation to the goal, a Christian Vedanta that is also an Indian theology.

Chapter 3 really concerns Bede's epistemology, metaphysics,

and contemplative theology, and is thus quite useful to the purpose of this book. Here I present his rather severe critique of the old science and the pervasive rationalism of life in the West as he conceived it. It is an attempt to awaken, or rather to reawaken, the intuitive dimension of consciousness present in all of us. His epistemological attack on the rationalism of scientific, technological culture is aided by his eloquent and coherent appeal to the new science, especially to the new physics, cosmology, biology, and psychology. Having clearly and forcefully demonstrated the intrinsic limitations of rationalism and the old scientific/materialistic outlook (scientism), we will then be in a position to present his view of what true knowledge is and how to attain it. This is the wisdom of the perennial metaphysics. It is also his method of contemplative or spiritual theology, which includes praxis (mystical realization through prayer, meditation in the Indian sense, and deep reflection) as well as vigorous metaphysical thought. I present, question, and clarify his contemplative methodology. The reasons he believed such a theology was the great need of the future will also be considered.

Moving into part two, chapter 4 treats of his theological scheme and especially his extraordinarily profound conception of myth as a form of symbolic consciousness that is actually a kind of symbolic theology. This chapter is rather important, since myth, in Bede's view, is a common, indeed substantial link between the biblical and Hindu traditions. Both have this mythic core, and to grasp this truth prepares the way for an appreciation of the notions of the Cosmic/Vedic Revelation and Covenant in the second half of the chapter.

Chapter 5 enters deeply into the Hindu experience of the Absolute, the notion of Brahman pervading the universe, and Ātman as the true Self discovered in the depths of interiority in meditation. It also elaborates the Hindu discovery of Advaita and Saccidānanda, a crucial link with Christianity. From this quintessential mystical awareness, we will then be in a position to enter the Christian contemplation of the Trinity. We must try to discern these mysteries from within this contemplative realization grounded in an enlightened faith.

In chapter 5 we also come to the most essential and interesting part of this chapter and of the entire book: the explication of the inner relationship between the awareness of Saccidānanda and the personal consciousness of the Trinity. It must be established whether Bede indeed found the primary point of contact between the two traditions. The emphasis here is to show how these two approaches can be grounded on a metaphysical and mystical continuum—the former because of the latter—in which we are able to reach deeper and deeper levels of interiority, and where we will find the Spirit at the center of consciousness, in the abyss, or "cave of the heart." This is also "where" we will discover, according to Bede, the crucial encounter and confluence of Hinduism and the Christian faith, and from it determine whether a Christian Vedanta is possible and, if so, what form it will assume.

Included in chapter 5 is a brief consideration of the feminine dimension of the Godhead. This was Bede's notion, following Hinduism, of God as Mother. Here is the domain of Tantra, which is the feminine or intuitive approach to the divine Reality. It involves the intuitive capacity, the sympathetic, which is an active passivity rather than the aggressive rationalism of Vedanta and Western metaphysics. We will find that this doctrine of God as Mother is in harmony with the Christian principle of Divine Providence, and Spirit as somehow the feminine aspect of God, or the Holy Spirit as Mother God.

Chapter 6 explores Bede's understanding of Christology, Tantrism, and Christian *sannyāsa* as the ideal of an Indian monasticism. It pursues the point that *sannyāsa* is perhaps the preeminent way to the mystical goal of life: union with Ultimate Reality, with God. That is what constitutes true liberation. The chapter examines *sannyāsa* as the context of those spiritual break-

throughs in consciousness that represent knowledge as a knowing wisdom, as contrasted with theoretical knowledge based on
reason alone. And according to Bede and others, the real meeting
of Hinduism and the Church, the Christian faith, is in the depths
of spiritual awareness, in the center of the mystical consciousness
that is the whole purpose of *sannyāsa* —that is, to actualize that
awareness within—and this is also the purpose of Christian monasticism. Chapter 6 also considers Bede's ecclesiology, how he
viewed the Church' s future and her role, task, and relation to the
other traditions. We will see how he placed the Church squarely
in the center of this movement toward convergence, and how the
Church is actually becoming the focus for the Asian religions as
she opens up to them in dialogue and sharing. Only in this way,
and as she assimilates the spiritual values of other traditions, will
she actualize her larger universality.

In chapter 7, the last one of this study, the emphasis is on
critical evaluation, conclusions, implications, and creative contributions. It presents my own evaluation of Father Bede's attempt
to integrate the Christian faith and Hinduism in a new theological vision that is "totally Christian and totally Indian." I discuss
the positive and negative points for his impressive achievement.
Then the implications for the future will be considered, chiefly
the implications of existential convergence for interreligious relations, what this principle is based on, and the way in which the
various world religions might be related to the Church.

2

The Historical Context as Sannyasic Monasticism

THE HISTORY OF the movement to which Bede Griffiths belongs has yet to be written.[1] It is a relatively modern development, beginning only in the seventeenth century with Roberto de Nobili, and acquiring definite shape and direction in the latter half of the twentieth century, with such figures as Jules Monchanin and Abhishiktananda, after having passed through the incipient groping stage with the Indian Carmelites in the first half of the nineteenth century, and in Brahmabandhab Upadhyay at the turn of the twentieth century.

The literature dealing with the relationship of Hinduism and Christianity is rather vast, particularly if this relationship is viewed on a scholarly or missiological level. When the two traditions are related on their deepest level, however, the literature is far less extensive. But when that common depth-dimension is situated within the sannyasic monastic context, then the available tomes on the subject become extremely rare indeed. It is precisely this element of the relationship, that is, the sannyasic as the continuous thread in this historical movement, that determines the use of certain figures in this brief historical sketch. It is a fact, an existential truth, and not a product of theoretical speculation, that the actual encounter of Christianity and Hinduism has occurred and continues to occur around the institution and state of *sannyāsa*. This is the praxis dimension and the focal point of the historical context.

Commitment to the way of *sannyāsa* is the common denominator in de Nobili, Upadhyay, Monchanin, Abhishiktananda, and Bede. All of these leaders have assumed the sannyasic state, to some extent for different reasons. Bede was greatly influenced by his predecessors' example of embracing the condition of a *sannyāsi*. And Abhishiktananda, for instance, emphasizes the essential equality in the ideal of Hindu *sannyāsa* and Christian monasticism. He claims they have the same goal: "the profession of a Christian monk certainly implies, at least in its roots, the full renunciation and radical transcendence which shines out so clearly in the tradition of Hindu *sannyāsa*."[2]

Both Monchanin and Abhishiktananda had a strong impact on Bede's understanding of monasticism in the Indian situation, and this impact came from a direct knowledge of each of these seminal figures, specifically in regard to *sannyāsa* and the whole attempt to "translate" Benedictine monasticism into a sannyasic form in India, which is really to find a synthesis between them. Bede agreed with Abhishiktananda's assessment, and this is evident in typical statements like: "the goal of monastic life East and West is essentially the same. Saint Benedict requires of a monk that he should 'truly seek God,' and it is this search for God, or Quest of the Absolute...which remains always and everywhere the characteristic mark of the monk."[3]

It is only natural, then, that Hinduism and Christianity would discover a deeper foundation to their relationship in *sannyāsa*, for the Christian monk and the Hindu *sannyāsi*[4] are both seeking Ultimate Reality and meaning: both are striving for unity with the Absolute, with the Divine One. In each tradition it is in the life of the *monachos*[5]—be he or she a Christian monastic or a Hindu renunciate—that this union with Ultimate Reality is pursued wholeheartedly and in many cases is attained.

Sannyāsa in Hinduism has had a strange history (discussed in greater detail in chapter 6). Originally it was the fourth *āśrama,* or stage in a man's life, after *brahmacarya,* or studentship (sort of like being a novice); *grihasthāśrama,* family life, or the stage of a householder; and *vanaprastha,* a period of retirement to the forest spent in solitude, penance, and meditation. After this time of intense spiritual preparation in the forest, one came out a *sannyāsi,* a man of renunciation, mystical experience, enlightenment, and wisdom, living solely on alms, usually in a mendicant lifestyle. In a *sannyāsi*'s travels and otherwise, he would exhort people on right living and the way to enlightenment.[6] In addition to the fourth *āśrama* of life, *sannyāsa* also emerged as a lifelong commitment. Originally, *sannyāsa* or religious life as a lifelong commitment was not a Hindu institution but was peculiar to Jainism and Buddhism, which were, in the first place, monastic religions, formulated as ways of life for monks, and only secondarily for laypeople. So when a Hindu took the radical step of becoming a monk, he also automatically relinquished his caste privileges and became an outcaste as far as the Hindu social structure was concerned.

Sannyāsa in Hinduism in its original sense also had an activist connotation. Great sages or *sannyāsis* like Vasista and Visvamitra were counselors to kings. When Swami Vivekananda established his Ramakrishna Mission as a religious community, this activist orientation to public service in the educational, social, and academic or scholarly fields (competing with the Western Christian religious orders) was its main goal. Similarly, the Sabarmati Ashram in Gujarat founded by Mahatma Gandhi and the Pawanar Ashram founded by Vinoba Bhave in Wardha both stressed this original sannyasic ideal of public service.[7]

In the encounter, or *existential convergence,* of Hindu *sannyāsa* and Christian monasticism, the way has been opened to spiritual discovery for the Western monks and Eastern as well. In this historical movement there is a progressive clarification of what *sannyāsa* is for Christians in themselves, and in dialogue with Hindus. There is also the reality of the movement becoming conscious in the lives of Monchanin, Abhishiktananda, Bede, and others. So much is this the case that in the modern period we can speak of a new identity for the Christian monk in the Indian context, that is, the Christian *sannyāsi. Sannyāsa* thus becomes the way to enlightenment, liberation *(moksha)*, union with Ultimate Reality *(samādhi)*, mystical wisdom being the content of this enlightenment, the very substance of it, and the new identity itself.

Christian *sannyāsa* has evolved from de Nobili to Bede, and its vision of the relationship of Christianity and Hinduism has unfolded along with it. If we study this very significant movement in depth, we begin to see that there is more to it than just *inculturation* and *indigenization,* which are addressed more to the externals of adaptation and do not necessarily touch the essence: the inner life of mystical contemplation in both traditions.

Because these men walked the path of *sannyāsa,*[8] the life of renunciation, depth experience, and meditation, they were able to approach the question and the task of relating Hinduism and Christianity on a deeper level; they were enabled to grasp the point of encounter and convergence on an experiential basis. It is out of the realization of their experience, their profound encounter within their own being, that Upadhyay, Monchanin, Abhishiktananda, Bede, and others came to understand the relationship as involving and requiring a connection between the two notions and intuitions of Divine Reality. In Monchanin the relation is narrowed to Advaita and the Trinity,[9] while Abhishiktananda and Bede Griffiths concretize the intuition in their own contemplative experience. This is especially true of Abhishiktananda.

Thus, in this movement the substantive encounter of the two traditions becomes progressively more focused until there is an actual existential convergence in the experience of the latter three members of the movement and in that of others. The focus of this existential convergence is the deepest mystical insight present at the heart of both faiths: Advaita/Saccidānanda and the Trinity. It is from an experiential realization of their intrinsic reliability, in the contemplative awareness of Monchanin, Abhishiktananda, and Bede Griffiths, that the intuition of a Christian Vedanta emerges, and yet not only is it a further development of the Vedanta in the terms and categories of the Christian tradition, but it is also—so they maintain and hope—an Indian theology that expresses the Christian mystery. Consequently, the thrust of the movement is that *sannyāsa* leads to an experiential knowledge of the Absolute in both traditions, and this knowledge can be formulated in terms of Advaita/Saccidānanda and the Trinity, a relationship in the depths of the Spirit.

EARLY ATTEMPTS AT ADAPTATION

There were two significant attempts to incorporate the Hindu sannyasic ideal (or aspects of it) into Christianity, one in the way of strict adaptation, that of Roberto de Nobili, the other by way of assimilating and modifying the sannyasic ideal of contemplation, which was done by a few Indian priests under the Carmelite Rule, beginning in the early 1830s. Both of these "experiments" were prophetic of the later flowering of Christian *sannyāsa* in India.

Roberto de Nobili (1577–1656), the great pioneer of adaptation, was born in Rome of a noble family.[10] In 1596, at the age of nineteen, he entered the Society of Jesus, and from the very beginning of his vocation he dreamed of going to India as a missionary. This was really a longing for him. De Nobili realized his ambition, for on April 28, 1604, he set sail for India, arriving at the port of Goa on May 20, 1605.[11] In India, he eventually befriended some brahmins, and from them he learned about the problems of social interaction that resulted from the caste system. He came to appreciate that the life of a *sannyāsi* best approximated his idea of what a priest should be in the Indian context. De Nobili thus decided to adopt *sannyāsa* as his way of life, a move from which he derived two advantages: first, it would permit him to escape the designation of low caste, assigned to him because he was a non-Hindu, an outsider; and second, the sannyasic state would allow him to translate his religious life into Indian terms that would be readily acceptable to and understandable by the people.[12] He "came to the conclusion that to adopt the *sannyāsi*'s dress, diet and manner of living would prove the best means of opening the door of India."[13]

In November 1607 he received the approval of his superiors to wear the *kavi,* the garb of a *sannyāsi,* and to live as one. He fasted and prayed, ate only one meal a day, and never touched meat again. He took a solemn vow to remain a *sannyāsi* to the end of his life.[14] As the first Christian ever to embrace *sannyāsa,* de Nobili is important in this historical movement. He left his comfortable, European-style house and moved into a poor little hermitage. He quickly learned Sanskrit and could read Grantham, a Tamilian variant of written Sanskrit.[15] A brahmin friend, Śivadarma, who taught him Sanskrit, introduced him to the study of the Vedas. He was thus also the first Westerner ever to read the Vedas or to have any knowledge of them. He had a very practical interest in the Vedas. They put him in a position to understand the brahmins, which made it possible for him to engage in fruitful dialogue with them, and his aim in dialogue was to lead them to Christ.[16]

De Nobili wanted to adapt himself to the Hindus as Saint Paul had adapted himself to the Greeks. He even changed his way of thinking so that it would conform to Indian conceptions. He was passionately committed to Catholicism and its growth in India, but not to its European philosophical formulations or cultural forms. He never tampered with Christian doctrine but was always flexible in regard to customs.[17]

I do not think de Nobili can be dismissed as simply a "missionary" who adjusted himself to Indian forms as a tactic of evangelization. There is this side of him, but there is also de Nobili the saint, the Christian *sannyāsi,* the man concerned with the needs and welfare of others; he was also an incomparable scholar and thinker. The lifestyle he assumed he believed in. Indeed, he came to see himself as an Indian, and his commitment to *sannyāsa* was genuine. Father Ferroli, the Jesuit historian, says of him: "He was in the true sense of the word a pioneer ... [who] broke the barriers of Hinduism and Brahmin exclusivism."[18] His significance lies in the fact that he incarnated the Christian faith in Indian form and showed quite cogently that it could indeed be thoroughly Indian. Furthermore, de Nobili coined a terminology for Christian theology in the Indian context, and created a theological structure for communicating the Christian faith.[19]

Bede Griffiths, who addressed the issue of de Nobili's methods of evangelization, emphasized two essential elements of de Nobili's witness. In the first place, he learned the principal sacred languages of Tamil and Sanskrit, which then enabled him to study the Hindu scriptures in depth, and most important, he *lived* as a *sannyāsi.*[20] This gave him entry to the brahmins and other spiritual and temporal leaders of South India. Both of these elements are also normative in the movement we are considering here, for all subsequent figures of the movement will be intimately familiar with the sacred texts of Hinduism, after having studied Sanskrit, and all will embrace the sannyasic state.

Even though Roberto de Nobili adopted *sannyāsa* primarily as an apologetical and catechetical method in order to attract converts, nevertheless it is no exaggeration to say that he is the father of Christian *sannyāsa* and the forerunner of all who seek a relationship with Hinduism from the vantage point of Christianity. Of course, de Nobili never dared to suggest a synthesis between the two faiths; if he wondered about it from time to time, he kept it to himself.

The second great attempt at creative assimilation of the spirit of Hindu *sannyāsa* occurred with Catholic diocesan priests who were themselves Indian. They were three priests of the Syro-Malabar Rite, which has been dominant in South India for centuries: Father Thomas Palackal, Father Thomas Porukara, and the Venerable Servant of God Father Kuriakos Elias. In 1831 they decided to establish religious life in the Indian form, which had always been discouraged and opposed by ecclesiastical authority, de Nobili notwithstanding. The three sought an eremitical life, a life of total seclusion from the world, like many *sannyāsis,* but their bishop, who was himself a Carmelite, advised against it and instead invited them to a more balanced life, that of contemplation, renunciation, and action.[21]

They established a house of contemplation and spiritual counsel that was easily accessible to all people who sought their guidance, especially in spiritual matters, or who wanted a place for prayer and meditation. From its inception, this community—the Carmelites of Mary Immaculate (C.M.I.)—has followed the ideal of contemplation and active service to others, and they have done so with modified elements of Indian *sannyāsa.*[22] This was a noble attempt, but it retained many Western monastic elements, and to this day the *kavi* is not worn, while the Carmelite habit is. With Upadhyay, however, a more radical adaptation arises.

BRAHMABANDHAB UPADHYAY

Brahmabandhab (or Brahmabandhav) Upadhyay (1861–1907) is a crucial person in this movement and in the Indian struggle for independence, yet he is all but unknown outside the subcontinent. He was a brahmin convert to Catholicism who also took upon himself the life and responsibility of a *sannyāsi.* He was thus a link with the Carmelites and de Nobili, but closer to our own time and to the modern movement.

Upadhyay was born on February 11, 1861, in Khanyan, Bengal,

not far from Calcutta.[23] His name at birth was Bhawani Charan Banerji[24] which he changed to Brahmabandhab Upadhyay when he became a *sannyāsi* in 1894.[25] *Upadhyay* means "assistant-teacher," and *Brahmabandhab* means "Theophilus," or "friend of God," his Christian name.[26] He became a Catholic in September 1891.[27] Upadhyay was educated in the Hooghly Collegiate School and the Metropolitan College in Calcutta.[28]

He had a very subtle intelligence and was an extraordinary metaphysician and scholar. He was an intrepid lecturer and a prolific essayist who ran a number of journals at different times, chief of which was *Sophia.* This journal in particular, along with *Twentieth Century,* became a vehicle for the proliferation of his political and religious thought. More important, however, it was Upadhyay who pioneered the approach of Bede Griffiths and others to uniting Christianity and Hinduism, or the Vedanta, and he also furthered the adaptation of Christian monasticism to *sannyāsa.*

Upadhyay sat at the feet of Ramakrishna Paramahamsa (1824–1883) along with Swami Vivekananda (1863–1902), the founder of the Ramakrishna Mission, who was an influential figure, like his great teacher, in the Hindu renaissance. Upadhyay and Vivekananda became good friends. He also knew and was close to the Indian poet Rabindranath Tagore, who was associated with him and the others mentioned above through the Brahmo Samāj (Society of the Worshipers of Brahman), which was founded by Ram Mohan Roy (1772–1833), leader of the reform movement in Hinduism. Mohan Roy wanted India to return to the purity of the Vedas and the Vedanta, although he accepted the moral teachings of Christ.[29]

From the time he assumed *sannyāsa* in 1894, Upadhyay became an ardent advocate of adaptation. He was convinced that only when the Church appeared in "Hindu garb" could she have any hope of reaching the soul of India. He felt that even missionaries should dress and behave like *sannyāsis.*[30] Indeed, he was certain that only the Christian *sannyāsi* was able to present the teachings of Catholicism to the Indian people,[31] because of their spiritual authenticity and the extraordinary respect for the state of *sannyāsa* among the people. Influenced by de Nobili's example, he proceeded to found an Indian monasticism that would become a means for the evangelization of India's people.[32] In this way he became a true monastic pioneer.

In an article in the August 1898 issue of *Sophia*, Upadhyay elaborates the extent of adaptation. He asserts that the Catholic faith has to be preached in the language of the Vedanta, that liturgical celebrations should reflect Hindu customs, and poverty should be practiced in the same way as it is in Hindu asceticism. This way, in Hinduism, is the radical poverty of the *sannyāsi* with the vulnerability of wandering and solitude, while Christian asceticism and poverty is practiced normally in the relative comfort and security of a supportive community. Upadhyay says: "When the Catholic Church in India will be dressed up in Hindu garments then will our countrymen perceive that she elevates man to the universal kingdom of truth by stooping down to adapt herself to his racial peculiarities."[33] In this way, he is trying to suggest, Hindus will know that Christians are serious and worthy of attention because they respect Indian culture and tradition; play by the rules, and they will show that even this culture can be inserted into the bosom of the Church, the universal culture and tradition of humankind. The ideal of establishing Christian monasticism in an Indian form was of critical importance to him, and this lofty project, accompanied by his interest in a synthesis with the Vedanta, absorbed all of his time and energy.[34]

In the January 1899 issue of *Sophia*, Upadhyay announced the foundation of his Kasthalic Matha, or Catholic Monastery. He describes the purpose and principles of the ashram, and he equates the Trinity with Saccidānanda; indeed, he was the first to suggest this connection. Upadhyay also extols the hope of seeing Vedanta take its place in Catholic wisdom. His statement—one of many—is a precise summary of adaptation and assimilation: "Here in the midst of solitude and silence will be reared up true yogis to whom the contemplation of the Triune Saccidānanda will be food and drink. Here will grow ascetics who will, in union with the sufferings of the God-man, do penance for their sins as well as for the sins of their own countrymen, by constant bewailing and mortification. Here will be trained the future apostles of India ... here will the Vedanta philosophy be assimilated to universal [Catholic] truth."[35]

His monastery-ashram was established in 1900 but was later ordered to disband because of a lack of ecclesiastical approval, and open opposition from Church officials. The seed of his vision, however, was to bear fruit many years later, with the opening of Shantivanam in 1950. Commenting on the occasion of the founding of this Christian ashram, Abhishiktananda said: "Some sixty years ago, the intuition of what Indian Christian monasticism ought to be exploded from the heart of Brahmabandhab Upadhyay."[36]

Upadhyay espoused a Christian Vedanta, and he never tired of defending it. He was of the opinion that Śankara's Vedanta could be used to explain Catholic dogmas to the Indian mind. He wanted to use Śankara's thought much as the West has employed Saint Thomas's metaphysics in the formulation of Catholic philosophy and theology in the medieval synthesis. Upadhyay was convinced that "attempts should be made to win over Hindu philosophy to the service of Christianity as Greek philosophy was won over in the Middle Ages."[37] This insight is an integral part of the subsequent movement, especially prominent in the lectures and writings of Monchanin, Abhishiktananda, Bede Griffiths, and others.

Upadhyay believed that faith in Christ completed the Vedanta and that the theistic doctrine of the Vedanta, which he saw as its authentic core, could be a firm foundation for Indian Christianity.[38] He interpreted Hindu thought as essentially complementary to Christianity and as having a similar end. In an article that appeared in *The Tablet* (London), he says: "Hindu thought has reared up a magnificent theism which in its essential conclusions agrees wonderfully with the philosophy of St. Thomas."[39]

Upadhyay saw and expressed the reality of the Divine in terms of the Hindu formulation of Saccidānanda *(sat-cit-ānanda)*.[40] But he went much further than holding to the notion, since he regarded it as a term for the Trinity. For the "Triune Saccidānanda" is the Trinity in his thinking. This is quite a radical step, and the subsequent theological activity in India will not follow him all the way in this, but he did indicate an important possible link between Hinduism and Christianity in his equating of Saccidānanda[41] with the Trinity.

Upadhyay died on October 27, 1907, at the age of forty-six. Although he did not complete his seminal work, his impact on the movement has been incalculable. Vattakuzhy sums it up best when he says: "It is no exaggeration to say that all modern efforts of adapting Christianity to Hindu thought are to a great extent inspired by the example of this daring pioneer."[42] His emphasis on *sannyāsa* or adaptation, the development of a Christian Vedanta, and the Trinity/Saccidānanda connection all passed into the thought of the subsequent leaders of the movement, with some important variations, as we will see.

JULES MONCHANIN

Although there was considerable interest in Hinduism and Buddhism in the West, particularly among scholars and some popularizers, during the latter half of the nineteenth and early twentieth centuries, little actual progress[43] was made in the area of Hindu-Christian assimilation after Upadhyay's death until the time of the saintly Abbé Jules Monchanin (1895–1957), who is regarded as a pivotal figure, indeed, one of the founding pioneers of the Christian sannyasic movement in its more modern expression. He is also an important link in the development of an Indian Christian theology and the attempt to reconcile the Hindu and Christian mystical doctrines, Advaita and the Trinity.

Abbé Jules Monchanin was born on April 10, 1895, in the little village of Fleurie in the Rhône region of France, not far from Lyons. He had frail health as a child. He studied for the priesthood and was ordained on June 29, 1922, then went on for advanced work in theology and taught for some years. He was quite popular as a spiritual director.[44] He joined the Société des Auxiliaires des Missions in July 1938 and, responding to the promptings of the Spirit, went to India that same year. At the invitation of Bishop Mendonca of the diocese of Tiruchirapalli, in Tamil Nadu, he served as a parish priest for ten years (1939–1949) in villages of South India. Then in 1950 he and Henri Le Saux (Abhishiktananda) founded Saccidananda Ashram on the banks of the river Kavery in Kulittalai, a hermitage dedicated to the adoration of the Trinity. He died on October 10, 1957, in Paris.[45]

One of the great themes of his Indian "experiment" was given to him by his old friend Father (later Cardinal) Henri de Lubac before he was to set sail for India. Shortly before his departure from Marseilles in May 1939, he met in Lyons with de Lubac, who reaffirmed their friendship. Monchanin recorded the substance of their conversation and the task de Lubac envisioned for him: "to rethink everything in the light of theology and to rethink theology through mysticism, freeing it from everything incidental and regaining, through spirituality alone, everything essential.... He believes that it is in coming into contact with India that I will be able to rework theology...."[46]

With this remark, Monchanin defined one of the important ideals that will guide the sannyasic-monastic movement. This "task" was picked up and incorporated into Bede Griffiths's own vision, becoming a central element in his lectures and writings. Monchanin the seeker, in his relentless quest for the Absolute,[47] accepted the challenge from his old friend, and this task took a definitive form—a concrete embodiment of the ideal, which was an experiential approach—when he and Henri Le Saux together founded Saccidananda (or Shantivanam) Ashram in Kulittalai on March 21, 1950, the old Feast of Saint Benedict.[48]

Monchanin wanted a Christian monasticism in India that would be "totally Indian and totally Christian," an ideal that has come to be accepted by the Church in India[49] and is another theme that has influenced Bede, as we shall see. Now, part of this vision of an Indian monasticism included the insight of de Nobili and Upadhyay on *sannyāsa*. And it was their intuition that inspired the establishment of Shantivanam by Monchanin and Le Saux, the first Indian Catholic ashram to receive canonical recognition.[50] Both Monchanin and Le Saux embraced the state of *sannyāsa* and took Indian names. Monchanin adopted the name Swami Parama Arubi Ananda, which means "a man of the supreme joy of the Spirit—the Formless One," and Henri Le Saux adopted the name Abhishiktananda, which means "bliss of Christ," or "joy of Christ,"[51] a name by which he has been known ever since. This was the first recorded case of Christian *sannyāsis* taking Indian names,[52] with the possible exception of Upadhyay.

Monchanin and Abhishiktananda saw monasticism as playing a vital role in the attempt to reach Hindus. For monasticism— in its Indian sannyasic form—aims at the purest realization of Hinduism's goal; the pursuit of and union with the Absolute. And they recognized a basic similarity between *sannyāsa* and Christian monasticism. Together they write: "But there is too, in the Indian legacy, a gem hidden under a bushel ... namely a deep desire for the knowledge of God, anxious yearning for union with Him, and keen dissatisfaction at the instability and worthlessness of whatever is not eternal. Are not these basic principles the very source of monasticism, its very heart?"[53]

Moreover, they were convinced that it is on the monastic level of both traditions that India and the Church will meet[54] and embrace each other. The features that Indian Christian monasticism must possess, and that were (and are) pursued at Shantivanam, are two: solitude for contemplation, and assimilation of Indian standards and practices.[55] All of Indian tradition is open to this careful process of assimilation. Thus, at Shantivanam they came to embrace Upadhyay's ideal of Indian Christian *sannyāsa* and adopted most of its elements, especially those of poverty, renunciation, vegetarian diet, sitting and sleeping on the floor, and wearing the *kavi.*

Monchanin was an extraordinary metaphysician and theologian. He had an exceptionally keen and subtle intellect and was capable of extraordinary depth. The focus of his metaphysics, his contemplative theology, his very life, was the Trinity.[56] This concern had been central to his life, long before going to India. India only drove it deeper into his heart. Like Upadhyay before him, he regarded *Saccidānanda* as a term for the Trinity—a fact attested to by naming the ashram at Shantivanam after the Trinity under the designation of "Saccidananda." At the same time, Monchanin did not mix the two approaches; he kept to a pure Trinitarian doctrine, which passed into the formulations of Abhishiktananda and Bede Griffiths. In a lecture at the All-India Study Week in Madras, December 1956, Monchanin was uncompromising in his commitment to the purity of the Trinitarian intuition/doctrine: "Christian mysticism is trinitarian or it is nothing. Hindu thought, so deeply focused on the Oneness of the One, on the *kevalin* [One, or the Alone] in his *kevalatua* [Oneness, or in its Aloneness], cannot be sublimated into trinitarian thought without a crucifying dark night of the soul. It has to undergo a noetic metamorphosis, a passion of the spirit."[57]

Although Monchanin rejected an easy syncretism—and this is also true of Abhishiktananda and Bede—he did work untiringly for the reconciliation of the two traditions in their deepest dimension, that of the contemplative or the mystical. He came to realize that in that depth was where the two mystical paths could meet, and their meeting would bring together or relate Advaita and the Trinity. But such a meeting requires that Christians must assimilate the Hindu experience. Monchanin wrote to a nun: "Advaita and praise of the Trinity are our only aim. This means that we must grasp the authentic Hindu search for God in order to Christianize it, starting with ourselves first of all, from within."[58] This is a formula Monchanin always used when trying to conceptualize the task for people by expressing it in its simplicity. This will also be Abhishiktananda's focus, but he will lean toward identity between the two states of mystical consummation. In another context, when talking about Ruysbroeck's mystical doctrine, he also sums up his own approach: "What is striking in Ruysbroeck's mysticism is the perfect synthesis of extreme apophatism with the deepest trinitarian vision."[59] Furthermore, he was convinced that a fruitful dialogue between Hinduism and Christianity had to be, on the deepest level, that of the Trinity,[60] the interpersonal reality of the Godhead; it had to have that metaphysical quality, that essential depth.

Monchanin and Abhishiktananda were very close, and the former had an enormous impact on the life and thought of the latter. After Monchanin's death in 1957, Abhishiktananda wrote a memoir of his dear friend and collaborator. In it he paid tribute to Monchanin and his prophetic role in India: "And many... understood that there was a secret in that priest and in his heart a hidden treasure, which once opened and spread would prove a priceless asset for the blossoming of the Church in India."[61]

ABHISHIKTANANDA (HENRI LE SAUX)

One of the greatest influences on Bede Griffiths was the example of Henri Le Saux, known as Abhishiktananda (1910–1973). Abhishiktananda went farther than any other Christian in his penetration and assimilation of the Hindu ascetical/mystical ideal. He became a living symbol of dialogue and convergence, and, one can also say, of struggle, the struggle and pain of birth. He incarnated in himself the quest for the transcendent mystery that is so clearly the focus of every serious Christian monk and Hindu *sannyāsi*, as well as Buddhist, Jain, and Zen monks. For Christianity and Hinduism fused in his inner experience, in the depths of his mystical contemplation in profound interiority.

Henri Le Saux was born on August 30, 1910, in Brittany. After his early education he entered the Benedictine Abbey of Saint Anne de Kergonan. He made his solemn profession in 1935 and was ordained a priest in 1939.[62] He started writing to Jules Monchanin in 1947, and arrived in India on August 15, 1948. On March 21, 1950, he and Monchanin established Shantivanam, as was mentioned above, and from here on he was known as Abhishiktananda.[63] In 1960 he became a citizen of India, and in 1961 his hermitage at Gyansu in Uttarkāshi was built. On March 21, 1968—exactly eighteen years after the founding of Shantivanam—Abhishiktananda left the ashram for good and went to the North to his hermitage. Marc Chaduc, a Frenchman and close disciple of Abhishiktananda, joined him, becoming his disciple in 1971. Abhishiktananda engaged in a considerable amount of writing and lecturing, until illness overtook him; after a convalescence of three months, he died on December 7, 1973.[64]

His life as a Christian *sannyāsi*, which he embraced in a totally radical way, has to be seen as the meaning of his life and message, just as much as his themes of dialogue and Trinitarian Advaita. He was well prepared for the transition from Benedictine monk to Indian *sannyāsi*—both of which he saw as complementary, as was pointed out—since he had studied Tamil and Sanskrit in France, long before his move to India.[65] From the very beginning of his new life in India, Abhishiktananda was alert to the depth experience. In January 1948 he went to Arunāchala and experienced the *darśan* of the great Hindu master Sri Ramana Maharshi. Ramana Maharshi had a profound effect on him that was to last for the rest of his life. He was able to awaken in Abhishiktananda, through a silent communication, the mystical life of depth in the "cave of the heart."[66]

Abhishiktananda was the first Christian known ever to sit at the feet of an Indian master, that is, to submit to one as a disciple. For he did not just study the Hindu contemplative tradition, he lived it in an ultimate sense and with an extreme intensity of concentration. If Ramana Maharshi awakened him, it was Sri Gnanananda who became his guru and taught him the way of meditation *(dhyāna)*, which is essential for the commitment to *sannyāsa.*[67]

Part of the reality of being a monk in the Indian or Hindu context is to receive initiation from a spiritual master, and this involves a knowledge that far exceeds our normal, everyday sense and rational consciousness. The meeting with the guru does not happen on this plane of reality. Abhishiktananda elaborates his own experience of it: "in the meeting of the guru and disciple there is no longer even fusion, for we are on the plane of the original non-duality. Advaita remains forever incomprehensible to him who has not first lived it existentially in his meeting with the guru."[68]

Sannyāsa embodies the quest for the Absolute and concretizes it in a person's life. It is the ultimate call *to be,* to live in the realm of transcendent consciousness, the abode of the Divine Reality. The sannyasic life is a way that transcends all social ties and responsibilities, and is a symbol of that deeper dimension of experience to which we are all destined in our humanity. As Abhishiktananda puts it: "The *sannyāsi* is the outward expression of man's ultimate freedom in his innermost being."[69] And this freedom is to pursue the wellspring of being in the depths of interiority, in that which is beyond all signs, that is, all manifested reality in this world.[70] For *sannyāsa* exists in the fullness of realization beyond signs. Abhishiktananda lived in this beyond as a Christian *sannyāsi,* and he saw in the *sannyāsi*'s commitment to renunciation, solitude, and spiritual freedom a complementarity with the values of the Christian monk,[71] for both the Hindu *sannyāsi* and the Christian monk or *sannyāsi* have the same goal: union with Divine Reality. The life of the Christian *sannyāsi* which in Abhishiktananda's experience[72] united the two traditions, allowing for the necessary detachment, created the environment for spiritual exploration through meditation. Concerning the importance of meditation, he says: "Meditation helps toward concentration and the quietening of the mind and leads to that interior silence, without which nothing can be achieved."[73]

Sannyāsa is rooted in inner experience; it is life in the Spirit. This was Abhishiktananda's foundational methodology, an experiential methodology, the justification of which he discovered in the Upaniṣads. They formed the basis of his later realization of Advaita, his experience of it. Evaluating the essential importance of the Upaniṣads, he maintains: "Their aim is to help the disciple himself to reach the fundamental experience which defies every attempt at conceptual expression, to put him into the attitude of mind and heart which will make him capable of this experience."[74] The Upaniṣads teach the primacy of the experiential over the merely speculative. Again, he declares: "Upanishadic formulations have no other function than to lead to an experience.... It is a kind of consciousness, an awareness...."[75]

This awareness, this explosion of transcendent consciousness in one, is Advaita, the experience of nonduality, the experiential awakening into pure unity in being, the realization that, in a certain sense, one *is* it. In one of the last things he wrote before his departure from this life, Abhishiktananda characterized the experience of Advaita in the most stark of terms. With intellectual acuteness, honesty, and theological "asceticism," he asserted: "In this annihilating experience, man is no longer able to project in front of himself anything whatsoever, to recognize any other "pole" to which he will refer himself and give the name God. Once he has reached that innermost centre, he is so forcibly seized by the mystery that he can no longer utter either a 'Thou' or an 'I.'"[76]

But then Abhishiktananda holds that beyond God—in the depths of the interior silence—is the experience, the reality, of the Father.[77] This is a constant theme of his more mature writing. Beyond even unity, or in the ultimate depths of it, in the inwardness of the Spirit, there is an experience of the Word entering back into the Source, which is the Father. Whenever Abhishiktananda gets to the limits of language in discussing these matters, he lapses into Eckhartian terminology and expression; he tries, at these times, to convey his own penetration of the Ultimate Reality in the mystico-theological categories of Meister Eckhart. This is especially true when he reflects on the Trinity.

The Trinity was the other pole of his contemplative theology, something that undoubtedly was reinforced for him in his relationship with Monchanin, who was totally centered on the triune mystery. Abhishiktananda struggled for many years with the reality of these two poles—Advaita and the Trinity, and how to relate them, if indeed they are relatable. He was trying not only to reconcile them interiorly in his own contemplation, but also to reconcile two unique cultures, two civilizations. On the one side, that is, in Hinduism, there is the emphasis on unity or nonduality in the ultimate state, and on the other, at the heart of Christianity, in the Trinity, there is an emphasis on Being as essentially communion, of *koinonia,* of love which is actually a *co-esse.* So, the Divine Reality is generally conceived in the Hindu tradition as a Solitude, and in Christianity as a community of Being.[78]

Abhishiktananda is not satisfied with Advaita alone; his intuition and finally his realized experience tell him there is more to it. Eventually he comes to understand that Advaita has different levels of depth to it, and that at the deepest—which is the pure unity of the Spirit—the Trinity shines forth out of the fullness of Advaita itself, and that fullness is Saccidānanda. He conceives of Saccidānanda—Being *(sat)*, Consciousness *(cit)*, and Bliss *(ānanda)*—as essentially an adumbration of the experience of the Trinity, but he also seems to identify them.[79] I say "seems" because he experiences or intuits the Trinitarian mystery as deeper but wants to use the term *Saccidānanda* to represent this mystery of the Godhead as communion. How far he takes the equating of the two is unclear. This conception will be taken over by Bede Griffiths in his own contemplative theology, as we shall see in chapter 5, when we come to the heart of this book, and when we will have the opportunity to examine the difference between the approach of Abhishiktananda and that of Bede on this central issue.

In this historical movement to which Bede Griffiths belongs, Abhishiktananda is the most influential figure because he achieved a profound clarity (and obscurity) in his assimilation of *sannyāsa*, and in his understanding of how the two traditions relate on the deepest level, in the *guhā*, the "cave of the heart." As Vattakuzhy remarks: "He became a Hindu-Christian meeting point.... In him, the interior experience of *Advaita*, the Christian experience of the indwelling of God and the knowledge of Western philosophy and theology fused into a transcendent unity."[80] He showed that it was possible to have an authentic Christian *sannyāsa*, but he was himself a rare, perhaps new kind of spiritual figure, a genuine hybrid of two traditions, but a hybrid who opened up the two to each other in the depths of his own heart. He lived with the extreme tensions and paradoxes of his truly fascinating spiritual journey. It does not seem possible to understand him on a conceptual level only, for that misses the whole context of his own very deep *experience*.[81] He built the modern foundation of the movement with his own life, which was itself an eloquent witness to the future of not simply Christianity and Hinduism and their interaction, but of all faith systems that spring from an authentic contact with the Spirit.

BEDE GRIFFITHS (DAYANANDA)

All these figures who preceded Bede together influenced his adoption of *sannyāsa:* his assimilation of the Hindu mystical tradition, and his understanding of the issues involved in relating the two traditions, while attempting to develop an Indian Christian theology that in some sense is convergent with Hinduism as a cultural and philosophical matrix, and emergent from this synthetic situation. Since this work concerns Bede's thought and experience, I will limit myself in this section to a brief sketch of his life, work, and writings, for the remainder of the book will consider his thought and experience in considerable detail.

Bede Griffiths was born on December 17, 1906, in the village of Walton-on-Thames; he was the youngest of four children. He was related to the novelist Henry Fielding on his mother's side. Bede was brought up in the Church of England, for which he had a great love and respect. As a boy he was educated at Christ's Hospital, the so-called Blue-Coat school, which could boast Leigh Hunt, Coleridge, and Charles Lamb among its alumni. At school he read a great deal in all his spare moments.[82]

Bede always had a very deep love of nature, which owes its origin to a mystical illumination he had in the presence of and in relation to nature. During his last term at Christ's Hospital, he relates in his autobiography, he went for a walk as dusk was approaching, and he could hear the birds singing, only it was like the first time he had ever heard them sing. It seemed as if he had never noticed before. This experience really changed the course of his life because it awakened in him a sense of God's presence in nature, and is actually the beginning of his interest in the spiritual dimension of life. Bede describes the nature of his experience in idyllic terms:

> Now I was suddenly made aware of another world of beauty and mystery such as I had never imagined to exist, except in poetry.... I experienced an overwhelming emotion in the

presence of nature, especially at evening. It began to wear a kind of sacramental character for me. I approached it with a sense of almost religious awe, and in the hush which comes before sunset, I felt again the presence of an unfathomable mystery. The song of the birds, the shapes of the trees, the colors of the sunset, were so many signs of this presence, which seemed to be drawing me to itself.[83]

This experience was formative in his own quest for the Absolute. Thirty years later he realized that this Presence in the natural world is God.[84] This was an important experience for him, because it shook him out of his skepticism, and perhaps was the basis for his appreciation of the Cosmic Revelation and mystery. In chapter 4, I will explore his notion of this natural revelation, a significant element in his worldview, and the place it had in his contemplative theology.

In October 1925 he began his studies at Oxford, in Magdalen College, with a Classical Exhibition (a partial scholarship). There he befriended his brilliant tutor C. S. Lewis, who had been through a similar phase of romanticism in relation to nature.[85] Lewis later guided his study of philosophy through a regular correspondence, and through him Bede was led back to Christianity.[86] It was during this period that he began to read Eastern thought, particularly the Bhagavad Gita, the teachings of the Buddha, and the Tao Te Ching. And so began his long effort to relate the Eastern traditions to Christianity.[87]

Bede Griffiths formally entered the Catholic Church on Christmas Eve 1931 and about a month later was received into the monastic life at Prinknash Abbey. He was clothed as a novice in December 1933.[88] Then on March 9, 1940, he was ordained a priest.[89] The influence of his friends and his reading of the historian Christopher Dawson convinced him that he should do a serious study of the Asian religions, and so he began a systematic study of Indian and Chinese philosophy. Already, while still in England, he was beginning to see the possibility of a synthesis of sorts between the Vedanta and Christianity.[90] It was also during this period that he began to realize that if the Christian faith were ever to penetrate into the heart of the Orient it would "have to find a correspondingly Eastern form, in which the genius of the peoples of the East will be able to find expression."[91]

Bede stayed at Prinknash Abbey until 1947, at which time he was sent to St. Michael's Abbey, Farnborough, as prior. He left there in 1951 to become novice master of Pluscarden Priory in Elgin. In 1955 the opportunity to go to India presented itself, as he was invited by an Indian Benedictine monk to help establish a Benedictine community on the subcontinent. So he went out to India in 1955 and lived in a monastery near Bangalore for two years. It was during this period that he started to dialogue in depth with Hindus. But then in March 1958, he and Father Francis Mahieu, a Belgian Cistercian, founded Kurisumala Ashram in the mountains of Kerala in South India.[92] There they entered profoundly into the tradition of Indian *sannyāsa* along Christian lines but had a deep sensitivity to Hindu traditions.[93] Bede remained at Kurisumala for approximately ten years and then went to Saccidananda Ashram, where he became the superior and spiritual master in 1968, upon Abhishiktananda's departure for his hermitage in the Himalayas.

In his many years in India, Bede (also known as Dayananda, "Bliss or Joy of Compassion") had engaged in the study of the Sanskrit language and the sacred texts of the Hindu tradition. He had traveled widely, lecturing in India, Europe, America, and Australia. He also wrote and had published numerous books and well over a hundred articles. In all of his activities—including dialogue—he always tried to advance the new understanding of Catholicism's relationship with Hinduism, Buddhism, and other Asian traditions. Bede carried on a large correspondence with people all around the globe. It can be said with genuine insight that he was a truly universal man, yet while retaining his Christian identity; indeed, it was his Christian faith that was the essential focus of his life, the reference point in his attempts to relate the various traditions. These travels brought him to America in 1963, 1979, 1983, 1990, 1991, and 1992 and to Germany, Britain, and Australia as well. The last twenty years of his life saw Bede patiently guiding the growth of his community at Shantivanam, reaching out to people from all over the world, and engaged in numerous writing projects. A great turning point for his spiritual life occurred in early 1990 when he suffered a stroke that led to a major mystical experience, a process that lasted for months and one that he says awakened him to the Divine Feminine. Father Bede died on May 13, 1993, at Shantivanam after an illness brought on from two serious strokes.

Among his works are the following.[94] His autobiography, *The Golden String* (1954), has some important indications of his eventual direction, the seeds, if you will. *Christ in India* (1966) is important for the history it covers. *Vedanta and Christian Faith* (1973) is a serious attempt to relate the two traditions. *Return to the Center*, first published in Britain in 1976, is a more subtle work than *Vedanta and Christian Faith*. *The Marriage of East and West* (1982) is really his most mature work to that time. After this he wrote *The Cosmic Revelation* (1983), a reworking of his lectures at Conception Abbey, Missouri, in the summer of 1979. It is a fine introduction to the issues involved in relating the two traditions. *The Bhagavad Gita: A Christian Reading* provides a valuable tool in evaluating his understanding of the Hindu scriptures. In relation to the goal of a possible Christian Vedanta and Tantra, *Return to the Center, The Marriage of East and West,* and a number of his lectures are significant.

Bede Griffiths was the latest, most contemporary figure to come along in the Christian sannyasic movement. What essentially defines this evolutionary development in consciousness is its wholehearted commitment to the possibility of a creative and valid synthesis of some kind: a convergence, an inner encounter between Christianity in its ultimate meaning and Hinduism on the profoundest level. The encounter comes to relating the experience of Advaita/Saccidānanda and the mystical intuition of the Trinity, a preeminently experiential path. And *sannyāsa* is the way chosen to embrace that path and its pure realization.

In the next chapter, we will explore Bede Griffiths's epistemology and how it prepares the way for and leads into his metaphysics and his contemplative theology, which I will go into in some detail. This will allow us to see how his particular genius lay in his capacity for *synthesis*, his ability to grasp the implications of various insights from a number of movements, including the world religions, but in our focus here is the essential, ultimate intuition of the Hindu and Christian traditions. This is actually a consideration of his methodology, a methodology that is really a "theological epistemology." But his epistemology aimed at a higher form of knowing than the merely philosophical, hence its theological character. Yet it is not a theoretical kind of theology; it is intrinsically a product of contemplation. It is mystical theology, and the theological epistemology leads to an understanding of this experiential way. This is all part of Bede's contemplative theology. In chapter 3, I will pursue this discussion under three terms: *epistemology,* which will aim at this more ultimate way of knowing that is the heart of metaphysics, and this *metaphysics,* or perennial philosophy, is based on an ultimate experiential awareness and intuition, that which becomes the generating source of Bede's contemplative or *spiritual theology.*

In summary, I wish to stress that Bede Griffiths was very much a product of the history of what I have called *sannyasic monasticism,* the term that identifies the evolution and formation of a Christian *sannyāsa* in India. He is squarely in that tradition and a very significant figure in its continued growth and development from Abhishiktananda and before: that is, the Kurisumala period, up to and including the recent time in which he was the dominant spiritual leader of the Christian sannyasic movement, one of the most extraordinary breakthroughs in history.

3

Epistemology, Metaphysics, and Contemplative Theology

THE ULTIMATE CONCERN of this chapter is Bede Griffiths's contemplative theology and how it relates and contributes to the reconciliation of the two traditions of Christianity and Hinduism. Before we can get to that point, however, we must first pass through his epistemological considerations, which are quite general, relating as they do to the role of reason in what is regarded as knowledge and the cultural perspective or mentality derived from a certain narrow use of reason. Bede's critique of reason and the old science will be presented briefly. Then will follow a section on the *new science:* the new physics, biology, psychology, and other sciences as contributing, in Bede's vision, to a rediscovery of the cosmic unity behind all things and lending itself to the intuition of the mystics. This will clear the way for a discussion of Bede's metaphysical tradition, which is a variant of the *philosophia perennis* as articulated by Seyyed Hossein Nasr in his book *Knowledge and the Sacred.*[1] The perennial philosophy is the universal metaphysics, a metaphysics that expresses the intuitions, experiences, and insights of Bede Griffiths, at least in their general outlines.

This metaphysical tradition is called upon to support and invigorate Bede's contemplative theology, a theology that is rooted in spirituality, in mystical experience; reflection on this experience and on the sacred texts of Hinduism and Christianity as they inform the contemplative heights and depths. Contemplative theology is also a spiritual theology that includes both asceticism and mysticism, and it is a monastic theology as well. I will explore this dimension of his method, using Jean Leclercq's *The Love of Learning and the Desire for God*[2] as a focus of comparison. With this chapter, the background to Bede Griffiths's efforts at relating and reconciling the two traditions will be complete, and we will be in a position to proceed to a presentation of his vision and a critical evaluation of it.

CRITIQUE OF RATIONALISM AND THE OLD SCIENCE

Rather early on in his life Bede had experienced a subtler form of knowing than was conventionally available through reason, common sense, and science. It began with his encounter with the mystery behind and surrounding nature. The discovery of this mystery, this other world of meaning, was crucial for Bede's intellectual and spiritual development. It was, in a sense, the first indication for him of the inadequacy of reason and science in terms of the larger picture of life and its meaning and purpose as evidenced in nature and being. I say "in a sense" because in his early life this sense of inadequacy was not fully articulated. Clearly, though, the seeds of dissatisfaction with conventional knowing were there. This experience of nature was part of his journey to God and ultimate enlightenment. He expresses his fascination with the natural world and its secrets in this way: "I liked the solitude and the silence of the woods and the hills. I felt there the sense of a Presence, something undefined and mysterious, which was reflected in the faces of the flowers and the movements of birds and animals, in the sunlight falling through the leaves and in the sound of running water, in the wind blowing on the hills and the wide expanse of earth and sky."[3]

This experience, which was a constant theme in his studies of the poets and philosophers, in the literature and theology he was exposed to, was religious for him, and it showed him that there was indeed more to existence than he had thought, or was led to believe by his own somewhat skeptical bent of mind and independent nature, the prized possessions of a young English intellectual who was in temperament affected by the spirit of the Enlightenment. His experience of the Divine in nature was the cornerstone of all his subsequent experience and thought, and only later did he come to comprehend its significance: "Always it has been understood that our life in this world, as Keats said, is a 'perpetual allegory'; everything has meaning only in reference to something beyond.... We only begin to awake when we realise that the material world, the world of space and time, as it appears to our senses, is nothing but a sign and a symbol of a mystery which infinitely transcends it."[4]

It is precisely this sense of nature, being, and life as having a symbolic meaning, of being *theophanic* in function in their deepest reality, that has been virtually lost in the West, where a limited notion of reason and science has dominated culture and life. The West has no awareness of the sacredness of nature and the human, for science has demolished every trace of it, "so that Western man finds himself in a universe in which both man and nature have been deprived of any ultimate meaning."[5] This emphasis on reason and science over intuition, imagination, and spiritual art has resulted in an imbalance, a terrible lack of equilibrium in Western civilization, according to Father Bede.[6] And this imbalance is further characterized by a pervasive experience of alienation, an estrangement of human beings from God, nature, and themselves. Reason has broken the original sense of unity that we once knew. Rational consciousness—as Bede saw it—is a divided consciousness. It is the source of our alienation. Bede laments: "Never before has man felt so isolated, alone in a vast, impersonal universe obeying mechanical laws, shut up in his own individual consciousness divided both from nature and from God."[7]

"Rationalism," as Bede employed the term in his lectures,[8] connotes this alienating kind of reason stemming from the Renaissance and fixed with Descartes and his dualistic doctrine, his bifurcating universe. Bede held that there has been a steady disintegration from the fourteenth century onward because of the dominance of rational consciousness. It is almost exclusively a mental or cerebral consciousness, which is also highly analytical. The type of consciousness that is limited to the mental sphere of experience is this "rationalism," and in his view it was always dualistic, for dualism is the mark of rational consciousness in the extreme.[9] Dualism is one of the reasons why people experience this dreadful alienation from themselves and the world. If mind and world are separated, as Descartes assumed, then it is difficult to see how we can feel at home in such a reality. Dualism has even colored our sense of the body, and this in such a way that more attention is given to the mind, the rational compact, than to the body. Dualism has thus done enormous harm to our self-understanding and has put us on the road to destruction in terms of technology. But Bede felt that dualism and the notion of the universe as an extended substance outside the mind is an illusion. This is what *māyā* is, the principle of illusion in Indian philosophy.[10]

But science, the "old" science that has held sway over culture for generations, is also alienating. It is wedded to the same "rationalism" as its basis of justification. Scientific knowledge, in Bede's opinion, can greatly increase our efficiency through its application to technology, and can even make our practical knowledge more precise, and yet "it alienates man from nature and creates an artificial world."[11] It brings into being a world far removed from the ultimate concerns of humanity and the natural rhythms of human existence, a world that insulates us from the secrets of nature and being.

The old science is alienating for other reasons as well. Not only is it removed from actual, existential reality in the life environment that it makes possible, but it is removed in its very language. This is an epistemological point. Scientific language is steeped in abstraction and an unreal world. Bede put it this way: "Scientific language, above all in its most typical form of mathematics, is the most abstract and unreal language that is, furthest from the total concrete reality."[12] Science abstracts certain aspects of reality and generalizes about the whole; this is what its world is, what constitutes its approach to knowing. It only deals with those aspects that are amenable to measurement in time and space.[13] And it leaves behind all that does not conform to its way of knowing reality. In doing so, science misses other dimensions of experience that are nearer to the ultimate mystery than the method that it follows. The poet and the mystic are closer to the totality of vision that the scientist aspires to achieve. Bede elaborated: "The poet is nearer to a vision of the whole, the world begins to be transfigured in him, but it is only the mystic who is present at the final transfiguration, who catches a glimpse of the world transfigured in the divine light."[14]

Long before the advent of modern scientific methodology, the ancients and medievals had achieved a systematic understanding of reality, had penetrated the secrets of nature by grasping its symbolic, revelational, or sacramental character. Nature opened itself up to their gaze. We have to recapture that consciousness of the unity of being and life that we once knew. This is the way to a higher understanding of the mystery of existence. Primitive humanity had this knowledge, this experience, and expressed it in terms of myth.[15] I will take this point up in the next chapter. Epistemologically speaking, in Bede's view, the approach of the West has prevented us from coming to know ourselves and the cosmic order better; it has blocked us from an access to the Divine Reality, which comes through intuitive knowing.

Bede's earlier experiences of the Divine Presence in nature and his later mystical intuitions convinced him that the way of reason, and more specifically of science, is a lesser way of knowledge, and that very little of ultimate value is known in this way because of the limited way in which it regards reality. He was critical of reason and the old science primarily because they are not equipped to allow us to see the larger picture of things or to give us access to metaphysical and mystical truth. Reason and science must serve wisdom and the quest for Ultimate Reality. Bede expressed it in this way: "The discursive reason which seeks to dominate the world and imprisons man in the narrow world of the conscious mind must be dethroned, and must acknowledge its dependence on the transcendent Mystery, which is beyond the rational consciousness."[16]

If reason and science are cast into a new and creative role as servants of contemplative wisdom, then there can be a "marriage" between intuitive wisdom and scientific reason. Bede maintained that this is one of the greatest necessities of the future, if we are to survive and progress.[17] Reason, which Bede regarded as the active intellect, has to be united with the intuitive mind, which is the reflective knowledge of the self, in order for a positive change to occur. When this happens, reason itself then becomes intuitive.[18] This marriage of reason to intuition does not mean the abandonment of the positive values of reason and science, of systematic organization of thought and logic, but their integration in a higher matrix of value. In such a marriage, reason surrenders itself to the more profound values and intuitions of the Spirit.[19] The capacity of reason is greatly expanded, and the human is once again given access to the Ultimate Reality of the Divine Life. As we shall see, the very weight of modern science's discoveries have pointed in the direction of a larger view of things, of a metaphysical and mystical view that undergirds all reality, life, truth, and thought. Thus, modern science, the "new" science, is aiding the process of growth, if not by reform in its method, at least by dint of its own investigations into the structure of the cosmos, the living organism, and the human psyche.

THE NEW SCIENCE

The "new" science is a set of radically novel approaches to old problems: the nature and structure of the universe (physics, mathematics, and cosmology), the formal causes of organic structure in biology, and the evolution of the human from a physical level to a spiritual one, into a divine or "deified" being, the aim of some advocates of the new psychology. So, actually, the new science is an attempt to find a more subtle understanding of reality in general, and the interaction of the human reality and the cosmos in particular. It is not only the discoveries and approaches that are new, but the spirit of openness in theoretical considerations that border on metaphysics and mysticism. There is no longer a fear of trespassing the boundary between science and the metaphysico-mystical realm of experience. Furthermore, it is in this element of the new science in Bede Griffiths's thought that we can discern his particular genius for synthesis, for seeing the long-range implications of scientific developments, and developments in society, culture, religion, and philosophy. He, more than any other contemplative theologian, showed an enthusiastic interest in the various currents of contemporary thought.

On an epistemological level, the first or primary fact of the "new" science is that of a shift in models, a shift from an atomistic to an *organic* one. Bede felt that this had momentous implications across the board. For one thing, there is a rediscovery of the cosmic unity occurring in science on various levels, and an appreciation of the bonds that unite religion and science. The old antagonism is becoming a thing of the past as scientists make discoveries and see new relations that tend to confirm the ancient metaphysical and mystical wisdom systems. This is immensely significant for the future. In an important lecture given at Tantur in Jerusalem on May 3, 1984, Father Bede made this assessment of the new science: "The sciences which for centuries have been opposed to religion and spirituality are discovering links with it.... The scientists are beginning to see the cosmic whole, as the Vedic revelation sees it, as a physical, psychological and spiritual reality, which forms an interrelated and interdependent whole."[20]

It is the cosmic unity that is emerging again into human consciousness, though doubted and denied by some for centuries. In our time, advanced scientists in most fields are conceiving the universe as an *organic* whole,[21] a system of totality in which all the parts are interrelated. This is the new vision of science. The new science is profoundly aware of the cosmic unity not simply as an ideal in theory but as an actuality. It has a sense of the totality, of knowledge and being. Moreover, it seeks a larger vision of reality and truth, one that is complementary to and supportive of mysticism or contemplative experience, not because of a newfound tolerance that allows science to condescend to it, but because science is itself discovering the essential truth of mystical knowledge and metaphysical wisdom. And so, the new science is becoming a bridge between conventional (or commonsensical) knowledge and contemplative spirituality. Here I would like to present some examples of the new science that Bede often drew upon, especially in his lectures.

Bede usually began with Einstein and his theory of relativity and with quantum mechanics, in order to show the breakdown and collapse of the old Newtonian model of the universe as composed of discrete particles of matter, or atoms in motion, following mechanical laws, an objective system in a universe independent of consciousness. As noted above, such a universe is an illusion; it is not, nor can it be, independent of mind. Einstein demonstrated, and his theory predicts, that the space-time continuum is dependent on the observer's position at any given moment, and that both time and space are part of an integrated whole that is related in consciousness. This discovery was a terrible blow to Newtonian physics. The final blow to this system of physics came with the advent of quantum theory, for it was shown that the atom is not solid or absolute, is not the basic building block of the cosmos. The atom could be split, and the behavior of the subatomic particles simply does not fit into the Newtonian scheme. This was the real turning point, as Bede understood it, "the decisive moment when the mechanistic model of the universe finally broke down and scientists were forced to conceive of matter not as an extended substance, but as a 'field of energies.' In this view, the universe has been described as 'a complicated web of interdependent relations.'"[22]

Matter is a form of energy, and all energy is interrelated in the totality; the universe is one integrated system. In other words, there *is* a cosmic unity behind reality; reality itself is one.[23] In his knowledge of the new physics, Bede relied heavily on Fritjof Capra and the innovative work of the physicist David Bohm. Both of these figures profoundly influenced Bede's thinking about science, especially Capra. Capra sums up the discovery of the new physics: "Quantum theory has abolished the notion of fundamentally separated objects, has introduced the concept of the participator to replace that of the observer, and may even find it necessary to include the human consciousness in its description of the world. It has come to see the universe as an interconnected web of physical and mental relations whose parts are only defined through their connections to the whole."[24]

Bede agreed with Capra's assessment and drew two essential insights from it. The first is that the cosmos is conceived as an interdependent organic whole, a totality. It is not a machine but an *organism,* and the whole cannot be comprehended by analyzing any of its parts, even all of them; for the parts are intelligible only in relation to the whole, from which they have their being, and in relation to one another.[25] Second, Bede felt that this view entails that the universe be seen as "a dynamic system subject to perpetual change," which allows the organism of the universe to continually grow, as all organisms do, by a continual change of its elements.[26] He regarded this discovery as a *recovery* of the ancient view of the cosmic unity, the cosmic whole of which we are a part.[27] So here is an example of the new science rediscovering something of the ancient spiritual wisdom.

But Bede Griffiths was convinced that David Bohm's vision of the universe was the deepest view yet into its structure. This is the view of the *implicate order,* which is unfolded or *explicated* over the full range of the universe's development. The hologram is a good metaphor or analogy of how the explicated reality of the implicate order is present in every part: the whole is present in every part and vice versa. Bede detailed this:

> In his [Bohm's] understanding the whole universe is originally an integrated whole, which is "folded up," as it were, and what we see is the explication, the "unfolding" of this whole. This means that the whole is present in every part. This has been illustrated by the analogy of a hologram. A hologram is a lensless photo, which shows simply waves of light, but when a laser beam is focused on the photo a three dimensional figure appears and this figure is present in every part of the photo. This suggests that the universe is a field of energies, of waves of light which presents itself to our senses as a three dimensional world. What we see is not the reality itself but the reality reflected through our senses and the instruments which we use to further the senses, interpreted by the observing mind.[28]

The hologram is a model of the nature and structure of the universe. It reflects the ultimate principle of how the cosmos develops, but also the principle of the microcosmic-macrocosmic relationship, as suggested by the hologram itself. Bohm was certain that the hologram, the phenomenon it illustrates, has significant implications for mathematics and cosmology. He maintained that it requires a different way of looking at the universe and indicates a different structure at work. For the hologram is symbolic of the nature of the universe itself and reveals a basic law at work, which contemporary physics must take into account. It is also consistent with the notion of the origin of the cosmos in the so-called Big Bang cosmology. Bohm explained the importance he perceives in the hologram analogy:

> What is being suggested here is that the consideration of the difference between lens and hologram can play a significant part in the perception of a new order that is relevant for physical law. As Galileo noted the distinction between a viscous medium and a vacuum and saw that physical law should refer primarily to the order of motion of an object in a vacuum, so we might now note the distinction between a lens and a hologram and consider the possibility that physical law should refer primarily to an order of undivided wholeness of the content of a description similar to that indicated by the hologram rather than to an order of analysis of such content into separate parts indicated by a lens.[29]

The hologram itself shows us something of the cosmic situation. It reveals the relationship between the parts and the whole, and how the whole is reflected in each part because the parts are one with the whole and have been *explicated,* or unfolded, from the same implicit or *implicate* order, the ground of later manifestation in space-time. So there is here a confirmation of sorts of the ancient and medieval notion of the microcosm-macrocosm relation, and to some extent also the *rationes seminales* of Augustine, the seminal reasons being part of the *implicate* order, the principles, natures, and essences of things bound up with the original unity from which they spring. Bede found Bohm's presentation most persuasive.

The discoveries of modern physics, as illustrated by Capra and Bohm, also indicate that mind or consciousness is part of the whole and the process of its unfolding in the spatial-temporal realm, the realm of becoming. The cosmos is quite unintelligible apart from consciousness. The knower is always engaged with the observed or the known. The cosmos cannot exist of itself apart from consciousness, as Bede saw it. Bede remarks: "We ourselves are a part of the field of energies which we observe; energy and consciousness, mind and matter, are interdependent. This leads to a recognition of the limits of science. Science can never give knowledge of reality in itself. It gives knowledge of reality as reflected in human consciousness, that is, through the senses and the reason."[30]

A further development in the new science, specifically in the field of biology, Father Bede found in the seminal work of the English biologist Rupert Sheldrake. This work is articulated precisely and exhaustively in his book *A New Science of Life*.[31] Sheldrake was a personal friend of Bede's and in fact wrote this book at Shantivanam. Bede held that Sheldrake reintroduced formative causes into biology, which he calls *morphogenetic fields* and which are responsible for structuring energy, since energy as such is without form.[32] Bede echoes Sheldrake when he says: "The attempt to explain life in terms of physics and chemistry is totally impossible."[33]

These morphogenetic fields, as formative causes, bring to birth a *morphé* (the Greek word for "form"), which then gives structure to the formless energy. Bede felt that the implication of Sheldrake's discovery is that he has shown that formative causes have to exist because the universe cannot at all be explained by chance and necessity, as some have tried to do in the past. Form gives order, intelligibility, and purpose to the universe, what in fact we discover in its actuality. And it gives this meaning and purpose to the cosmos on all levels.[34]

The formative causes of Sheldrake impose an order externally in terms of space and internally in terms of structure. They are responsible for the structure of all entities that have a recognizable form, or *morphé*. By having a structure or formal organizing principle inherent to them, entities become morphic units. Sheldrake describes his notion of *formative causation:* "a further type of causation is responsible for the forms of all material morphic units (sub-atomic particles, atoms, molecules, crystals, quasi-crystalline aggregates, organelles, cells, tissues, organs, organisms). Form, in the sense used here, includes not only the shape of the outer surface of the morphic unit but also its internal structure."[35]

These formative causes are akin to Aristotle's causes, the formal and final ones. And so, through the advance of scientific research, discoveries are made that corroborate the ancient wisdom on many levels. An important implication of all these discoveries, according to Bede, was that the Cartesian distinction between matter and consciousness has broken down. We are, as he said, *conscious organisms.* We cannot separate matter from consciousness, for consciousness pervades all.[36]

Another crucial area of the new science is that of psychology, and in particular, the work of Ken Wilber. Bede was quite impressed with this man's achievement and often introduced his insights in lectures. The new psychology, as represented by Ken Wilber, is open to the spiritual wisdom and vast range of psychological experience found in Eastern mysticism. In his major studies[37] Wilber has tried to bridge the gap between clinical psychology, which is based on the study and treatment of pathological states of consciousness, and the Eastern doctrines that study and enter into the higher, more subtle planes of consciousness. This, as Bede saw it, "opens the way to a comprehensive vision of the universe as an integrated whole."[38] The universe then becomes understood as the place of the evolution of consciousness[39] from body to mental consciousness, and from mental consciousness into spiritual consciousness, where we transcend the body and the mind (the psyche), and open up into the infinite and eternal Reality. At that point, we are united with the whole, with the totality, the transcendent consciousness that comprehends the totality. This is really the link with Eastern mysticism.[40]

The new science is assuredly more dynamic and responsive to

aspects of experience than its predecessors would have dared to take seriously. It has broken the bonds of the old science by encountering the metaphysical and mystical reality. We might ask, however, with what kind of mysticism is the new science compatible? What form of mysticism is it? Capra provided us with a rather clear answer. After characterizing the significance of the new physics and its important consequences, he links these discoveries with Eastern metaphysics and mystical wisdom by way of a citation from Lama Anagarika Govinda's book *Foundations of Tibetan Mysticism* and sees a similarity between the worldview described in the new physics, atomic physics, and Tibetan Buddhism. The world that Lama Govinda characterizes sounds very much like that of atomic physics. Capra quotes the lama: "The Buddhist does not believe in an independent or separately existing external world, into whose dynamic forces he could insert himself. The external world and his inner world are for him only two sides of the same fabric, in which the threads of all forces and of all events, of all forms of consciousness and of their objects, are woven into an inseparable net of endless, mutually conditioned relations."[41]

Capra was obviously at home with Eastern mysticism and perhaps knew little of other mystical traditions. For if he did, he would probably also have found them compatible with the new physics. The *typos* of mystical consciousness that Capra followed is definitely in the tradition of the impersonal ultimate reality. He did not seem to look beyond the East in his search for parallels between atomic physics and mysticism—the subtitle of his book, after all, is *An Exploration of the Parallels between Modern Physics and Eastern Mysticism*. Father Bede himself was aware of this deficiency and sought in numerous lectures to show how Christianity and its mystical tradition fit in, primarily through the intuitions of Trinity, Godhead, and the Incarnation. He labored these points in most of his books, and we will be studying that material in chapter 5.

What made the new science significant for Bede is that it continues to discover other states of consciousness beyond the merely rational and analytical level. It is finally realizing that other modes of knowing are possible and do exist. There is a marriage between intuition and reason taking place, or rather, a recognition of the role and value of the intuitive mode of knowing. Capra himself admitted this in relation to Eastern mystics, but it has validity universally. Capra comments: "I see science and mysticism as two complementary manifestations of the human mind; of its rational and intuitive faculties. The modern physicist experiences the world through an extreme specialization of the rational mind; the mystic through an extreme specialization of the intuitive mind."[42]

This understanding was also true of Bohm, Sheldrake, Wilber, and others. It should be noted also that their visions of reality are compatible with Western as well as Eastern mysticism, even though Wilber himself has a penchant for the East and the formless Void, for the ultimacy of consciousness over Godhead.[43]

Bede followed the development of contemporary instances of the new science with great interest and did years of study of this fascinating area. His gift for synthesis was alert to the possibility of a marriage between rational science and intuitive wisdom, as we saw above. He was one of the first Christian thinkers to see the potential of the new science to break fresh ground epistemologically, which would permit a reconciliation between science and religion, and an active cooperation between them. He saw that through the recent scientific discoveries of the new physics, biology, psychology, and so on, we are finding our way back into a knowledge of the ancient wisdom or the perennial philosophy.[44] It is to this, as his metaphysical tradition, that I wish now to turn, before going on to a consideration of his contemplative theology.

METAPHYSICS

Bede Griffiths had never systematically written about or developed his metaphysical position, but all his works depend on an unspoken metaphysics. In his Tantur lecture he explicitly identified himself with the *philosophia perennis* and mentioned that the new science is aiding the rediscovery of the ancient wisdom that comes under this title, not the modern term popularized by Leibniz. Bede says that the *"perennial philosophy* [is] the ancient wisdom of Hinduism, Buddhism, Taoism, Sufism and traditional Christianity, [that] it had a unified vision of the cosmos as an organic whole pervaded by consciousness, in which man had a central place as the 'eye' of the universe."[45]

As the "eye" of the cosmos the human being has a faculty of intuition that puts us into contact with the Divine Reality in a direct way. It is a higher form of knowing than is available to reason, and is in fact a kind of illumination in and through the Divine Intelligence. Since I had no texts written or spoken by Bede Griffiths that elaborated the nature of his metaphysical view, I asked him to reflect on the question and provide me with his position. He wrote back a rather lengthy reply in which he clearly stated his view, one that is articulated so well by Seyyed Hossein Nasr. Bede states emphatically:

> I accept almost in its entirety the metaphysical doctrine of Hossein Nasr in his *Knowledge and the Sacred.* It is based on the view that there is in man a capacity of intellectual intuition. That is a capacity to know ultimate reality not by means of images or concepts but by direct intuition. This is a *capacity*, that is, a potentiality, but for this potency to be actuated there is required a movement of faith and of revelation. In his view the different religious traditions all give access through faith to this ultimate knowledge, which is an illumination of the human mind by the divine Truth itself.[46]

Bede thus gave us here the substance of his metaphysical doctrine, which is the same as that of Nasr. By the emphasis placed on a direct kind of illuminative intuition as a way of knowing

Ultimate Reality, Bede presented us with the very epitome of his metaphysics, which is found to be based on a mystical illumination. Hence the basis of his metaphysical approach is a spiritual epistemology. His intuitive epistemological doctrine rests on the *philosophia perennis,* which also rests on this intuitive experience of the Divine Reality. They mutually reinforce each other. In order to highlight some of the characteristic elements of this metaphysical approach, I am going to introduce Nasr's formulation here. This will grant us a better understanding of Bede's metaphysical foundation, which in turn will aid us in understanding his contemplative theology.

The perennial philosophy is also the *scientia sacra,* or sacred knowledge, which is the heart of revelation that defines or encompasses tradition. It is the universal metaphysics, the primordial wisdom, the original revelation. The source of this knowledge is twofold: revelation and intellectual intuition, which is an illumination of the mind and heart, an illumination that gives rise to an immediate experiential knowledge that is *sapience,* a "tasting" knowledge. It is a sapiential knowing of Ultimate Reality, the Absolute.[47] Father Bede concurred in this view, and remarks: "Truth itself can only be known by a pure intuition which is beyond all language."[48]

Scientia sacra is a pure gift from the Divine Intellect; it is not produced by a process of reasoning from experience, which then would approximate the vividness and reality of the inspired state; it *is* the inspired state itself. One has sacred knowledge directly from the Source, from God's Intellect. Nasr is very clear on this point. He asserts:

> *Scientia sacra* is not the fruit of human intelligence speculating upon or reasoning about the content of an inspiration or a spiritual experience which itself is not of an intellectual character. Rather, what is received through inspiration is itself of an intellectual nature; it is sacred knowledge. The human intelligence which perceives this message and receives this

truth does not impose upon it the intellectual nature or content of a spiritual experience of a sapiential character. The knowledge contained in such an experience which is the (Divine) Intellect, the source of all sapience and the bestower of all principal (Metaphysical) knowledge....[49]

This means that the human intellect plays only a passive role, and that the knowledge obtained from inspiration and spiritual experience is untainted by human reason and the errors and fragmented notions to which such a reason is heir. This is a mystical way of knowing, a knowing in and through the Divine Intellect. It is totally opposed to the doctrine of abstraction of the Scholastics, popularized by Saint Thomas and taken in large measure from Aristotle. Bede Griffiths agreed with this assessment and said so in the letter quoted above. Furthermore, he believed that Saint Thomas went astray on this point because he followed Aristotle too closely.[50]

Scientia sacra is metaphysics, and this term must be "understood correctly as the ultimate science of the Real,"[51] says Nasr. And notice that he does not define metaphysics in terms of Being. He regards Being as the object of ontology, since Ultimate Reality is even beyond Being, and ontology is a branch of metaphysics.[52] When Nasr finally comes to present a more precise definition of metaphysics—the *philosophia perennis*—as the science of the Real, he states that it is "the knowledge by means of which man is able to distinguish between the Real and the illusory and to know things in their essence or as they are, which means ultimately to know them *in divinis.*"[53] This is to know God, to have a participation in His own Knowledge of Himself. This "consciousness ... is the goal of the path of knowledge and the essence of *scientia sacra.*"[54] Thus, *scientia sacra,* the perennial philosophy, ultimately issues from mystical experience, or mystical illumination. Furthermore, the Absolute is the Supreme Good, the Infinite One who manifests or generates the created order out of goodness, and this is done through the Logos, the source of the archetypes, essences, forms, cosmic perfections, the Word through whom all things came into being.[55] Moreover, to know this God who is "Absolute Necessity and Infinite Possibility,"[56] faith is crucial, since it activates the intellectual intuition without which such knowledge would be quite impossible. Nasr says it is essential to keep in mind "the important metaphysical principle that integral intelligence is never divorced from faith but that, on the contrary, faith is necessary in the actualization of the possibilities of intellection within the cadre of revelation."[57]

We saw above in the quotation from Bede's letter that he was in substantial agreement with Nasr's formulation of the universal metaphysics. He also agreed with the requirement of faith as the activating element of intellectual intuition. It is like Augustine's dictum, echoed later by Anselm: *credo ut intelligam* (I believe in order that I may understand). Bede saw this intuitive knowledge as an integral knowledge, one which embraces the whole being of the person.[58]

This intuitive capacity of the intellect, which gives us access to Ultimate Reality, is like "a little spark," a divine ray of light that shines in the depths of the soul, in the "cave of the heart," the abyss of interiority, where we are touched by God's mystery. This ray of light, this divine spark, according to Bede, "awakens us to this transcendent mystery"[59] that is at the center of our own being and of all reality. The fullness of *scientia sacra* is mystical realization, which is present in seed form in intuition itself, for "the ultimate mystical experience is only the flower of that intuition which was hidden in the root of matter."[60] We have seen how the heart of Bede's epistemology and his metaphysics involves intuition, and that this intuitive knowledge is itself an illumination in the divine mysteries. Now we must turn to consider his contemplative theology, which simply brings together all his concerns around the necessity for spiritual life and a knowledge (contemplative wisdom) that flows out of such a life. It is in fact his contemplative theology that is the medium of his attempt to relate Christianity and Hinduism.

CONTEMPLATIVE THEOLOGY

Bede Griffiths's contemplative theology was grounded on a very deep faith, an enlightened faith that is a form of illumination, the *photismos* of the Greek tradition. His faith was alert, awakened to the mystery.[61] His theological reflection, his writing and lecturing, seemed to be the results of his creative faith illumined by the graces of contemplation. His creative efforts grew out of a need to bring theology back to its roots in experience: in life and in mystical consciousness. Bede's contemplative theology is a mystical theology, and he emphasized the necessity for this kind of theology today:

> Many of us think today that Christian theology has to become a mystical theology once again. Henri de Lubac, a great friend of one of the founders of our ashram, Jules Monchanin, once wrote to him, "Your task is to rethink everything in terms of theology, and theology in terms of mysticism." Many feel today that that is what the Church needs. Christian theology has become a scientific, philosophical, theological system, but it has lost that dimension of contemplative wisdom which St. Thomas Aquinas and Augustine and all the Fathers had.[62]

It is this dimension of contemplative wisdom that characterized the essence of Bede's theological approach. His theology was experientially based; it was always presented as the fruit of a deep penetration into God's being and actuality, and God's indwelling in us. This was the ideal and the reality as Bede communicated it in his various efforts at verbalization and sharing. His contemplative theology seemed to be the creative result of his own mystical prayer, or meditation and realization. It flowed out of contemplative awareness and illumination, which evolved from his practice of meditation, mystical experience, and reflection.

Bede's contemplative theology was also a *spiritual theology* in Jordan Aumann's sense of the term.[63] Aumann uses the term to include both ascetical and mystical theology as part of the same system of one's ascent to God and the process of spiritual perfection.[64] I employ the term interchangeably with *contemplative theology* because I think it is more accurate and precise to consider asceticism and mysticism together, for they are part of the same system of Father Bede's experience. The ascetical is the praxis, while the mystical is the experiential content, the realization. This praxis, the ascetical discipline, is called in Sanskrit *tapas,* or austerity, and *sādhanā,* the spiritual practices or exercises followed in order to achieve enlightenment. Both terms appear to be equivalent in meaning to what we have come to understand by asceticism in the Christian tradition and so can be employed in contemplative theology in the Indian context. But unlike Aumann's treatment of spiritual theology, which is highly academic, speculative, and systematic, Bede's contemplative theology, his spiritual theology, is practical, personal, and nonspeculative but reflective, experiential, existential, and synthetic. I will return to these elements at the end of this section. Suffice it to say in the meantime that Bede's spiritual theology was oriented toward mystical realization.

His ascetical practices, his *sādhanā,* involved *tapas,* chanting, scripture reading or *lectio,* liturgy, and, most important, meditation, contemplative prayer, or what the Indian tradition calls *dhyāna.* This is an important term in that tradition, and I believe also in Indian Christian contemplative theology. It is a more precise term for what the Christian tradition signifies by the word *contemplation* or, more specifically, *contemplative prayer.* So I think the term is not only appropriate but useful as well. It was certainly part of Bede's vocabulary in his spiritual theology. It is this practice of *dhyāna* or meditation that leads to mystical illumination, to enlightenment, or *samādhi,* the final awakening that comes after death. This is the ultimate goal of *dhyāna* and is like the Beatific Vision, but of course it is not appropriate

to use the term interchangeably with "the Beatific Vision," because we are not certain if the states are essentially equivalent.
Basically, *dhyāna* aims at *advaita*, the experience of nonduality or
unity. I will be scrutinizing this term more closely in chapter 5.
Meditation aims at an experiential realization of the divine mystery within one's own being, in the *guhā*, or "cave of the heart."
Father Bede used this term to express the depths of interiority
where we meet God, the Ultimate Reality. I think it is the best,
since its poetic nature is clear, and it does express the deep reality
of God's inner presence to the person, in his or her "heart." It is
a metaphor akin to our own usage.

Father Bede's contemplative theology was based on this inner
experience, this interior awareness that is a secret knowledge,
a *gnosis* in the Greek sense, and *jñāna* in the Hindu sense. Bede
said that *jñāna* and *gnosis* are essentially expressing the same
experience and awareness, the same level of depth. Bede mentioned how the roots are the same: "The root *jna* is the same as
our English 'know' and the Greek 'gnosis.'"[65] *Jñāna* is spiritual
wisdom arising from experiential realization in meditation, or
illumination. It would seem to be an equivalent word for *contemplative wisdom*. The *jñānī* is the one who has achieved *jñāna*,
or is always achieving it. *Jñāna* is a kind of transcendent knowledge that comes to a person who is united with the Absolute,
with God.[66] It is the same as *gnosis*. Bede's spiritual theology was
grounded in *jñāna*, his own mystical wisdom.

This *jñāna*, or contemplative wisdom, that is the heart of his
spiritual theology is a knowledge of God's inner being; it is *brahmavidyā*, knowledge of Brahman, especially in the depths of the
soul. It is also *atmavidyā*, knowledge of the Self, the presence of
Brahman in the "cave of the heart." This knowledge of Brahman
and knowledge of Ātman gives us true self-knowledge, according
to Bede's understanding. "That is the supreme knowledge we all
seek."[67] *Brahmavidyā* and *atmavidyā* are profoundly experiential
and so are quite similar to union with God in the Christian mys-

tical tradition, at least in the way that these forms of spiritual knowledge are described in the Hindu tradition. They point to the same quality of depth that is achieved in the heights of contemplation. I think it can stand as a term for knowledge of God in contemplative theology. Of course, all these Sanskrit terms acquire new meanings within the context of a Christian's experience, and Bede was certainly aware of this fact. He was also aware that many terms are used rather loosely.

Contemplative, spiritual, or mystical theology is also an experience of the Godhead, the Nirguna Brahman (Brahman without attributes), the transcendent One beyond being and knowledge who is known in the darkness, like the Absolute in the system of the Pseudo-Dionysius. This is also the śūnyatā, or the Void in Buddhism.[68] Jñāna includes this experience of the Godhead. It is perhaps a useful term for Bede's contemplative theology, but it should be noted that the concept of the "Godhead" occasions confusion; it is very obscure in the Christian mystical tradition. Pseudo-Dionysius and Eckhart both speak of the Godhead, following the lead of Plotinus, who refers to the transcendent One, free of attributes, formless and ineffable. The notion of the Godhead is more elaborated in the Hindu tradition. Perhaps Hinduism via assimilation can teach our tradition the nuances of this very elusive dimension of mystical consciousness. At any rate, it is part of the contemplative tradition of both faiths and so should have a place in our theology.

Bede's contemplative theology was also the fruit of a knowledge by way of *connaturality*—a special knowledge that happens through love—for theistic mysticism is ultimately personal communion between God and the individual soul. There is no mediation by a concept, but a direct experience of the Divine Reality by way of a participation in it. Saint Thomas, quoting the Pseudo-Dionysius, says that a spiritual man comes to know divine things through connaturality by "suffering them."[69] Such a one is exposed to them from within the Divine Subjectivity and known in and through God's knowledge of Himself. God "does" the knowing for him. In other words, he knows through a pure intuition. Nor can he tell you how. Jacques Maritain says that mystical experience produces a connatural knowledge through love, a love that participates in Love Himself.[70] Bede's spiritual or contemplative theology suggests a profound understanding of mystical intuition, a knowledge by way of connaturality.

His contemplative thought/experience was also a monastic theology. We saw this emphasis in chapter 2, when considering *sannyāsa* as normative of his movement. *Sannyāsa* is a monastic institution. All of Bede's creative efforts at communicating his ideal and experience—the experience of India—were within the monastic context peculiar to India: the sannyasic vision of monasticism, but also—in his case—having a continuity with monastic theology as it has been pursued in Christian Europe. Let me mention some of its elements. The monastic theology of the Middle Ages, which is just as relevant today as then because it has perennial values crucial for the Church and for humankind, had a profound respect for mystery, God's Mystery and the mysteries of life and faith.[71] It was characterized by a "holy simplicity" that sought God single-mindedly rather than being preoccupied with disputes and questions. The ideal was "to seek God, not to discuss Him...."[72] Thus there was great value put on personal experience of and union with God, and this came to distinguish monastic from school theology. The experience of God "in the cloister is both the principle and the aim of the quest."[73] Contemplation, or spiritual *gnosis,* is the aim of monastic theology, the type of understanding for which the monks are striving, and *gnosis* is a mystically enlightened faith.[74] Monastic theology is eminently practical, for "what occupies them [monastic theologians] is less the mode according to which the mysteries are accomplished and made known to us, than their end, which is the loving union with the Lord in this life and in the hereafter."[75] Monastic theology is a spiritual theology. Leclercq sums up so eloquently the goal of this theology: "Their [the monks'] principal purpose is not to reveal the mysteries of God, to explicate them or derive from them any speculative conclusions, but to impregnate their whole lives with them and to order their entire existence to contemplation."[76] And then he goes on to say: "Monastic thought is less affected by the concerns of the moment: rather it is governed only by the enduring necessities of the search for God."[77]

Bede's contemplative theology is just as much a monastic theology, although with a different cultural and geographic context: India. It has the same characteristics of respect for the Mystery, simplicity as evidenced by its end, which is mystical contemplation, and the goal of union with Ultimate Reality, with God. It is more experientially oriented, which is discernible in its commitment to meditation, or *dhyāna*. The explicitly experiential element of his theology is ordered to an existential convergence between Christian and Hindu mysticism. His monastic *lectio*—one of the pillars of his contemplative theology—is considerably wider than European monastic theology was. We have seen above his interest in science. He had an equally keen interest in spirituality, comparative religion, philosophy, new age culture and literature, and ecology, not to mention politics. His meditative reading of scriptures drew primarily on Hindu and Christian texts. Even the aim of assimilation of Hindu contemplative values was different from the assimilation of classical culture by the monks. The monks sought to Christianize and subsequently to humanize this cultural complex, while Bede maintained that the need to introduce Eastern mysticism into Christian theology was governed by the necessity to discover a new way to "express the Christian faith in contemplative terms."[78] Furthermore, his contemplative theology served the larger purpose of the evolving Indian theology. Bede said of this latter theological enterprise: "We seek to express our Christian faith in the language of the Vedanta as the Greek Fathers expressed it in the language of Plato and Aristotle."[79]

Bede's contemplative theology arose out of his community experience in India, from a concrete situation, a human situation. His contemplative community was totally integrated with the culture in which it found itself in South India, and it reflected the life of the people there. This is how a contemplative theology comes to birth: a community existing in another culture, reflecting on that experience in the light of Christ and the scriptures of that tradition. Out of this grows contemplation and contemplative theology. A theology evolves as we relate the two traditions, Bede maintained. A monastic or contemplative theology can evolve as monks write commentaries on the scriptures of other traditions, relating them to Christ and to the Christian tradition. And these commentaries are themselves the fruit of *lectio divina*, deep meditative reading. This describes Bede's experience of the formation of his contemplative, spiritual, or monastic theology.[80]

The contemplative theology of Bede Griffiths was also integrative, taking into account the three levels of reality: the physical or material world, the sphere of the body; the psychological dimension, the realm of the soul or psyche; and the domain of the spiritual and of the human spirit. As should be clear, the three levels of reality also have their corresponding analogues in human nature, as we have a body, a soul (psyche), and a spirit. This was Bede's anthropology, and it corresponds somewhat to that of Saint Paul, who makes similar divisions. This is the doctrine of the "three worlds,"[81] and it is also a part of the perennial philosophy.

Again, Bede's spiritual or contemplative theology is (1) practical, (2) experiential, (3) existential, (4) reflective, and (5) synthetic. It is not, however, speculative in the pejorative sense of the term, nor is it systematic, although one may wish it were so at times. Like traditional monastic theology, Bede's theology is quite practical in goal and practice; it is based on spiritual discipline. Its aim is contemplative and dialogical; it seeks to express the essential value of life: union with Ultimate Reality, with God. It is a living theology; it flows out of praxis, particularly meditation. It is dialogical because it attempts to advance mutual understanding and cooperation between the traditions and, where possible, convergence. It is a theological vision nurtured by the springs of experiential awareness of God within, in nature, and in others. Its very heart is experiential, as it seeks always the sapiential, connatural knowledge of the Divine Mystery. And because it strives for a common meeting point in contemplative wisdom and experience—and perhaps achieves it to some degree—it is also existential. In a certain sense it can be called a theology of *existential convergence.* It is highly reflective, and self-reflective, as it tries to understand reality, the dialogical situation, the Indian culture and civilization. In the quality of its reflection it is capable of great metaphysical and mystical heights, of subtle nuances and sharp insights, but it is neither verbose nor tedious. It is, rather, compelling, inspiring, and challenging. Finally, Bede's contemplative theology is synthetic, and I believe this to be one of its marks of genius. It is able to bring together and see the implications of a large variety of currents of thought, experience, and culture. Always the circle gets wider as it finds room to accommodate fresh insights, discoveries, and faith systems.

The question can be asked whether or not Bede Griffiths's methodology was syncretist. His wide scope of thought and its variety would seem to indicate syncretism. He seemed to unite so many incompatible lines of thought—Christian theology, modern science, Indian mysticism, the perennial philosophy, and preoccupations with monasticism—without any real coordination. His approach appeared so loose and unsystematic that one wonders if it all really belongs together. I think that Bede's method was not syncretist but actually emphasized convergence. His method of convergence was based on an openness to and acceptance of truth in these various strands of thought and experience, an openness that permits an organic, natural assimilation of all that is of value in other traditions and that somehow enriches and illumines the Christian mystery without contradicting its essential meaning and value. His method of convergence presupposed unity behind the diversity of religious and cultural experience. And it is this unity that he sought to express in an expanded vision of the Christian faith.

In the next chapter Bede's method will be apparent in his notion of myth and the Cosmic Revelation, as these are found to link together the biblical and Hindu traditions, and it will be especially evident in chapter 5 when considering the essential convergence of the Christian and Hindu faiths in Trinity and Advaita/ Saccidānanda, and in chapter 6 when treating his notion of Christian *sannyāsa*. What emerges is a rather composite picture that yields greater intelligibility very much like a hologram.

PART TWO

The Possibility
of a Christian Vedanta

4

Bede's Theological Scheme, Myth, and the Cosmic Revelation

I n this chapter, I will present Bede Griffiths's theological "system" or scheme in its general outlines. It is important to note, however, that Bede was not a systematic thinker in the sense that a Karl Rahner, a Bernard Lonergan, or a von Balthasar was.[1] Rather, he was a highly intuitive thinker, but rational within this context. Bede was also quite evocative and could be very precise when necessary. After outlining his general theological scope, the elements of his framework in its Christian character, I will take up the issue and ideal of theology's task as he conceived it, following Monchanin and de Lubac: to rethink everything in terms of theology, and theology in terms of mysticism.[2] This is a crucial issue to consider because Bede's whole enterprise and creative effort presupposed the truth of this project, ideal, and statement. It was an underlying presupposition in all his writing, lecturing, and dialogical exchanges, and it is also a basic principle of the movement to which he belongs.[3]

Next I will deal with his notion of myth as symbolic or intuitive thought because myth is a first instance of convergence. For mythic consciousness was a significant preoccupation of his theological reflection and experience, and it is a bridge concept, whose purpose will become apparent as we proceed. Following the discussion of the mythic element of his thought, we will then be in a position to explore his insight of the Cosmic Revelation, another important element in his theological vision and one of the chief objects of myth. It is this revelation and covenant that establish a permanent *link* between the Christian faith and Hinduism, and among all faiths. Then we will find that the Vedic revelation is part of this primordial Cosmic Revelation. We will see how, and then ponder the nature of this revelational experience in Indian antiquity. These considerations will bear fruit for us in chapter 5 when they will culminate in a careful examination of Hinduism's ultimate mystical wisdom, which has come through this pristine revelational experience. I want to turn now to a brief outlining of Bede's theological structure, which should serve to orient us in his thought and permit us to see how in fact he was truly a Christian contemplative theologian of great subtlety and, one can say, of orthodoxy as well.

THEOLOGICAL SCHEME

From Bede Griffiths's writings, lectures (taped and otherwise), and personal correspondence, we can glean the essential theological themes that are part of the overarching structure of his thought and experience, his intuition, and his creative breakthroughs in the area of interreligious dialogue. It is also wise to realize at the outset that his theology, in its general terms, is the expression of his deeper, more experientially based contemplative thought, his contemplative theology. It is this experiential theology that was the focus of his efforts. His theological structure is itself rooted in tradition, but its elaboration and understanding are informed by his contemplation. Father Bede was not in Europe or America; he was in India and so must have sought to relate his faith and experience to the Indian context, which is contemplative and experiential. His audience was at once Indian and Western, and so he must have strived to communicate a spiritual vision that satisfied both audiences. His theological vision is thus in continuity with the Christian tradition in its European form, and in dialogue with the Indian tradition, particularly with Hinduism. It is this complex relationship that has to be remembered when attempting to understand his thought. Because he lived in India, in a situation that put him at the heart of the development of an Indian Christian culture, a culture that assimilated the Hindu ideal and practice, his theological experiments centered on ways to express the Christian faith in terms and categories understandable to the Hindu, the Buddhist, and the Jain as well as the Christian. But his scope is broader; it embraces the notion of complementarity, which becomes the horizon of his cross-cultural theology. In this notion, Bede conceives of the reconciliation of not only the Hindu and Christian traditions, but all of them, because the ultimate mystery is present and revealing itself in each tradition. Bede elaborates:

> The view which is gaining ground in theology today is that of complementarity. The one divine Mystery, which is beyond word and thought, reveals itself in different ways in each religious tradition. Each religion manifests the one Reality, the one Truth, under different symbols, a symbol being defined [as] a sign in which the reality is really present. In this sense it is true to say that Jesus Christ is a symbol of God. The human nature of Christ is a sign in which the divine reality, the ultimate truth, is personally present. Each religion has its own set of symbols, of ritual and doctrine and spiritual path, in which the one is revealed in different ways....[4]

At the same time, the theological development to which Bede Griffiths belongs has a long history in modern terms, especially since the time of Upadhyay when it began in earnest in the twentieth century. The point is, Bede did not write his theology in a vacuum, or in isolation from other figures preceding, following, and contemporary with him. He is part of a corporate effort, which in historical terms has just begun; it is a task that will consume centuries. In addition to the important figures in the Christian sannyasic movement—de Nobili, Upadhyay, Monchanin, Abhishiktananda, Francis Mahieu (Acharya), and others—there is a long line of theologians, philosophers, missiologists, and philologists who continue to contribute to the formation of an Indian Christian theology. The list includes people like S. Anand, C. M. Cherian, J. B. Chethimattam, P. De Letter, R. V. De Smet, M. Dhavamony, J. Dupuis, A. Gomes, X. Irudyaraj, J. Mattam, J. Neuner, R. Panikkar, C. B. Papali, V. P. Thomas, I. Yesudasan, and countless others.[5] Father Bede's own theological attempts always took this contemporary activity into account, and he was influenced on numerous issues by many of these and other writers. Again, it is a corporate enterprise, like all genuine tradition.

The central focus of his theology is of course his doctrine of God. This doctrine includes the obscure notion of the Godhead, obscure in the Christian tradition, but not in others, notably in Hinduism. Godhead and Trinity go together, but there is a real sense in which he associates the Godhead with the Father[6] rather than seeing it as off by itself as some of the mystics do.[7] His doctrine of God is explicitly and emphatically Trinitarian, a fact that is confirmed again and again in his books, articles, lectures, and letters, as well as in a number of personal conversations I had with him in different years. (I examine his view of the Trinity in chapter 5.) His notion of God is as a dynamic community of being, which is what the Trinity signifies, among other things. It is a personal Reality whose essence or essential nature is communion.[8] The Father is Source and Godhead; the Son is Logos and Divine Pattern, and the Holy Spirit is the goal and unifying principle of the divine nature. The Holy Spirit as spirit is the point of creation, as all things are evolving into spirit, or spirit is emerging from creation and consciousness, in which it was present from the beginning. It is in the Spirit that we meet God.[9]

Creation itself is another category of Bede's theology, and he had quite a lot to say about it. He explored its relationship to the Divine Reality and saw it as essentially in process toward completion in that spiritual transformation which first occurred at the Resurrection of Jesus. Creation is thus real for him. He did not regard the Hindu notion of the created world as either adequate or accurate as an explanation. He felt that the Hindu understanding of Creation devalued it and life, making them seem unreal. In Bede's vision, the whole cosmos is in transit toward Spirit.[10]

Creation is in need of redemption, along with the human being, and the Incarnation functions as the cosmic event that triggers this transformation of the human and everything into spiritual being, or spirit itself. Incarnation, creation, God, and humanity are all closely linked, but the Incarnation is the key to uniting them in the Spirit. The human being, as icon or image of God, as spirit, is the term of Creation, and the task of Redemption is essentially one of spiritual transformation. In his notion of humanity, Bede follows the Pauline doctrine of the person as a composite, a unity of body, soul, and spirit, which is consonant with the Hindu doctrine of the three worlds. Bede incorporated into his theological anthropology this notion that there are three levels of reality. The first two are the material cosmos of multiplicity and the psychological realm of psyche or soul, the place of the unconscious and the collective history of not only the cosmos but of every human life as well. The person is transformed at the end into spirit, the third realm, just as Christ's body and consciousness were transformed at the Resurrection and the Ascension. The entire universe is sharing in the spiritual transformation begun at the Resurrection, a cosmic event.[11] In a very real sense, in Bede's theological understanding, the Incarnation is the summit of the evolutionary process, unveiling the goal of the process as Spirit.

Bede was also profoundly interested in the ultimate destiny of the person, in salvation, or *moksha,* final liberation. This is also to some extent connected with the notion of the spiritual transformation at the end. He was thus concerned with last things, with death and resurrection, but not too much interested in a literal interpretation of the Eastern doctrine of reincarnation. He found this notion too simplistic if taken literally. He hardly ever dealt with it, except in some of his public lectures, or in question-and-answer periods following his talks. I believe his view on reincarnation was subtle and original, but he had not yet developed it in his writing.[12]

The Church is also an enduring theme of his theological reflection, and he perceived a central role for her in the future.[13] Along with Bede's strong endorsement of the Church was an equally strong commitment to the whole sacramental structure of the Christian faith, including the hierarchical element, but both have to be adapted to new conditions and new opportunities. Bede envisioned the Church as becoming truly universal by finding other expressions in the various cultures. She has to realize her universality and her relationship with all the religious traditions of mankind.[14]

Another category of Father Bede's theology is contemplation, and we have seen this at work above in chapters 2 and 3. In a very real sense, contemplative theology, or mystical theology, justifies Bede's entire theological and metaphysical enterprise. It is absolutely central to his understanding of human life and religious experience. This is the practical side of his theological efforts. Everything he wrote aims at awakening others to the contemplative dimension in themselves. His contemplative theology—as well as his entire theological "system"—emphasizes the ultimate value of the experiential approach to the Divine Reality. To this end, he encouraged a rigorous *sādhanā*, or spiritual practice. This practice includes meditation *(dhyāna)* and asceticism *(tapas)*, and Father Bede practiced both with extreme assiduousness as the way to come to mystical realization and identification with the Absolute, to have knowledge of God *(brahmavidyā)*, which is like the *gnosis* of the Christian tradition or *jñāna* in the Hindu contemplative way.[15]

In all of Bede's theological works he was attempting to find parallels between the main doctrines and experiences of the two traditions. For instance, in his doctrine of God, he can equally use *Godhead* and *Brahman* for the transcendent One beyond being and manifestation. He can use the term *Ātman* for the Self, especially as it is united to God, the Brahman. He sees the possibility, in his theological vision, of employing the term *Puruṣa* for Christ, particularly in the function of Logos and Cosmic Person. And he wonders about the possibility of adopting the word *Saccidānanda* as a symbol of the Trinity, just as it is a symbol of the Ultimate Reality in Hinduism. These parallels are part of his attempt to express the Christian faith in language accessible to the Hindu mind and heart.

Of course this work concerns, among other things, the possibility of using Hindu theological categories and language to formulate the Christian faith, and this with the ideal—if it is feasible—of developing a Christian form of the Vedanta and a Christian Tantra. These were constant concerns of Father Bede's. A Christian Vedanta would be an Indian Christian theology, and this feasibility, or the lack thereof, is one of the primary points to be pursued in chapter 5. The issue of a Christian Tantra is also a point to be discussed.[16] In the context of his Indian experience, it was the relating and creative interaction of Hinduism and Christianity that became the focus of his efforts. This relationship is conceived around the essential teaching of both traditions: Advaita and Trinity; but the means or lifestyle that allows for the experiential realization of the Divine in both is *sannyāsa*, and *sannyāsa* is a lived theology. Thus, *sannyāsa* is another theme of his theology, especially of his contemplative spirituality, and it will be discussed in chapter 6.

Other elements in his theological framework include a very profound understanding of myth and its nature. Here his insight is myth as intuitive thought, or a kind of symbolic theology. The

mythical element plays a large role in his theological structure
and worldview, as we will see in the next section of this chapter.
Furthermore, his notion of the Cosmic Revelation/Covenant is
closely related to that of myth. We will examine this theme in the
final section of the present chapter, along with a consideration
of the Vedic revelation, since all three—myth and the Cosmic
and Vedic revelations—are crucial links in this book and are intimately related to the primary focus of the topic: the relationship
of Hindu mystical intuition, Advaita, and Saccidānanda to the
Christian faith and experience, expressed in the mystery of the
Trinity.

The horizon of Bede's theological endeavors extends rather
far and is indeed quite wide. For beyond his concern with the
Indian Church, the formation of an Indian Christian theology,
the renewal of spiritual life in the universal Church, he addressed
himself to humanity at large. This is the global dimension of his
theology. He sought the emergence of a new synthesis that would
include Western science in its new form, the rational/analytical
component, Eastern and Western mysticism, and Christian faith.
In a powerful series of lectures given in the summer of 1983, at
which I was present, Father Bede characterized this new synthesis and the need for it. He said that civilization has come to
the end of the Greco-Roman rational, abstract conceptual, linear
thought. There is the task of renewing Catholic theology by re-
turning to the sources in the Old and New Testaments and the
Fathers. This has to be integrated with the new science and then
opened to the East and its experience of contemplation. He emphasized the necessity of renewing Catholic theology in the light
of this new science and the Eastern religions.[17] This program is
also an accurate description of his own theological method: creative synthesis based on contemplative experience, comparative
study, and reflection.[18]

Before moving on to a consideration of myth, I would like
to return to the ideal and statement of rethinking everything in

terms of theology, and rethinking theology through mysticism, alluded to above. Again, this is what, in a real sense, Bede's thought actually represents. Bede had not written much on Monchanin's principle, but he certainly accepted it. Indeed, in the preface to a study of Monchanin's life and works, Bede expressed his support and appreciation of this ideal, which Cardinal de Lubac had inspired in Monchanin years before Bede's coming to India.[19] Although Bede did not use the same language in describing the ideal, he did practice it and had a deep attachment to it. He related it to contemplative theology—on which he had a lot to say—and an Indian Christian theology. We have seen something of the depth and richness of his contemplative theology in the preceding chapter. Bede maintained that the task Monchanin came to embody in his life and example still remains to be achieved, and he felt that it could best be achieved in an ashram.[20] Like Monchanin and Abhishiktananda, Bede Griffiths shared the "vision of a Christian contemplation which shall have assimilated the wisdom of India, and a theology in which the genius of India shall find expression in Christian terms."[21] It was always within the context of contemplative theology that Bede interpreted the task of "rethinking everything." And this was also his favorite term for mysticism, that is, contemplation. So, to rethink theology in the light of mysticism is to rethink it in the light of contemplation. For Bede, contemplative theology *is* mystical, and this means, further, that it is essentially intuitive and symbolic, precisely also the characteristics of mythic thought. He says that scriptures, poetry, and other literary forms are highly symbolic and intuitive, and that the New Testament itself is an example of a contemplative theology.[22]

There are other reasons we may adduce for the validity of this position, the recasting of everything in terms of mysticism or contemplation. First of all, it makes sense in the Indian context, at least sociologically, since mysticism or contemplation and meditational practice are the essential values of Indian spirituality and culture. India's civilization is steeped in mystical wisdom. Second, it is reasonable because the mystical dimension, contemplative spirituality, is common to Christianity, Hinduism, and all genuine religions. Every authentic religious tradition has a depth dimension, which is the realm of the ultimate and the eternal. And third, rethinking everything through the vision of contemplative theology brings us to the deepest level of reality, the hidden springs of Divine Life, which nourish the self in the presence of the Presence. These are a few practical reasons for supporting Bede's ideal and task, which became for him and are becoming for many today an actuality. The principle is proving itself existentially as people seek to lead a deeper life, a life of ultimate meaning. One part of recognizing this meaning involves mythic thought. It is also an extremely important element in Bede's "system" and in the substantive relating of the two traditions.

MYTH

There is an important sense in which myth holds one of the keys to an adequate understanding of Bede Griffiths's subtle approach to the relationship of Hinduism and Christianity, and the whole cultural matrix of which the Christian faith is a part (Judaism, etc.). Myth is a comprehensive category for him, which is even involved in the most advanced forms of philosophical and theological reflection. And so it is necessary to examine how Bede regarded myth. At the outset we must put aside the pejorative sense of myth as connoting untruth, illusion, and a lack of civilizational sophistication. That attitude is simply the white man's prejudice, a form of ethnocentricity. Indeed, it is a bitter pill for Westerners to swallow that the peoples of other cultures, notably more primitive than their own, have genuine insights into ultimate matters, and moreover, that these so-called primitives may actually have more wisdom as well.

First, Bede maintains—and I think rightly—that all genuine religion has its origin in mystical experience. This experience is beyond the range of thought, and it is given expression or form in the social organization, ritual, and language of a particular people.[23] The encounter with Ultimate Reality from which religion derives its force and life transcends the capacity of the mind to know in the ordinary sense. It is then that myth serves the crucial function of providing a form in which these experiences can be communicated. Bede Griffiths remarks: "Myth is the language of primitive religion; it is the poetic expression of a mystical experience. Myths can only be understood as poetry. They spring from the depths where man encounters the ultimate Mystery of existence and interprets it in poetic form."[24]

Mythic thought is the product of the creative imagination that strives to convey the primordial truth, the Ultimate Reality experienced in mystical states of consciousness. This form of consciousness is concrete, symbolic, and intuitive, rather than abstract, logical, and rational.[25] Because myth is the vehicle of primitive humanity's experience of the divine mystery it is also a form of "theology," but a kind of theology that is symbolic in its form and intuitive in its content. Indeed, ancient peoples had a deep experience of being and consciousness as undivided, as a unity, and they formulated this experience in mythic terms.[26] Bede puts it more succinctly: "Myth in its origin is the symbolic expression of the one Reality experienced as a living unity in an undivided consciousness."[27]

Furthermore, myth is genuine insight into the nature of reality, an insight arising out of the innate genius of the imagination. It is real knowledge, indeed wisdom, but presented under the compelling and charming guise of symbol, and allowing the one who encounters it to enter into the consciousness of the original sage who discovered the Source of wisdom, life, and beatitude. Father Bede writes that "myth is the language of imaginative insight into ultimate reality, which not only reveals the truth under a symbol, but also enables those who receive the myth to participate in the experience of the poet or prophet who communicates it."[28]

And yet the truth of myth eludes the modern mind, caught up as it is in the allurements and promises of science. In fact, science has blinded us to the real nature and value of mythical consciousness. Science has prejudiced the West against myth and instead espouses a realm of "fact," something accessible to measurement and the various other tools science employs.[29] But myth is in touch with hidden meanings, values, and truths. Bede puts it rather eloquently: "It is myth that opens the mind to ... higher states of consciousness, while the scientist remains shut up in his little world of 'facts.'"[30] Science, with its influence on culture, life, and education, has greatly limited modern humankind in its understanding of life and reduced its field of action as a consequence.

Let me now give some examples of myth and the intuitive wisdom present in it. One comes from the experience of ancient Israel, another from the event of the Incarnation, and a third from the Hindu tradition, involving Hanuman, the monkey god, and Ganeśa, the elephant god. In the first instance of myth as a deep spiritual truth embodied in a symbolic form, we find this meaning mixing with the historical experience of the Jews. Myth inspired history and the Jews' understanding of history. As Bede points out: "The Promised Land was the land of Canaan, to which the Israelites were passionately attached ... but it was also a symbol of the 'heavenly country,' the land of heart's desire."[31] This "heavenly country" is the spiritual truth encountered in the intuitive experience of their prophets, patriarchs, and sages, but in time it becomes associated with the historical situation and the Jews' longing for a material homeland. The original insight concerns something much more profound, something conducive to their eternal happiness, the ultimate level of truth. That is the mythical level, the dimension of intuitive wisdom and mystical illumination.

Revelation, in its Christian acceptation of the term, occurs when myth and history converge and combine in the process of the Divine-human interaction. This is also a definition that accurately reflects the religious and historical experience of the Jewish people. Myth communicates the essential truth of human existence in relation to God, or Ultimate Reality, but history, according to Bede, only has form to the extent that it is *informed* and structured by myth, by the essential truth about humanity and God, or the Absolute. This process reached its perfection in Christ, when the meaning and value of the Divine-human relationship was clarified in historical actuality. Bede Griffiths elaborates: "In Jesus myth and history meet. Myth reveals the ultimate meaning and significance of life, but it has no hold on history and loses itself in the world of imagination. History of itself, as a mere succession of events, has no meaning.... When historical events are seen to reveal the ultimate significance of life, then myth and history meet."[32]

The mythical gives the historical content and direction, while the historical gives the mythical a vehicle of concretization; it is a step forward in the application of the ultimate truth in the human situation. History then reveals the truth in concrete actuality by allowing a spiritual event, defined by supernatural experience and illumination, to enter through it into life and memory. History is the external medium of myth's articulation in time, and its integration with all of human life in this world. Without history, myth remains powerful but unconnected, and yet history without myth is blind and devoid of purpose. Myth is the meaning of life, history, and time, while history is its vehicle of concrete communication to us. The Incarnation expresses the ultimate meaning of humanity and the cosmos in relation to God; it is the mythical and the historical giving birth to the plenitude of the revelational, a process in which God communicates Himself to us in a concrete and specific way, not in the general way of natural revelation through the cosmic order. The Virgin Birth, the Transfiguration, the Resurrection, and the Ascension are historical events that manifest the ultimate significance and reality behind life.[33] They are historical events whose meaning is spiritual or mythical, which is the deepest level of truth, that of intuitive wisdom and mystical consciousness.

In our third example of the nature of myth, we are taken into the Hindu devotion to the personal gods, the animal gods. We focus on Hanuman and Ganeśa because they were used by Bede Griffiths as examples. Hanuman and the 330 million other gods and goddesses of Hinduism have a mythical reality, which has a metaphysical and spiritual meaning. Hanuman, the monkey god, is a symbol of the incarnation of the *bhakti* principle; he is a perfect expression of devoted love, service, and care. And Ganeśa, the elephant god, signifies the union of God and us, as well as of the human and the animal kingdom. As Bede says: "in Hinduism the myth is given metaphysical meaning and this in turn leads to the ultimate mystical reality."[34] We can also observe that it usually works the other way as well: the mystical life expressing itself in myths that are also richly endowed with metaphysical meaning. In any event, we are now in a position to present and understand Bede Griffiths's notion of the Cosmic Revelation as an object of mythological creativity and the pristine link among the religions, particularly as a bridge between the Hindu and the Christian traditions.

THE COSMIC REVELATION AND COVENANT

The notion of the Cosmic Revelation is a central element of Bede's integral vision, and it is certainly indispensable for understanding his approach to Hinduism, and Hinduism itself as he estimated it. Indeed, he regarded Hinduism as preeminently a cosmic religion in which God is worshiped through the *devas*, the cosmic powers, or powers of nature, what we in the West would call the angels.[35] There is a sense of a Presence or presences in, through, and beyond nature and the entire cosmic order. I think that Bede Griffiths's early childhood experiences of this Presence in the natural world and his extensive reading of the Romantic poets prepared him to receive the insight of the existence of a Cosmic Revelation, a primordial revelation, that is still going on now, and will always go on, as long as the cosmos exists. His intuitive discovery of the Divine in nature grew progressively profound in his life and reached a great depth in his many, many years in India. The notion of the Cosmic Revelation is a vision of the Divine Reality manifesting itself in nature, being, and life and in the depths of interiority. Insofar as the first half of the revelation is concerned, that is, the natural world, it is quite universal, evidence of which can be found in all ancient and tribal cultures. It is very strong in the American Indians, especially in the eloquent expressions of the Dakota Indians, who speak of the Sacred Mystery as the Taku Wakan, which, as Bede points out, is "the supernatural and mysterious."[36] This Sacred Presence in our experience of nature is celebrated in the myths of the various cultures of the ancient and not so ancient world. The myths of origin are often related to a primordial encounter with the Divine in the surrounding reality of the natural realm, and the fact that the myths make the sacred time present through recitation—a commonly known truth—perhaps means that the Cosmic Revelation is always happening, the recitation being a vehicle of awakening us to it. Through the myths and their frequent recitation, a people becomes sensitive to and participates in the reality of the Cosmic Revelation.

And so the primordial experience of the Divine Presence in the natural world, the cosmos, life, and being, an experience of an encounter that is the matrix of all ancient cultures, preserved in symbols, signs, myths, ceremonies, and rites, is the Cosmic Revelation. It is, as Bede maintains, "the revelation of ultimate Truth, given to all mankind through the Cosmos, that is, through the creation."[37] Bede Griffiths was certain that it is this Cosmic Revelation that Saint Paul refers to in his Letter to the Romans (1:20): "Ever since the creation of the world His invisible nature, namely, His eternal power and divinity have been clearly perceived in the things that are made."[38] Moreover, Bede held that the knowledge of this primordial revelation, in the Hebrew tradition, is preserved for historical memory "in the story of the Covenant with Noah, who is represented as the Father of all mankind."[39]

From the dawn of human consciousness, Bede says, humanity has had an awareness of a hidden power or Presence in and behind all natural phenomena. Human beings saw themselves, their own consciousness, and the created order external to them as part of a cosmic unity, a cosmic whole that completely "enveloped" them. This is the constant experience of archaic humanity.[40] Indeed, it is a realization of this cosmic unity that is the basis of Vedic tradition, and the seers of the Upaniṣads recognize the source of this revelation of cosmic unity; they give it the names of Brahman and Ātman, and find a method through meditation of knowing this Divine Mystery in an experiential way.[41] In a very real sense, the depth experience of interiority, of pure unity or Advaita, is the culmination and ultimate refinement, experientially, of the original awareness of the cosmic unity and its relation to the Brahman/Ātman formulation of the Divine Mystery. At least this is the clear implication of Bede's understanding as I see it from a close reading of this section of the text.[42]

Bede Griffiths felt that there is a sense of the Cosmic Revelation, the primordial experience, in the biblical tradition. The fact of a covenantal relationship between God and humankind also attests to the existence of a Cosmic Revelation as the foundation of this covenant. How can there be a covenant between the Divine Reality and humanity if the human being has no sense of his or her existence and reality? Bede sees in the covenant with Adam a relationship with all of humanity and believes the covenant itself is a strong indication of the existence of a primordial revelation. After all, in the Book of Wisdom (13:1–9) there is a beautiful reference to this revelation of God's Presence in the created order, and this is perhaps where Saint Paul derived his knowledge of it, at least initially. Here is what Bede has to say concerning the Cosmic Covenant: "This covenant with Adam is the covenant with Man.... However far we have to extend the creation of man, maybe to millions of years, it is still covered by this Cosmic Covenant where God has related Himself to mankind. The word *adam* in Hebrew simply means 'man.' God has been calling man from the beginning of time, and that is the Cosmic Covenant."[43]

Through the experience of the Cosmic Revelation, it would seem, Bede is suggesting that God has been inviting us into a deeper relationship with Him. The Cosmic Covenant is predicated on and comes through the Cosmic Revelation; they are two aspects of the same reality. One side is knowledge—the acknowledgment of the Divine Reality in nature, being, and life, as God reveals Himself in the three, and the other concerns love—the response of the human person to God's loving care, shown in everything that nature does for our well-being. So the Cosmic Revelation is presupposed in the biblical tradition and others, since the Cosmic Covenant is the remembrance and the fruit of this revelatory experience so characteristic of the ancients.

Now, the Vedic tradition is also an integral part of the primordial revelation. It is, among other things, a product of the Cosmic Revelation, of which it is a more celebrated and eloquent instance. Indeed, it is one of the oldest articulations of natural revelation. In the Vedic universe everything is sacred; everything is sacramental. Cosmic religion is a sacramental system, and the cosmos itself is the chief sacrament, the vehicle of the divine mystery. In the Vedic revelation the entire world is permeated by the divine mystery, as in the many other instances of the Cosmic Revelation, but there is more subtlety in this Hindu approach, especially in the articulation of the nature of reality. The Vedic mystics had discovered the threefold character of reality, something that also underlies all ancient thought as part of the perennial philosophy, the original metaphysical tradition of archaic humanity, but the clarity of their vision is so extraordinary. Bede elaborates the Vedic view of reality:

> The Vedic seers had reached an understanding of the three-fold nature of the world, at once physical, psychological and spiritual. These three worlds were seen to be interdependent, every physical reality having a psychological aspect, and both aspects, physical and psychological, being integrated in a spiritual vision. The cows and horses of the Vedas were not merely physical cows and horses, they were also cows and horses of the mind, that is psychological forces, and beyond that they were symbols of the cosmic powers, manifestations of the Supreme Spirit.[44]

In the Vedic revelation, as a paradigm of the Cosmic Revelation, there is the further subtlety of a more interior realization. This is the second essential aspect of the Cosmic Revelation. It is the Cosmic Revelation in the depths of the heart of the person, the revelation of the eternal One who is present in the cosmic order, the whole of it, the *guhā*, the "cave of the heart." The God who is immanent in the entire universe and all of nature, being, and life also dwells at the center of one's own being. Bede expresses this insight in terms of the god Śiva Nataraja, the Dancing Śiva. Bede says of Śiva and his relation to Creation: "He is represented with four arms dancing in a circle of fire, dancing at the heart of creation. It is a cosmic dance; it represents the power which permeates the whole universe. The idea is that God is dancing in the heart of creation and in every human heart. We must find the Lord who is dancing in our hearts; then we will see the Lord dancing in all of creation."[45]

This is a compelling image, and I think it conveys so well, in such poetic depth, the twofold thrust of the pristine revelation, a revelation that is always going on in every time and in every person who cares to take the time, through meditation and other forms of prayer, to look.

The notion of the Cosmic Revelation was a way Bede Griffiths related the various world religions in his theological vision and synthesis. This is especially true of how he relates the Hindu and Judeo-Christian traditions. For through the fascinating and pervasive idea of a Cosmic Revelation and Covenant he is able to find a very significant bond that unites both Christianity and Hinduism (and all genuine faith systems) in a common religious and human experience. This allows him to speak seriously of a deep connection between the two traditions on the cosmo-contemplative level, and if here, then why not on the profoundest level of mystical realization in both? For, in a very real sense, each is in continuity with its original inspiration, and what exists at the zenith was perhaps present in the beginning; what the oak tree is in its maturity was already present, in some sense, in the acorn. In the same way, can this not be the situation with the two traditions: the incipient mystical awareness developing into that profound contemplative consciousness characteristic of them both?

At this point a few questions are appropriate concerning Bede's theology. Since Bede was not a systematic thinker, what is the rational validity of his theological "system"? How are we to determine the validity and integrity of his method of complementarity? Is mythologizing a valid theological method? Of course Bede was an intuitive thinker, a mystical theologian, thus the rational validity of his "system" rests more on its approximation of universal themes that represent authentic experience and insight, which can be communicated reasonably well. I do think Bede succeeded in this, but not without some obscurity.

The second question, which concerns the validity and integrity of his method of complementarity, is not so easy to answer. The approach I would emphasize in trying to determine this issue would involve how closely Bede followed the corporate effort and collective insights of the movement to which he belongs and the larger dialogical movement. I believe it can accurately be maintained that Bede did follow these developments very faithfully in his own thought, and also that his theologizing is consistent with his Christian faith.

The third question also is not easily answered, because myth had a special meaning for him. Insofar as myth is intuitive thought in contact with genuine experience of a spiritual order, and insofar as all theology, no matter what tradition, includes this mythic dimension so defined, it is a valid way to present theology. Bede was at least able to make sense of the Christian and Hindu faiths in this way, and so he was also enabled to relate them. One might add, however, that this mythic dimension of relating the two traditions is preliminary to the more specific and profound encounter on the contemplative level.

In the next chapter we will discover how the intuitive, mystical perception of the Vedic seers reached a deeper level of formulation in the Upaniṣadic tradition, and what the mystical wisdom of Hinduism is, that which must be related to the depth tradition of the Christian faith. This will ultimately involve Advaita/Saccidānanda and the Trinity, and the exploration of the issue of whether a Christian Advaitic doctrine is possible. If this can be shown to be possible, as Bede conceived it, then a Christian Vedanta could become a reality, and this would also be a form of an Indian Christian theology.

5

Christian Vedanta: Advaita, Saccidānanda, and the Trinity

In the preceding chapter we examined Bede Griffiths's general theological scheme in order to orient ourselves to the richness and depth of this thought and to acquire insight into the precise nature of his focus and concerns. This was done to give us a sense of how he envisions the Hindu-Christian encounter theologically and to determine how it shapes his "system." We also explored his profound notion of myth as symbolic or intuitive thought, the thought mode so characteristic of the ancient cultures, which grew out of a continuous experience of the cosmic unity, the cosmic whole. Then we delved into the notion of the Cosmic Revelation and Covenant in Bede's vision and saw how these are quite universal, since they are part of a primordial revelation experience in extreme antiquity, but a revelation that is always going on in nature, being, and life. It is this Cosmic Revelation/Covenant experience that is one of the primary objects of mythic consciousness. This was found to be important in Bede's system because it links together all the traditions through an original revelational event/process, especially the biblical and Hindu traditions.

Furthermore, we found that the Vedic revelation is part of this primordial tradition, a tradition that emphasizes the double thrust of encountering the Divine Reality in the cosmos and its order, and within the depths of the self, in the mystical dimension of interiority. The Vedic revelation seems to plunge deeper into the inner mystery of the Self and has a more refined understanding of the inner way, but this is balanced by its view of nature as revelational and sacramental. Bede reminds us that it is primarily a sense of the cosmic unity that is the foundation of the Vedic tradition, as he sees it.[1] Unity is indeed the essential category of Hindu thought, and we shall see how this intuition grows more subtle in Hindu mystical consciousness, as Bede interprets it.

It is in this chapter that we come finally to the heart of the issue in Bede Griffiths's attempt to relate Hinduism and Christianity on a deep contemplative level, the crucial issue of the essential terms of the encounter, which really can be summed up in two words: *Advaita* and *Trinity*. Moreover, this echoes Jules Monchanin's oft-repeated statement of the ideal of what constitutes the Christian sannyasic life: "*Advaita* and praise of the Trinity are our only aim."[2] Bede embraced this ideal with wholehearted commitment. It is one of the primary themes of all his writing and lecturing. The question of course is: Is it actually possible to relate them in this way, and then to reconcile them? Or is this only an arbitrary connection?

In considering these questions, this chapter also deals with material that is either preparatory to the task in the form of additional background information, notably concerning the development of Hinduism's early understanding of the Absolute, or part of the larger issue of developing an Indian Christian theology.[3] The notions of Brahman, Ātman, and Puruṣa are discussed, indicating how they can be related to the Christian faith as Bede conceived the relation. Advaita and Saccidānanda are considered in some detail, and I also focus on the crucial question of whether or not a Christian Advaita is possible, again, as far as Bede was concerned. And if a Christian Advaita is possible, what is Bede's conception of it? These are important questions that will be addressed.

Then we will explore his understanding of the Trinity, which was a constant theme in his writings, talks, and conversations. We will see just how he attempted to relate Saccidānanda and the Trinity in his new synthesis; what precisely he was claiming, and whether or not it is plausible and can stand up under scrutiny. These themes are all dealt with here in this pivotal, indeed seminal chapter, because together they constitute the substance of his contemplative theology. Near the end of the chapter, I will try to answer these questions, which I believe clarify his main points; bring together these themes in a more systematic formulation; and determine whether his theological project is viable in whole and/or in part.

BRAHMAN, ĀTMAN, AND PURUṢA

Hinduism has always had a deep knowledge of the cosmic order and the underlying unity of all reality. It has always emphasized, more or less, the unity over—and often at the expense of—the multiplicity. From the earliest times in this tradition, there was an awareness of the Divine Power immanent in all things and governed by the cosmic powers, or personifications of natural forces, the *devas*,[4] what we might call angels in Western religion. The *devas* are actually personified divine powers who are responsible for maintaining the universe. In addition, Hinduism has 330 million gods and goddesses, and some of these are cosmic powers, like the *devas*. And yet these divine beings are only manifestations of the One Reality; they are forms of the Formless One. They are "names and forms" *(nāmarūpa)* of the Divine Unity, which is beyond all names and forms, beyond all multiplicity. Hinduism is thus not really polytheistic at all. There is an abiding recognition that a unity keeps all things together, that everything is ultimately one. Everything stems from a unitary principle, and this is acknowledged in the notion of the *ekam sat,* "the one being."

So, though there are many "gods," "goddesses," or *devas*, many creatures and a multiplicity of other entities and things, there is a ground of unity from which they arise and in which they endure. This unity is the *ekam sat*, the "one being" that "the wise call by many names."[5] The various deities or *devas* are manifestations of this "one being." They are the "names and forms" under which it is expressed in the phenomenal world. There is an original experience of unity behind the multiplicity, and the multiplicity is itself seen as the creative expression of the metaphysical unity of being. This "one being," the *ekam sat*, eventually received the name of Brahman.[6] Brahman is the one reality, the one principle that penetrates all and is immanent in everything, and yet, as the Godhead, it is beyond all, transcending every determination, including being. It is the Source from which derives the universe and all creation.

The term *Brahman* originates from the root *brh*, which has the connotation of "to swell." It was at one time a mantra used in prayer, in worship. The understanding was that as those who were engaged in public prayer at a sacrifice gave themselves to the act of sacrifice in worship, the mantra or word rose up spontaneously within, swelling, so to speak, and concretized the significance of the sacrificial action. Brahman was thus regarded as the power or energy immanent in the sacrificial act itself. This understanding evolved and became refined over time. Since the ancient Hindus saw their liturgical sacrifice as the heart of the cosmos and the origin of all things, they conceived Brahman as the origin of the creation and all things in it.[7] In order to emphasize the nature of Brahman as the Source, destiny, and purpose of life, Bede quotes a passage from the Upaniṣads that expresses what he is trying to convey: "That from which beings are born. That by which when born they live. That into which when dying they enter. That you should desire to know. That is Brahman."[8]

Brahman is the immanent presence of the Divine Reality

indwelling in the created order, in all creatures, and the transcendent ground, inaccessible to conception and sense experience, imagination, and any thought process. It is the principle of unity, the cosmic unity that is the underlying intuition of all Indian speculation. Brahman is the name for this principle of unity,[9] the experience of which so profoundly inspired the *rishis*, the forest-dwelling sages at the beginning of Hindu tradition. As creator, He is called Brahma, but nothing is more ultimate than Brahman, the Godhead. Alluding to Upaniṣadic metaphors that evoke a sense of Brahman, Bede comments: "The whole world, the earth, the water, the air, the sun, the moon, the stars, the gods (the cosmic powers) and their creator, are all 'woven' on this Brahman. He is the 'honey,' the subtle essence of everything. In a real sense he is everything."[10]

This sounds curiously pantheistic and reductionistic but is neither, as far as Bede was concerned. What the language of the Hindu tradition suggests, especially as articulated in the Upaniṣ ads, is that the Source, the Divine Reality is, as Bede says, "totally transcendent and totally immanent."[11] He felt that this is the deeper meaning of the Hindu doctrine on the Brahman.[12] It is a mystical realization that comes through meditation, or contemplative living. Brahman is experienced as the indwelling Divine Presence in nature, being, and life. Bede formulates the matter more succinctly: "It is not the transcendent creator from above but the inner principle, from within. Brahman is within the creation and creates from within."[13] And yet, being "totally transcendent," He must also be completely beyond that which He creates. But when the Divine Presence, or Brahman, is experienced in the depths of the soul, in the *guhā*, the "cave of the heart"—that is, as indwelling, or as the very basis of selfhood—then it is called Ātman.

The word *Ātman* is derived from the Sanskrit root *ān* and *tmān* which originally meant "breath," among other things. Gradually it acquired the more definite meaning of the Self, the

Divine principle present in the heart, and the individual self or soul, "the unseen inner essence of an individual."[14] Ātman is both the immanent Divine Reality, or Ātman, present in all beings, and *Ātman*, the unique individual self of each person that is grounded on the great Self, the Ātman as such. And as the Absolute, Ātman is, as Radhakrishnan observes, "the foundational reality underlying the conscious powers of the individual, the inward ground of the human soul. There is an ultimate depth to our life below the plane of thinking and striving. The Ātman is the super-reality of the *jīva*, the individual ego."[15]

Furthermore, very early on in the Upaniṣadic tradition, the identity of Ātman and Brahman was experienced in the depths of meditation by the mystics. The Divine Reality was not simply the transcendent Source, the Brahman, but also the immanent Presence in the "cave of the heart," the Ātman giving being and reality to the individual *Ātman*, the divine spark, imperishable life of the person. Thus, the identity of each person as a self in the one Self, an *Ātman* in the Ātman, was regarded as a central intuition of the seers of the tradition, and it was asserted that this Ātman, the basis of the *Ātman*, the self, was *one with* Brahman. This intuition, this profound mystical realization is formulated concisely in the *mahāvākyas*, the four great utterances, sentences, or sayings of the Upaniṣads.

The first *mahāvākya* pertains to Brahman but is important for Ātman. It is: "Brahman is consciousness."[16] The transcendent Source, Ultimate Reality, or Brahman is pure consciousness. The factor of consciousness is necessary for an identity between transcendence and immanence in order to relate them in the same unity; they must be like. And so the second *mahāvākya*, which follows from the first, is: "This self (Ātman) is Brahman."[17] This can refer to both senses of self, to Ātman and *Ātman*, but probably more so to the Ātman. The third *mahāvākya* definitely refers to the *Ātman*, the individual self as one with the Self, or the Divine indwelling, and because of this, it is also one with

Brahman. It goes like this: "Thou art That!"[18] *Thou,* which is the individual *Ātman,* the human person, *art That,* are one with That which is the Self, the Atman, and one with the Brahman. This is the famous formula *tat tvam asi.* Radhakrishnan mentions that this applies "to the inward person, *antah purusa,* and not to the empirical soul with its name and family descent."[19] You and I and all of us are part of the Brahman through the Ātman. The fourth and final *mahāvākya* proclaims a unitive identity with Brahman. It exults: "I am Brahman."[20] But this statement "I am Brahman" *(aham brahmāsmi)* refers to the Brahman itself as knowing itself as the Absolute, or as Brahman. This is quite clear from the context. But then it says that whoever knows this "I am Brahman" becomes it.[21] By realizing that level of mystical consciousness, one becomes identified with it, because one is knowing in and through the Divine Consciousness.

Bede points out that the *mahāvākyas* are mystical experiences. They cannot be interpreted literally. That would lead to false conclusions and misunderstandings. In the depths of interiority, in the depths of the self, we are united with the Source, the totality. Commenting on the third and fourth *mahāvākyas,* Bede maintains: "In the depth of your own consciousness you are one with that power which creates the tree. You are one with the Brahman. So in the depth of our own being each one of us can experience this reality of Brahman, the source, the ground of all existence and of all consciousness. That is the Hindu mystical experience."[22]

It is this experiential element that chiefly characterizes the Hindu approach to religion. Brahman and Ātman are names for an intuition of the Absolute that is still accessible through meditation, so goes the Hindu approach. Although there is a speculative, even Scholastic dimension to Hinduism, its emphasis is upon the inner way of contemplation, a "tasting" knowledge, a living gnosis, what is called *jñāna,* an experiential wisdom. It is thoroughly mystical wisdom that is the goal of life itself. This is not a mere postulate but an existential fact, and it is something that has always been recognized and eagerly pursued by Christian contemplatives. Bede points out again and again how insistent the Hindu tradition is upon the necessity of the way of inner experience. One has to dwell in the innermost reaches of interiority in order to encounter the Presence. He cites a text from the Katha Upaniṣad to make his point more forcefully: "The wise man, who by means of meditation on the self recognizes the Ancient, who is difficult to be seen, who has entered into the dark, who is seated in the cave, who dwells in the abyss, as God, he indeed leaves both joy and sorrow behind."[23]

This is a form of liberation, of *moksha,* a liberation from *māyā,* the illusion of the world and of an egoistic life. One's existence is fulfilled by opening into the limitless realm of the Divine Self and merging into an awareness of unity. The question is raised by Bede concerning the relationship of the human person, the human spirit, the *Ātman* or *jīvātman,* to the absolute or supreme Spirit, the Paramatman.[24] Some would assert that individuality is finally lost in the ultimate state of unity, but Bede does not accept this assertion as true. He maintains that the person only loses his or her separate existence, not identity, for that remains. The person is transfused with the Divine Light "and participates in the very being and consciousness of God."[25] That state is Saccidānanda, the mystical condition of experiencing pure being, in pure consciousness and complete joy or bliss. More will be said on Saccidānanda later, but suffice it to say that one who enters this state, according to Bede, retains individual being.[26] That can never be lost, Bede felt.

The third essential term in the Hindu notion of the Absolute is that of the Puruṣa. It is part of the supreme Reality. Puruṣa is the Lord of Creation, the cosmic man, the archetypal human being who is perfect, like Adam Kadmon of the Jewish tradition, the one who is the son of Man, the first human.[27] Puruṣa is the primordial Person, the universal or supreme Person.[28] Panikkar mentions how this usage of the term *person,* or *puruṣa,* is not limited to the human sphere; indeed, it transcends it. It has a wholly metaphysical and spiritual meaning. Panikkar comments, and Bede follows him in this: "The person, for the Upaniṣads, is not phenomenal, but either universal Man or the interior, spiritual Man. Ultimately, it is the inner Man who is also the Lord of all...."[29] Puruṣa is the personal aspect of the supreme reality and is one with Ātman and Brahman.[30]

This Puruṣa, whose origin in human understanding goes back to the Vedas (*Rig Veda* 10), has a central place in the creative process of the cosmos and humanity. The Puruṣa is also an important part of the journey back to the Divine Reality. Bede elaborates: "Puruṣa is the cosmic person, who contains the whole creation in himself and also transcends it. He is the spiritual principle, which unites body and soul, matter and conscious intelligence in the unity of a transcendent consciousness."[31]

He is the Lord of creation and the ultimate term in the cosmic hierarchy. The basic structure of this hierarchy, of the universe, according to the Vedanta, following the philosophy, metaphysics of Sāmkhya is as follows. There are the senses and their objects, and beyond these is *manas,* the mind. *Manas* is like reason. Beyond *manas* is *buddhi,* the intellect. It is *buddhi* that can be illumined by the Divine Light. It is the receptive aspect of the person. Beyond *buddhi,* the intellect, is *mahat,* or the Great Self. *Mahat* is cosmic consciousness, the cosmic order, and is important in the Vedantic doctrine. Beyond *mahat,* the Great Self, is *avyakta,* or the unmanifest, and beyond *avyakta* is Puruṣa, the cosmic Person, the Lord of Creation. He is the supreme goal, for there is nothing beyond Him.[32] And creation comes through Him, through His cosmic sacrifice.[33]

The person, the soul, must ascend through this hierarchy, must pass through it in the depths of the heart, the *guhā,* on the path to eternal life, or immortality. Immortality is the goal of Hinduism and of the contemplative life. Panikkar points out that immortality is achieved through divinization, or rather, "divinization amounts to immortality."[34] The Puruṣa, being the Lord of immortality, the soul or *Ātman*, must be united to Him. He is the way to Brahman, the Immortal, by knowing whom we become immortal.[35] The *Śvetāśvatara Upaniṣad* expresses this intuition/experience of the Vedic tradition in these eloquent words: "I have come to know that mighty Person, golden like the sun, beyond the darkness. By knowing him a man transcends death; there is no other path for reaching that goal."[36]

This Puruṣa, the cosmic Person and Lord, the archetypal Person through whom all things come into being, is the unity of pure being and consciousness, known in and through meditation or in pure contemplation. He can only be known in this way.[37] This is the way to the knowledge of the Self, the Ātman. Bede quotes the *Katha Upaniṣad* to describe the process in meditation of attaining to the Ultimate Reality of the Divine Consciousness. The *Katha* says that "a wise man should keep speech in mind, and keep that in the self which is knowledge. He should keep knowledge in the self which is the Great (the Mahat) and he should keep that within the self which is peace."[38] Commenting on this text as showing the path to knowledge of the Self, Bede details the process. First we have to rest in the silence, leaving the sense world outside, putting it aside. We must then bring quiet to the mind by allowing it to rest in the self of knowledge *(buddhi)*. This is where the personality finds integration. But then the individual self has to be surrendered to the Great Self *(mahat)* and to the spheres of consciousness beyond the mind *(manas)*. This is the realm of cosmic consciousness, but this too must be sacrificed since it belongs to the order of created being; it must be surrendered to Peace, the "self of Peace, the Peace which passes understanding."[39] Then Bede says: "At this point we pass beyond the created world, physical, psychological, the world of men and angels, and we enter into communion with the Supreme, the Puruṣa, the ultimate Reality. Brahman, Ātman, and Puruṣa are now known to be one."[40]

The sphere of consciousness experienced in meditation, which is beyond imagination and sense-bound contents, a sphere in which one acquires self-knowledge through turning in, is that of Puruṣa.[41] This Puruṣa is also the source and ground of personal being, where all beings discover their unity, their center. But this realm of the spirit is one, for all consciousness is established in one all-embracing, all-penetrating consciousness that unites them in itself. When this sphere of consciousness is known in meditation as the ground of all existence and being, encompassing everything, it is called Brahman. When it is known or experienced as the center of consciousness, as its ground, the basis of human consciousness, the inner life and spirit, then it is called the Ātman, the principle of both knowing and being. But when this sphere of consciousness is experienced as God, transcendent being, or the Lord, then it is called Puruṣa. Bede points out that this is how the idea of the personal god arises in the Hindu tradition.[42]

Brahman, Ātman, and Puruṣa are different dimensions of the same Godhead, but the notion of the personal god developed late in the Hindu tradition, even though Puruṣa is mentioned as far back as the Vedas. He is called a *person*, a center of conscious intelligence, but He is not like the *avatāras*, the personal incarnations or "descents" of the Divine into the realm of this existence, which are recorded in the later tradition, for instance, Kriṣna (Krishna) in the Bhagavad Gita, with whom we can have a personal relationship of love and devotion. But starting with the *Śvetāśvatara Upaniṣad*, which is late in the tradition, and acquiring a fixed understanding in the Gita and other works, the notion of the personal god gained ground in Hinduism. With this development, Bede holds: "The ultimate reality, the Brahman, is conceived as a personal being, the object of worship and adoration."[43] Bhagavan is the name by which the personal God is called all around India today.[44] He is also named Śiva (Shiva), which is used in the *Śvetāśvatara Upaniṣad*.[45]

Every religion and every cultural configuration, institution, and nation grows and evolves. We have been painfully aware of this fact in recent years in the Catholic Church, which some mistakenly thought could never change. If we take a casual look at the development of the Hebrew understanding of God, of Yahweh, we notice rather quickly its evolution from a very primitive idea—the God of revenge, anger, and jealousy—to a more refined one: the God of love, faithfulness, and forgiveness. I think the same is true of Hinduism, particularly in regard to the development of its notion of the Divine Reality from that of an impersonal to a personal being with whom one can relate, and yet without diminishing the truth of the transcendent Brahman and the immanent Ātman, as well as the cosmic Lord, the ground of all personal consciousness. Bede felt strongly that the two traditions, the Hindu and the Judeo-Christian, are complementary.[46] I think in many ways they are, but it is perhaps too soon to say so in a definitive way, until this can be established more and more by other writers and scholars. My intuition, proceeding as it does from a deep conviction of the unity of reality and truth, is that ultimately they are complementary.

Another important aspect of Hinduism's notion of the Divinity is its long-established view that God is both Mother and Father. Bede was convinced that Christianity is impoverished by its lack of a similar understanding. He characterizes the Hindu view: "Puruṣa is the active principle in the Godhead manifesting itself as light and life and intelligence. Prakriti is the feminine principle, which in the Godhead is the Śakti, the divine power or energy. In the Christian tradition there has been very little recognition of this feminine aspect of God. Yet God is both Father and Mother, and in Oriental traditions this has always been recognized."[47]

And yet the Divine Feminine, as a principle, is implicitly pres-ent in the Western religious tradition. For example, *ruach*, the Hebrew word for "spirit," is grammatically feminine in gender. Furthermore, the later Syriac tradition kept the same name, and in this tradition the Holy Spirit was referred to as Mother. The Divine feminine implication is also preserved in the Wisdom tradition (the religious tradition of personified wisdom, rooted in the literature of the ancient Middle East). In Hebrew it is called *hokhmah,* in Greek, *sophia,* and in Latin, *sapientia.* All of these indicate a feminine dimension to the Divinity. The Holy Spirit could well be considered the feminine Person in the Trinity, the Mother, because the Spirit is a principle of receptivity and giving, of receiving love and sharing or reflecting it in an unlimited way.[48] So Bede was convinced of the necessity of including the notion of the Motherhood of God in Christian theology, of restoring the feminine aspect to its place in our understanding of the divine nature. Also, I think it is possible to see in the Christian principle of Divine Providence, which comes from a feminine Latin word *(providentia),* an indication of the Divine Feminine in the nature of the Godhead.[49]

Can these terms, *Brahman, Ātman,* and *Puruṣa*—and many others—have a place in an Indian Christian theology? Bede was inclined to think so and to work toward that end. He often uses the terms interchangeably with Christian terms. *Ātman* is frequently employed for the soul or spirit, and *Puruṣa* is advocated as a synonym for *Christ.* He sees in the Vedic conception of the Puruṣa, the cosmic Person, an analogy with the biblical doctrine of Christ as the innocent Lamb led to the slaughter before the creation of the universe. In both cases, in that of Puruṣa and Christ, the world issues into being through their sacrifice.[50] Then Bede proclaims quite forthrightly: "We seek to express our Christian faith in the language of the Vedanta as the Greek Fathers expressed it in the language of Plato and Aristotle. Puruṣa will be one of the key words in an Indian Christian theology. Advaita would be another."[51]

I think Bede's suggestion is that these and various other terms taken from the Hindu tradition would have to be recast in Christian theological usage. I do not think he held that the connotation is the same in each case, with a particular Sanskrit word compared to a Latin or Greek term from the Christian tradition; rather, that the major Sanskrit words used to express the various aspects of the divine nature might also be used to express similar Christian theological doctrines and principles as these pertain to the Divine Reality in its different aspects. It seems to me perfectly reasonable to allow adaptation and refinement of Sanskrit terminology in order to express Christian mysteries in an Indian context. This is one way in which our knowledge grows, and a way that the Church acquires new riches of perspective and spiritual insight. Consider, for instance, the adoption of the Greek word *Logos* and its application by Christian writers to the mystery of Christ and His inner nature as the Second Person of the Trinity. Is it not possible, in our time, to have a similar adoption of the Sanskrit term *Puruṣa*, for instance, and allow it to be applied to Christ in order to express in Indian terms the mystery of Christ? This is a difficult issue, and I do not think it has been settled here.

ADVAITA AND SACCIDĀNANDA

Here, with these two terms, we come to the very heart of the Hindu mystical and metaphysical tradition. The proper understanding of these terms is absolutely essential, for they are to be inwardly related to the essential term of Christian mysticism: the Trinitarian mystery. In this section I want to examine with great care Bede Griffiths's understanding of Hinduism's quintessential mystical intuition/experience as expressed in the Advaitic doctrine and in the powerful symbolism of Saccidānanda. What is assumed is the authenticity of this whole experience and, of course equally so, the authenticity of the Christian mystical intuition of the Trinitarian nature of the Godhead. It is this element of authenticity that is the entire basis of attempting to relate the two approaches/experiences. This factor of authenticity is part of the domain of faith and mystical contemplation, not something that can be demonstrated to the satisfaction of reason. All that can be done is to present the two intuitional experiences as Bede Griffiths understood them and related them, and evaluate his attempt at finding a connection between them.

It is important to stake a distinction between *advaita,* as the name for the ultimate state of mystical consciousness and Advaita as a philosophical doctrine of the eighth-century Hindu founder of the Vedanta, Śankara. When a person transcends the ego (*ahankara,* the conception of oneself as separate), transcends the rational discursive mind *(manas)* and the pure intelligence *(buddhi,* the intellect), then he or she enters the realm of pure unity or nonduality that is *advaita.* We are drawn into the experience of nonduality, into pure unity, through a power of the soul, a power of unification, just as reason and intellect are powers of discernment and division, of analysis and discrimination. This experience of nonduality, and the process of understanding it and relating it to life, is the essential focus of Hindu thought. But we must approach the subject with care, Bede warns, because there is plenty of room for misunderstanding and misinterpretation. Bede maintains that the way in which Śankara formulated the doctrine of Advaita is quite misleading, because Śankara gives the impression that the world of phenomenal experience, the objective reality of the senses, is illusory, and has no reality. Bede rejects this interpretation of the Advaitic experience of Śankara, and he felt that this kind of statement, which claims the unreality of the objective world, is a particular danger of the Eastern traditions.[52] Bede could not be more categoric in his disavowal of this understanding of Śankara's doctrine, which interprets it in a monist way. Śankara recognizes only God (Brahman) as having reality. Bede repudiates this interpretation of Advaita. He strongly asserts: "that kind of *advaita* which denies any reality to this world and says that God alone is real is only one form of

Vedanta, and one which I certainly would never accept."[53]

The intuition of nonduality of Advaita—from *a-dvaita*, "not two"—developed from an actual mystical experience of the founders of the Hindu tradition, and this experience is common among Hindus and others in India and elsewhere even today. From the initial sense of the cosmic unity—the religion of the Vedic period—through an interiorization of this experience in meditation by subsequent ages, the mystical realization of an inner unity with everything—with Brahman, Ātman, and the created order—flowered in the lives of India's sages, especially those of the Upaniṣadic period. This has had a lasting effect on the spiritual doctrine of Hinduism and has become the essence of this extraordinarily profound tradition. It is this experience of unity, of nonduality, that is named in the spiritual doctrine/intuition of Advaita. It is, as Bede suggests, something that cannot be known by the rational mind but "by an immediate experience of the spirit, the Atman, in man."[54] And this realization is of the hidden Brahman, an intuition of which the Upaniṣads labor to communicate. It is the mystical intuition of Saccidānanda, which is the nearest the Indian tradition comes to expressing the ultimate state of reality.[55]

In a very real sense, the *mahāvākyas,* the "great utterances" of the Upaniṣads, grow out of this mystical consciousness of Advaita/Saccidānanda and really sum up the tradition. But it must be remembered that these great sayings are themselves mystical perceptions; they are products of illumination gained in the state of nonduality. They reflect, symbolically, the quintessence of the experience, but they neither exhaust it nor grasp it adequately, and they are themselves difficult to understand or interpret. It is, however, nonduality that is their foundational inspiration. Bede says that "non-duality ... is the name given to the highest experience of God in India.... 'I am Brahman' is the way it is expressed. 'I am that one Ultimate Reality.'"[56] To understand the latter two sentences, though, presents a problem. In what sense are you and I and all of us human beings said to be Brahman, or God? It seems that the distinction between subject and object breaks down, and one knows in a new and expanded way. That is why it is characterized as *nondualism*. Describing this profoundly subtle state of consciousness as most educated Hindus understand it, Bede elaborates: "The difference between you and God disappears. There is only one reality, which is Being-Knowledge-Bliss, or *Saccidānanda,* and the Hindu tends to say that when you reach that ultimate state, then all differences disappear. There is only one absolute, infinite, eternal Being, Knowledge and Bliss, and 'You are That,' *'tat tvam asi,'* 'Thou art That.'"[57]

Since this is a mystical utterance, it is difficult to determine precisely what it means. Does it imply that the creature and Brahman are the same identity? Or does it mean that the person participates directly in the Divine Consciousness in such a way that the person loses any sense of the individual self, his or her phenomenal identity? It is uncertain, but it seems more likely that the latter interpretation is correct. Panikkar provides us with a clue in his thoughtful definition of *advaita:* "Spiritual insight which sees ultimate reality as being neither monistic nor dualistic. It is the recognition that the merely quantitative problem of the one and many of the dialectical reason does not apply to the realm of ultimate reality."[58] This is because ultimate reality so conceived (and experienced) is above multiplicity as we know it in this world. It is a realm of unity in which distinctions are known in and through the unity that the Source is. It is not a monistic principle, because beings in fact experience it and are related to it, which would not and could not be the case if it were just a static One, like that of Plotinus. It is a realm of pure consciousness in which all the things that are known in a fragmented way are known together. And it is not a dualistic principle, for again we are related to it in an intimate way, which indicates union. What is absolutely distinct or dual cannot be one, in the mystical sense of the term, cannot achieve unity with another.

There has to be some likeness, and the Hindu tradition suggests precisely such a likeness in the notions of the *ātman* and the Ātman, or the *jīvātman*, the human spirit, and the Paramātman, the supreme spirit, or the Purushottama, the supreme Person. This is somewhat like the relation between God and the person as the image of God in the Christian, Jewish, and Islamic traditions. In both, whether Hinduism or Western religions, there is declared a likeness between the Source and creatures, and this is, I believe, the basis of unity between them.

Whatever our interpretation of the meaning of these mystical statements of the Vedic tradition, we can be sure that we are considering something for which there is no adequate language. Our language reflects ordinary experience, and this experience is dualistic, governed by the subject-object relation. But in the Advaitic experience, that relation is transcended. Bede quotes the *Brihadaranyaka Upaniṣad* in order to emphasize this point in what he considers to be the classical statement of Advaita: "Where there is duality, one smells another, one sees another, one hears another, one speaks to another, one perceives another, one knows another, but when everything has become the Self, by what and whom should one smell and see and hear and speak to and perceive and know another? By what should one know that by which all is known? How should one know the knower?"[59]

The knower, the known, and the act of knowing are one. There is no face-to-face but a knowing, which is the Divine's knowing in itself. This knowing is a direct experience of the Self, the Ātman, and Brahman as one, an experience in which "being and knowing are one."[60] This is what is called *Saccidānanda*, because, as Bede points out, "being *(sat)* is experienced in a pure act of knowing *(cit)* in the bliss *(ānanda)* of oneness, of non-duality. The knower, the known and the act of knowing are all one."[61] Here we are in a state of consciousness that knows itself and all things through the unitary vision of an eternal awareness. But to know in unity is not to obliterate others, the world, and distinctions generally; it is just to know in the fullest sense, and not through the limitations of earthbound consciousness. Giving a more dramatic account of the Advaitic experience, Abhishik-tananda proclaims:

> Engulfed in the abyss, he [the person] has disappeared to his own eyes, to his own consciousness. The proximity of that mystery which the prophetic traditions name God has burnt him so completely that there is no longer any question of discovering it in the depths of himself, or himself in the depths of it. In the very engulfing, the gulf itself has vanished. If a cry were still possible—at the moment perhaps of disappearing into the abyss—it would be paradoxically: "But there is no abyss, no gulf, no distance." There is no face-to-face, for there is only That-which-Is and no other to name It. "Advaita!"[62]

This is also difficult to understand, because of the line "God has burnt him so completely...." That line indicates not identity but an intimate union that obscures distinction. The rest would seem to imply a kind of identity, but it can also mean that the experience of unity with the Absolute is so deep and intense that it is *as if* only the Absolute really is. It seems to me—drawing on the Christian tradition of mysticism—that union can be so far-reaching with God, and the soul so dominated by His glory and His act of being, that the person seems to be God. But it is not so in the ultimate sense. In the issue of Advaita and Saccidānanda, as with the Trinity, it is a question of the inadequacy of language. We need a language and a hermeneutics with which to interpret these mystical insights.

Saccidānanda

Advaita can be said to be the *state* of unity, while Saccidānanda can be regarded as the *content*. If this is the case, that would explain the universality of the Advaitic experience.[63] I want now to turn to and discuss the nature of Saccidānanda as Bede Griffiths understood it. When I say Advaita is the state of unity and Saccidānanda its content, I do not mean to imply a distinction between the unity and the content. The distinction is made only to better grasp the mystical insight of the Vedic tradition. Advaita does not specify the nature of its content, other than to say that it is nondual, something that is neither pure unity nor dualism, but somewhere between the two extremes. Saccidānanda illustrates the nature of the unity, the nonduality, and it is in some sense a symbol of the Godhead that includes the chief attributes of the Godhead, or Brahman. These are *sat, cit,* and *ānanda,* Being, Knowledge, and Bliss respectively.

These are three "qualifications" of Brahman, of the ultimate mystical experience, an experience in which one discovers the ground of personal identity in the supreme identity of the Godhead, in simply being aware of being. This term *Saccidānanda* expresses for the Hindu, Bede tells us, something of what God is, but from within God's inner life.[64] In God's inner life there are these three characteristic moments, or permanent attributes. *Sat,* of course, means "being," and derives from the present participle of *as,* "to be": It can also mean existence, and the real. Panikkar remarks how Brahman only is *sat,* in the ultimate sense, "as pure Being and Ground of all existence."[65] *Sat* is actually the pure intuition and experience of one's own being in God's, or the experiential intuition of the Divine's being, the Brahman's, at the center of one's own existential act. Abhishiktananda maintains that it is in and through one's own being, when one has reached the very purity of it, that one encounters God. It is in that intuition of personal being, which is *sat,* that one comes to experience Being itself, or pure *sat,* pure existence in the eternal act of being. One's own existential act, in the depths of meditation, is the entrance into eternal Divine Being. Abhishiktananda expresses it more clearly: "It is precisely here that I meet God, in the mystery at once of my own being and of his. This in fact is the *sat* on which the Upanishadic seers made their meditations."[66] In the ultimate state of Advaitic consciousness there is an experiential awareness of absolute being or existence.

Awareness, or *cit,* is the second element or attribute of Brahman as one encounters It in the depths of interior life. *Cit* is derived from the Sanskrit root meaning "to understand," "to perceive." It implies knowledge, intelligence, and consciousness. *Cit* is the pure awareness of *sat,* "the self-manifestation of *sat* in the most inward centre of the spirit."[67] Abhishiktananda says that in the purity of self-awareness, one discovers the reality of *cit* itself, which is "the nonreflective presence of the self to itself, the light that depends on no source, but shines with its own radiance and by its shining makes all things luminous."[68] It is the eternal attribute of absolute consciousness that, as pure awareness, upholds itself with no support from outside itself. *Cit* also implies absolute knowledge, for it is the very fullness of all being in the act of knowing itself, as self-aware, and in this act of awareness, all knowledge is implicit.[69] Furthermore, Abhishiktananda tells us how *sat* and *cit* are not separate from each other, and could not be, because they are part of the same identity. He says: "*Sat* and *cit,* being and awareness of being, cannot be 'other' to each other; their relationship is irreducibly non-dual, and *advaita. Cit,* the awareness that I am, which I reach in my innermost depth, is not an attribute of *sat;* it actually is itself *sat.*"[70]

The third attribute of the Godhead, Brahman, experienced in the mystical state of advaita, is *ānanda,* bliss or joy, and as Panikkar observes, *ānanda* is "the highest spiritual bliss."[71] *Ānanda,* the bliss arising from the transcendent state of unity, is known when one knows the self, when one knows oneself as *cit* and *sat,* awareness and being, awareness of being. It is the bliss of self-aware being, being's self-knowing of itself.[72] Abhishiktananda explains: "Only by going beyond everything that I can call my own, can I taste—though it is not I that taste it—the savour of my ultimate depth. This is the bliss of simple being; and I am this very bliss, this *ānanda,* since I *am."*[73] Abhishiktananda is speaking from direct experience, and Bede follows his understanding of Advaita and Saccidānanda nearly to the letter. *Ānanda* cannot be measured or limited; it is the profoundest, most ultimate meaning of being and awareness, of *sat* and *cit.*[74] *"Ānanda* is the ultimate truth of Being, its inmost essence and complete revelation."[75] It is the pure bliss that comes from knowing the truth of one's being directly and resting in that deep awareness, which is resting in the Absolute itself, to which it leads.

Bede accepted this formulation of Hinduism's experience of the transcendent mystery, the ultimate reality of the Source. He had great respect for and trust in the authority of this profound experience, and regarded it as a genuine penetration by human consciousness into Divine Consciousness. In an eloquent passage from *The Marriage of East and West* he sums up his understanding of the Advaitic experience and its culmination in the Saccidanandan symbol and intuition. He says:

> When the mind in meditation goes beyond images and concepts, beyond reason and will to the ultimate Ground of its consciousness, it experiences itself in this timeless and spaceless unity of Being, and this is expressed in the "great sayings" of the Upanishads: "I am Brahman," "Thou Art That." The Ultimate is experienced in the depth of the soul, in the substance or Centre of its consciousness, as its own Ground or Source, as its very being or Self (Atman). This experience of God is summed up in the word *saccidānanda.* God, or Ultimate Reality, is experienced as absolute being *(sat),* known in pure consciousness *(cit),* communicating absolute bliss *(ānanda).* This was the experience of the seers of the Upanishads as it has been that of innumerable holy men in India ever since. It is an experience of self-transcendence, which gives an intuitive insight into Reality. It is this knowledge which Western man has to learn to acquire.[76]

Bede realized that this intuition can no longer be ignored

by Christianity because of the power of its truth. It is a living realization of a living tradition of spiritual actualization. Abhishiktananda attested to the authenticity of this tradition again and again in his numerous writings, reflections on paper that spring from his own long experience searching and knowing the depths of it firsthand. His life was a brilliant witness and symbol of the truth of the Advaitic and Christian traditions, as well as of the hope for their ultimate reconciliation through a deeper appreciation of the spiritual values present in each. Advaita is not something to be proven by argumentation or reasoning, but something to know through direct experience. And that is the whole point of it. The same holds true for Christian mysticism. Catholicism itself formally recognizes the existence of authentic spiritual intuitions and experiences, incomparable values in other traditions, and encourages us to "acknowledge, preserve, and promote the spiritual and moral goods found among these men, as well as the values in their society and culture."[77] Advaita and Saccidānanda are among these values and experiences that are treasures of the Spirit, which must be "acknowledged, preserved and promoted," because they have arisen from the depths of Hinduism's genius. These are the essential terms that Bede related in a substantive way to the ultimate depth of the Christian tradition, and perhaps of reality itself, the Trinitarian intuition. Before passing on to a consideration of Bede's notion of the Trinity and then to its relationship to Saccidānanda, I would like to examine briefly his vision of a Christian Advaita and what this amounted to in his view.

Christian Advaita

Bede saw in Christ's relationship with His Father a Christian instance of Advaita, of nonduality. For in Christ's consciousness of unity with His Father there is a nondual experience, as Bede interprets it. But this is not the type of Advaita where the distinction between the person and the Absolute disappears—in this case between Jesus and His Father—as with a figure like Śankara. As Bede comments: "He [Jesus] experienced Himself as one with God, the Father, and yet distinct."[78] It is an ontological unity that Jesus is referring to, but one that also preserves the identity of Jesus so that He can be said to be related to the Father and not swallowed up into a pure Advaita, a pure unity that obliterates difference. Bede based his idea of a Christian Advaita on the Gospel of John, especially chapters 10 and 17. In chapter 10, we read: "I and the Father are one."[79] And in chapter 17, we find it even more clearly expressed: "That they all may be one, as thou Father, in me, and I in you: that they also may be one in us."[80] Finally, also: "that they may be one, as we also are one. I in them, and you in me: that they may be made perfect in one...."[81]

Bede interpreted these statements in an Advaitic way, that is, as expressing the truth of a modified Advaitic experience in Christ's consciousness, but he is not referring to Ramanuja's "qualified" nonduality. Jesus is keenly aware of His ontological unity with the Father, but He does not claim pure identity with Him, Bede maintains. What Jesus is articulating, Bede says, is the principle of *unity-in-distinction, oneness-with-difference.* Bede elaborates this principle within the context of John's Gospel.

> But there [in John's Gospel], Jesus reveals this inner mystery of His oneness with the Father. This to me is the climax of it all, that this Son of Man, this man knows Himself in this unity with the Father. He can say, "I and the Father are one." And that is the mystery of *unity-in-distinction.* This is the point that is generally missed.... Jesus does not say, "I am the Father." That would be pure advaita, pure identity, but says rather, "I and the Father are one," which is unity-in-distinction.... And He also says, "I am in the Father, and the Father is in me." That is the proper way of expressing advaita in Christian terms.[82]

The starting point is the *human* consciousness of Jesus: Christ in His human consciousness sees His own divine self as being one in divinity with the Father and at the same time as a self or person proceeding as Son from the Father. This is unity-in-distinction. Bede followed this experiential approach through the inner consciousness of Jesus as a man. Bede applies his understanding of modified nonduality to Jesus' own experience in relation to the Father, and so is able to discover a Christian version of the triune identity. Advaita—and how to reconcile it with the Christian faith, particularly with the Trinitarian intuition—was also one of Abhishiktananda's constant preoccupations. He saw what he regarded as the Advaitic dimension of the Gospel in John's account, and in an essay entitled "The Johannine Upanishads" he makes this remark about the importance of John's Gospel: "That mystery which had first been glimpsed by the rishis is now revealed by St. John in all its splendour, seen in the clear light of the Word and in the depth of the Spirit."[83] He sees in chapter 17 of the Gospel of John what he believes to be the "crown and completion of the Upanishads," and although the language is different, "the profound experience it seeks to convey is the same—or rather, the experience of the Upanishads is here seemingly put to the test and reaffirmed in the light of Christ."[84] Bede agreed with this view, as we saw above, but his emphasis was different, since he stressed the relational element, the unity that, paradoxically, preserves distinction or Christ's unique identity. This relational element should become more evident in the next section.

BEDE'S NOTION OF THE TRINITY

Now we come to the other term in the relationship of Hinduism and the Christian faith, that of the Trinitarian insight. It is necessary for clarity's sake that we examine Bede's understanding of this great mystery before proceeding on to a consideration of it in relation to Saccidānanda. Bede's utterances concerning the nature and value of the Trinity are well within the tradition.

They were quite orthodox, but his whole approach to the mystery possessed a certain freshness and vitality that came, I believe, from a living intuition, a contemplative experience, rather than from mere abstract thought or conceptual and historical theological studies. There is the dynamism of mystical perception in it, which is usually rather fluid in language.[85] Indeed, the Trinity is for him not a static category of theology, but the living Center of all reality, the place of the meeting of the various religions and cultures of humanity.

We saw above that Christ's experience, His awareness of His unity with the Father, is the basis of a Christian Advaita, in Bede's view. We can elaborate Bede's understanding further and say that the Trinity's inner relations of oneness are also the foundation of Advaita in Christian terms. The Trinity is a mystery of unity; there is no duality to it. The relations of the Persons are all nondual. But they are nonetheless real relations. Bede declares: "It [the Trinity] is a total oneness, and yet there are distinctions within the One."[86] The distinctions are grounded in the unity, and the nondual relationship of the Persons preserves their distinctions. Unity-in-distinction is thus also the principle of the Trinitarian inner life and being, just as it is the basis of Christ's relationship with His Father. Bede underlines this important principle when he says: "In the Godhead itself, in the ultimate reality there is unity-in-distinction.... It is all interpersonal relationship. And personal relationship is one of knowledge and love."[87] On a human level, Bede points out how we come to know another, that through knowledge, we receive the other into our mind and heart. In this way, we distinguish the other or others from ourselves. But in love, we give ourselves to others, and others give themselves to us. Likewise, by analogy, "in the Godhead itself there is this movement of self-knowledge and self-communication."[88] The Son is the Father's self-knowledge, the full comprehension of His being, while the Father is the underived One, the Source, the Origin. He expresses Himself in the Word, in the Son, who is the Logos, and everything comes into being or manifestation through the Word, and everything manifests or reflects this Word and this relationship. Here is how Bede expresses it: "But all of this manifestation in creation and humanity is gathered into this one Supreme self-manifestation which is eternal, the Father knowing Himself in the Son, and the Son knowing Himself in the Father, so that this experience we have of the universe and of ourselves is a reflection of that knowledge which is eternal in the Ultimate, His self-understanding, self-reflection, self-manifestation, the Word expressing the Father, the Source ... and communicating Himself in the Spirit."[89]

The Spirit is what Bede called the power, or the Śakti of God. It is communicated to and revealed in the entire creation.[90] This Spirit, this Śakti is present as a power, an energy in everything. It is the eternal, uncreated energy of God, of the Father and the Son. And the Spirit "manifests itself in the energies in matter, in the energies of life, the energies in our whole human being.... The Spirit is manifesting through all this energy, and we receive this...."[91] The Spirit is the self-communication of the Father and the Son to us. And this Spirit is Love, for it is Love that is the energy manifesting itself in all creation, in us, and in the relationship of the Father and the Son, the Source to His Image. Bede elaborates his intuition, which also has traditional elements in it: "The Spirit is the Love of God acting in us as an energy, bringing us into being, and calling us back to Himself. Love is working in us to return. We receive our being, and we have to return that being in love.... The Father gives Himself to the Son; the Son gives Himself to the Father, and the Holy Spirit is that gift of Love by which the mystery of the Supreme Person (the Purusha) is revealed. The Ultimate Reality is a *personal* reality, involving personal relationship."[92]

There is interpersonal relationship among the members of the triune identity, and Bede brings this note out clearly. He thinks we have a profound revelation of this truth in Christ's relation to His Father, a relationship of knowledge and love, a distinction-in-unity. It is actually the Trinity that is the focus of Bede Griffiths's faith and commitment, and it is a commitment to a vision of a personalist approach to the Ultimate, to the *relationalness* of the Godhead. Bede was convinced that *communion* is the essence of God. Communion is how he translates the Greek term *koinonia,* from the experience of the Early Church tradition. God as Trinity is pure communion of being, and we share in that same communion, that *koinonia.* This communion is a dynamic, inner relationship of Love to Love.[93] Here he is following the eloquent formulation of Abhishiktananda, who says: "The mystery of the Holy Trinity reveals that *Being* is essentially a *koinonia* of love; it is communion, a reciprocal call to *be;* it is being-together, a being-with, *co-esse;* its essence is a coming-from and a going-to, a giving and receiving. All that is, is communion, extending from the Father, the Source of all, to the Spirit, the consummation of all, and transmitted by the Son; and again, extending from the human nature that was hypostatically united to the Word down to the lowliest elements in the universe."[94]

Communion, *koinonia,* is essentially a community of being in the triune identity, and this community of being at the heart of reality is eternally established in knowledge and love. The Trinity is pure relation in self-knowledge and in self-donation. It is the mystery of personal relationship in the Godhead. It is the revelation that the Ultimate is personal, personal or interpersonal relationship within the nonduality of the Absolute, the Godhead. And this personal relationship is itself love. Bede explains: "The Ultimate Reality is love, and love *is* relationship. You cannot have love with one (a static unity), and that is the weakness of a pure advaita. There is no love ultimately. There is pure consciousness, but no love. And yet in the Christian understanding there is pure consciousness and pure love: self-knowing and self-giving. The whole creation comes to its fullness in this intimacy of personal relationship. So, the personal God is *in* the Ultimate Godhead.

The Ultimate Godhead is both beyond person and integrates person."[95]

Bede maintains that because there is differentiation in the Godhead there is also love, and that only with differentiation or distinction can there be this love. And love is communion. There is distinction-in-unity in the Godhead's being. For Bede this is quite essential, since it becomes the metaphysical principle of difference or multiplicity in this world, and assures that this world, this cosmos, is *real*. It is not *māyā*, or illusion, nor is it *avidyā*, or ignorance. This is one of the dangers of Eastern thought, both Hindu and Buddhist, according to Bede, since both have a tendency to regard the world as unreal. The differentiation of the Persons in the Trinity grounds the differences here in the cosmos.[96] Bede puts it emphatically: "the Ultimate Reality is differentiated; the Son knows Himself in the Father. The Father knows Himself in the Son, and they are united in love in the Holy Spirit. And that is Ultimate Reality for us. That means all the differences of this world are *real* and meaningful...."[97] This is an important insight to stress because in Hinduism there is a general tendency to interpret everything in the light of the principle of unity and to disregard multiplicity. The Trinity, in Bede's understanding, seems to reconcile the one and the many, or to show how opposites can coincide, how unity and distinction are mutually inclusive, rather than contradictory.

In a real sense, in Bede's view, the Son or Word as the Logos is the actual metaphysical ground and principle of distinction and multiplicity. He is the paradigm of differentiation, the archetype of difference, the pattern for distinguishing. Of course this function that the Logos has operates eternally within the divine unity. But insofar as the Son as Logos is differentiated from the Father, the Source and underived Origin, He is paradigmatic of distinction, or difference, and how it is possible for the many— that is, this creation—to come out of the One. Because distinction-in-unity is actual in the triune Godhead, all phenomenal distinction, all multiplicity, is real, since it is made possible—and hence existent or actual—through a participation in the supreme actuality of the Logos. His actuality as truly distinct from the Father, and yet one with Him, is the foundation of distinction as such, as a metaphysical principle of differentiation. Thus, according to Bede, the Word is the source and juncture of distinction and unity. He is the conduit of the Father's knowledge, the living way in which the Father knows Himself and all things. And insofar as the Son, the Word, the Logos, is the foundation of all knowledge, forms, principles, and relations, He is also the ground of their cosmic manifestation in time/space, their concretization in the created order. Bede characterizes this process in the following way: "in the Logos, the whole creation, all humanity is gathered into unity, and is known by God. God knows Himself in that Word, that Son Who comes forth from Him as the Other.... The Word is the self-expression, the self-knowledge of God, and the Spirit is the self-communication of His being. And just as God knows Himself in the whole creation He has made, so He loves Himself [in it]. The Spirit is present in the whole creation.... In a real sense, we are loved into existence by God."[98]

This is that personalist tendency mentioned above showing itself, but it is united with a metaphysical acumen reminiscent of Thomas Aquinas and Bonaventure. The personalist and metaphysical inclinations go together; they are part of Bede's overall synthesis, and in terms of the Trinity, they are well expressed in this epigrammatic statement of his: "The Father knows himself in the Son and communicates himself in the Spirit."[99] It is fairly clear what Bede means by the first part of that statement, but the second part is a little vague. He provides an answer to this, however, indicating that what God communicates is His Love. He gives us His Love in giving us His Spirit, and this self-donation of Himself in His Love follows from His self-knowledge. And such an act of communicating Himself in His Spirit reveals a similar principle of self-donation in His inner being as triune identity, as Godhead. Bede conveys the insight in this way: "in the divine being, in the absolute reality, there is a movement of love, a self-giving, a self-surrender. God gives himself to man, communicates his own spirit, his inner self to man, but this in turn reflects a movement of self-giving, of self-surrender in the Godhead; the movement of self-knowing, of self-reflection, of self-consciousness in God, is accompanied by another movement of self-giving, of self-surrender, of ecstatic love."[100]

The Persons of the Trinity are bound together in a nondual relationship; this is the compelling depth of their unity. They are related through knowledge and love. But what is the basis of their unity? How are they one? What makes them to be one? This is a very difficult question, and in a sense, to know that is to understand the Trinitarian mystery. The answer that Bede gives to this important and deep question is quite interesting and comes from the tradition. The principle of their inner relationship is *perichoresis,* or *circuminsession.* The Persons are totally present in one another. Or, as Bede puts it, they are *dancing* in one another.[101] They are indwelling in one another. Both of these terms mean mutual penetration,[102] or indwelling. Bede describes perichoresis or circuminsession as a "perfect coinherence," and of this he declares: "The Father is in the Son and the Son in the Father in such a way that they have but one nature which is totally in each without any duality. There is no difference between the Father and the Son except that of relationship. Their nature or essence is one 'without duality,' without any difference whatsoever."[103]

Perichoresis is thus an expression of an Advaitic type of relationship, or rather an acknowledgment of a unity of being that is quite similar to Advaita. So it is, in a sense, the form of the Divine Advaita. But to understand the inner life of the Godhead, of the Trinity, Bede tells us, we must participate in the experience, the inner consciousness of Christ. This requires that we "receive the Spirit of God ... share in the divine life and so become the son of God, to be one with Jesus as he is one with the Father."[104]

SACCIDĀNANDA AND TRINITY

Now we come at long last to the crucial question of this whole study: the relationship of Saccidānanda/Advaita and the Trinity. How are they related? This was the central focus of Bede's contemplative theology, or rather, the assumption that they are relatable was a working principle of Bede's mystical theology, worldview, and spiritual practice. If these two intuitions are internally compatible, if they meet in the deepest level of consciousness and are symbolic expressions of this depth dimension they seek to name, then a Christian Vedanta would be possible. Then an Indian Christian theology would also be possible, one that draws its terms, symbols, and methodology from Hinduism in a carefully selective way. In a strict sense, an Indian Christian theology is not dependent upon the success of a Christian Vedanta, because such a theology is a response to the needs of the Indian Church and the Indian people, and it is a creation of that cultural/religious context. Furthermore, a Christian form of the Vedanta has to be recognizably Hindu in the profoundest sense; that is, it has to reflect the spirit of its mystical doctrine we have outlined and discussed above, and it must also be thoroughly Christian. In another sense, to develop a Christian form of the Vedanta that is a valid expression of both traditions is also to develop an Indian Christian theology. Can the Vedantic experience of the Ultimate Mystery as we have unfolded it here express the essential truth of the Christian tradition, the truth of the Trinitarian nature of the Godhead as Christ, the Son of God, experienced it? Can Advaita and Saccidānanda validly convey the Christian intuition?

Bede seemed to think so, and there is a history to his conviction that runs through the modern sannyasic movement as Christians have attempted to adopt and live this ideal. Brahmabandhab Upadhyay, Jules Monchanin, Abhishiktananda, and countless others have all considered this issue in great depth. Abhishiktananda's whole life, for example, was predicated on the assumption that the two traditions could be reconciled on the level of mysticism. Prior to both Abhishiktananda and Monchanin, in the late nineteenth century on into the early part of the twentieth, Upadhyay encouraged a synthesis between Vedanta and the Christian faith. Speaking within the context of evangelization, he makes this bold pronouncement concerning adaptation: "The European clothes of the Catholic religion should be removed as early as possible. It must put on the Hindu garment to be acceptable to the Hindus. This transformation can be effected by the hands of Indian missionaries preaching the Holy Faith in the Vedantic language, holding devotional meetings in the Hindu way and practising the virtue of poverty conformably to Hindu asceticism."[105]

From this statement we can discern that Upadhyay accepts wholeheartedly the missionary strategy, formulated in the sixteenth century by the Jesuit Roberto de Nobili, to translate the Christian faith into the language of Hinduism; but he goes beyond this point somewhat. He begins to take a synthesis for granted. For instance, when writing about his founding of a Christian ashram, he proposes this ideal: "Here in the midst of solitude and silence will be reared up true Yogis to whom the contemplation of the Triune Saccidānanda will be food and drink."[106] Such a synthesis seems to him a foregone conclusion, and it appears he did assert that "God is *Sat-Cit-Ananda.*"[107]

Monchanin, whose entire adult life was focused on the mystery of the Trinity as the Ultimate Reality, was far more cautious than Upadhyay. He saw the encounter of the two traditions as the work of contemplatives in both faiths, and he shared this view in common with Abhishiktananda, and with Bede Griffiths. Bede remarks: "Father Monchanin and Father Le Saux were both deep students of Hindu thought, but they also realized that the ultimate ground of meeting between the Church and Hinduism must take place not in the realm of thought but in that of contemplation."[108] But Monchanin was able to define the focus and ideal of the relationship of the two traditions, and to present the context, which is *sannyāsa*. In prophetic words, he declares: "We would like to crystallize and transubstantiate the search of the Hindu *sannyāsi. Advaita* and praise of the Trinity are our only aim."[109] But then he goes on to elaborate his meaning, and this, I think, shows the degree to which he, Abhishiktananda, Bede, and others take seriously the mystical intuition and doctrine of Hinduism. He indicates what is involved in this "transubstantiation," this inward relating of the two doctrines: "This means that we must grasp the authentic Hindu search for God in order to Christianize it, starting with ourselves first of all, from within."[110] This is a deeply significant statement, because it sets out the program that Abhishiktananda, Bede, and others have followed ever since.

It is Abhishiktananda, however, who goes the furthest in this process, and certainly the deepest. He symbolizes in himself that very depth of reconciliation to which Monchanin refers and which is a basic ideal of Bede Griffiths. Abhishiktananda lacks the caution of both Monchanin and Bede. At least this seems to me to be the case. He passes beyond the ideal stated by Monchanin and plunges into the heart of the proposed convergence. At first he does so slowly. In the introduction to the original French edition of *Saccidānanda*,[111] which also appears as appendix 3 of the revised English edition, Abhishiktananda states: "the Indian intuition of *Saccidānanda* seems to be truly the nearest approach of human thought in the direction of the Trinitarian mystery, which is also the most interior mystery alike in God and in man.... Sensitive Christian thinkers cannot fail to perceive in the intuition of *Saccidānanda* itself a kind of stepping-stone towards the Trinity and at the same time an invitation to lose themselves a little more completely in that divine Depth which summons them from within the self, and is even deeper than the self."[112]

But from this mild statement in the old introduction he moves to the point where he sees the possibility of an essential *convergence,* and he identifies the Trinity, the Three Persons, with Saccidānanda, or, more precisely, he suggests an identification, and this is very clearly put. He makes this powerful statement, which is also like a plea, out of a profound conviction of the truth of both mystical traditions, both Saccidānanda and the Trinity, but he does so from his own experiential awakening into an awareness of both. In his own experience he seems to have discovered the key to their relationship and compatibility. He tells us that what he is presenting here is not a matter of theological speculation about the terms in the relation of the two traditions. Rather, as he remarks, it is more "a matter of an awakening, an awareness far beyond the reach of intellect, an experience which springs up and erupts in the deepest recesses of the soul."[113] But what is that experience? What is that identity that he discerns between Saccidānanda and Trinity? It appears that he interprets Saccidānanda and the Trinity as essentially the same. Abhishiktananda evokes the identity of the two traditions in their core experience and doctrines in this way: "The experience of Saccidānanda carries the soul beyond all merely intellectual knowledge to her very centre, to the source of her being. Only there is she able to hear the Word which reveals within the undivided unity and advaita of Saccidānanda the mystery of the Three Persons: in *sat,* the Father, the absolute Beginning and Source of being; in *cit,* the Son, the divine Word, the Father's Self-knowledge; in *ānanda,* the Spirit of love, Fullness and Bliss without end."[114]

He is leading us to believe that Saccidānanda is the door, in Hinduism, which leads into the realization of the Trinity at the heart of being, and after passing through the Word, the Logos, allows us to understand the isomorphic relation between, on the one hand, *sat, cit, ānanda,* and on the other, the Father, Son, and Holy Spirit. Moreover, it is an experience, not a matter of theorizing; and, one gets the impression, it is Abhishiktananda's own experience, his realization. One also gets the clear sense that he is certain of the identity he asserts, of the ontological connection that he so courageously articulates with such grace and profundity. It was a position he did not come to lightly, and which he agonized over for years. He had an enormously significant impact on the thought of Bede Griffiths on this pivotal, even epochal relationship. But what is Bede's view of the matter? How does he regard the relationship of Advaita/Saccidānanda and Trinity?

It is clear that he considers Advaita/Saccidānanda and the Trinity as the focus and overarching relationship between the Hindu and Christian traditions. In this commitment he is in harmony with his great predecessors, Monchanin and Abhishiktananda. Bede had known for many years that if the two traditions were ever to meet in depth, it would have to be around that which is essential to both. That much is clear. From his statements in this chapter, recorded and discussed here, it should be evident that for Bede, Advaita/Saccidānanda and the Trinity are a mystical knowledge, and if they can be related, it will have to be similarly in a mystical way. It is not sufficient to relate them theologically, because that is speculative. If Abhishiktananda is correct, one has to tread the way of experiential realization and look for the point of internal convergence. Let us turn to what Bede Griffiths had to say on this fascinating subject.

Bede has a different approach. His concern is more practical: the development of an Indian Christian theology which is also a contemplative theology. He does not speak in terms of radical identity between the Advaita/Saccidānanda experience and the Trinitarian intuition. He is always careful not to let his enthusiasm run ahead of his common sense, nor to assert something that he is not sure about, or of which his experience is limited. My reading of his works and my studies do not indicate a position like that of Abhishiktananda, at least on the issue of the relationship of Saccidānanda and the Trinity. He accepts the focus on the relationship as the place of comparison and meeting, but not quite the same formulation as Abhishiktananda adduces. Bede's whole approach is somewhat circumspect; it is marked by prudence. He is convinced of the authenticity of the Advaita/ Saccidānanda experience, as we saw above, but his priority is whether or not Saccidānanda can be used as a term for the Trinity, that is, whether or not the Christian mystery can be accurately expressed through the categories of the Vedanta. His sympathy is with Abhishiktananda, even his admiration, but his way of framing the relationship between the depth terms of both traditions is modest.

Bede advocates a change in the theological language, for India, in the way in which the Trinitarian mystery is formulated and presented. He comments on the inadequacy of the Western development of Trinitarian theology and believes it to be too much dominated by Greek philosophical thought. He asks if it would be possible to interpret the Christian experience of the Trinity differently,[115] something more in line with Indian culture, language, and spiritual tradition. And he answers this question in the affirmative, suggesting the Saccidanandan experience as a good way in which to express the Trinity in an Indian context. That is the background of his formulation. Bede asks:

> Would it not be possible to interpret the experience of Jesus in the light of the Hindu understanding of ultimate reality? We could then speak of God as *Saccidānanda*—Being, Knowledge, Bliss—and see in the Father, *sat,* Being, the absolute eternal "I am," the ground of Being, the source of all. We could then speak of the Son, as the *cit,* the knowledge of the Father, the Self-consciousness of eternal Being, the presence to itself in pure consciousness of the infinite One; Being reflecting on itself, expressing itself in an eternal Word. We could then speak of the Father as *Nirguna Brahman,* Brahman "without attributes," the infinite abyss of being beyond word and thought. The Son would be *Saguna Brahman,* Brahman "with attributes," as Creator, Lord, Saviour, the Self-manifestation of the unmanifest God, the personal aspect of

the Godhead, the *Purusha*.... Finally, we could speak of the
spirit as the *ānanda,* the Bliss or Joy of the Godhead, the
outpouring of the superabundant being and consciousness
of the eternal, the Love which unites Father and Son in the
non-dual Being of the Spirit.[116]

What Bede is essentially asking is, first, can the inner experience of Jesus be expressed or communicated and so understood
in other than Western or Greek theological language? And if so,
is the Hindu formulation of Ultimate Reality, or Saccidānanda,
able to adequately communicate the Trinitarian mystery, the
heart of the Christian faith? If there is no real objection to creating a Trinitarian theological language that conveys the mystery in the terms of *sat, cit, ānanda,* or Being-Knowledge-Bliss,
that is, Saccidānanda, then this Hindu mystical insight can be
applied to a new formulation of the Trinitarian intuition and
experience. Furthermore, this would require that the notion of
Nirguna Brahman would stand in the place of the notion of the
Father as Godhead, the Source beyond manifestation and multiplicity, and that the notion of Saguna Brahman would express the
function of the Son as Logos, while the Puruṣa could convey the
personalism of the divine nature. Thus, what Bede is attempting
to do here is to give us an example of what is involved in a new
formation of a Christian theology that takes its language from a
different cultural and historical experience. He is confident that
such a new formulation would be valid. The implication is that,
although the metaphysical and theological terminology we employ in the growth of Christian theology is important, the more
crucial point is that the content of Christian faith is itself not
bound exclusively to any one culture or linguistic framework; it
is flexible and capable of endless variation of expression.

What is also immediately apparent is that Abhishiktananda's
influence is strong insofar as Bede comes to grips with the importance of the Saccidanandan intuition and sees the necessity to give
it some role in Christian theology. At the same time, Bede does

not openly identify the two experiences in quite the same way as Abhishiktananda; he does not reduce them to each other. His approach is more gentle, though in the long run it may have the same effect as that of Abhishiktananda. Clearly, insofar as Bede formulates the Trinitarian mystery in terms of Saccidānanda, there is an implication of an isomorphic relationship between these two intuitions. In some sense they must be seen as complementary. If this is the case, then they share in a mystical continuum that makes an existential convergence possible. That is one reason it can be said that Saccidānanda is a symbol of the Trinity, that Bede's ashram can be dedicated to the Holy Trinity under the name of Saccidānanda, and that Upadhyay could compose a hymn to the Trinity under the same name of Saccidānanda.[117] So, although an identity between Saccidānanda and Trinity is not claimed by Bede, it is perhaps implied. But I think the primary emphasis of Bede's thought here is on a theological adaptation and appropriation of Hindu or Vedantic terms, and only secondarily on an isomorphic relationship of the two mystical intuitions of Ultimate Reality. So the two terms are intimately related in Bede's understanding but expressed in a more concrete and practical way.

Although Bede does not compromise Christian truth, its principles, or its metaphysics, he does admit not only to the possibility of a convergence but really to its necessity, the necessity for the Christian faith to break out of its European conceptual habits and modes of expression, so that it can discover and appropriate what is of value in the Eastern religions and in this case, in Hinduism. This is what he understood by convergence, or the context of it: the growth of Christianity into an openness that allows for a universal assimilation of the values and intuitions of other traditions, making them part of its own heritage, and formulating the Christian mystery in their terms, those of other traditions that are relevant to the Christian way. This is his method of convergence that I glean from his approach, on the basis of his statements about Advaita and Saccidānanda. Referring to the universality of the future, he remarks: "We have to open ourselves to the revelation of the divine mystery, which took place in Asia, in Hinduism and Buddhism, in Taoism, Confucianism and Shintoism. Nor can we neglect the intuitive wisdom of more primitive people...."[118] These and other traditions all have something to contribute to the Church's self-understanding of her spiritual tradition, a tradition that embraces every culture and religion. The Eastern traditions and the primitive tribal religions are able, in Bede's view, to awaken new levels of meaning in the Christian faith.[119] This is the context of convergence, for him.

When the encounter of two or more traditions, through representatives of each, takes place on the ultimate level of depth—in the case of Bede, in the relation of Advaita/Saccidānanda and Trinity—then there occurs what I call an existential convergence, for it is an encounter that goes beyond mere dialogue and plunges into the mystical depths of each tradition, attempting to relate them in this very depth of spiritual realization. In existential convergence or encounter, there is an openness and receptivity to the other tradition and a sensitivity to how it can have an internal relation to one's own. This presupposes an experiential interest in the depth of both traditions represented.

Furthermore, an existential convergence also entails, especially in our present example, what can be called a continuum of realization. It requires that the two mystical intuitions, if relatable, are relatable because they are in continuity with each other by their participation in the one ontological mystery. In this mystical continuum of realization, an infinite depth is possible, accessible to the one who is dwelling there. In the light of Bede's understanding of a Christian Advaita as it has been presented above, I think it is not inappropriate to say that the Trinitarian intuition represents a deeper experience on this ultimate continuum of realization, because of its dimension of personalism, which is lacking in Hindu Advaita, at least insofar as this has been represented in the mainline literature of Hindu philosophy and spirituality, particularly in the interpretation of the Śankara school of Advaita. Because interpersonal relationship is the essential characteristic of the Trinity, and since this relationship is one of communion in knowledge and love, it is thus a fair assumption to suggest, on the basis of Bede's statements, that the Trinitarian doctrine/intuition is actually a deeper, more ultimate experience of the Ultimate Reality and mystery than the Advaita/Saccidananda doctrine/intuition and experience. And this is as it should be, for a Christian can never accept a doctrine as more ultimate than the revelation of the *personal* nature of Divine Being that has come to us in Jesus Christ. Without this quintessential, mysterious revelation, mystical life and metaphysical reflection on the basis of that experience is lacking. It lacks a more complete or integral understanding, for the interpersonal dimension is a very important part of human life, and as the Christian tradition shows, and Bede concurs, it is the essence of Being itself; it is the ground of human relations, the archetype of human relations in their perfection. And it seems that the Hindu doctrine, as Bede understood it, is actually somewhat limited in the Upaniṣadic period and only gains or discovers the personal God late in the tradition with the *Śvetāśvatara Upaniṣad* and the Bhagavad Gita.

So, with respect to the question raised above as to the possibility of the Advaitic/Saccidanandan formulation validly expressing the Christian intuition of the Trinity, a qualified "yes" can be given. This means essentially two things: appropriated term/symbol and respect. *Saccidānanda* is a term adopted from the Hindu tradition to symbolize the Trinitarian mystery, and it signifies a new application of this insight to the work of formulating the Christian experience in Indian language. At the same time, this qualified assent also signifies a profound respect for and sensitivity toward the Advaitic/Saccidanandan intuition as an authentic realization, a genuine mystical experience/insight. I think that is presupposed in existential convergence, and it should be clear from the above discussion. I think it is also reasonable to assume, on the basis of Bede's understanding, that this development represents a new page in the history of Vedanta, a Christian form of Vedanta. And it is also by this very fact an Indian Christian theology, because not only has it "Christianized" the Vedantic understanding, but it has also succeeded in formulating the Christian faith—the heart of it anyway—in Hindu or Indian terms. Since the Advaitic doctrine is the key to relating Hinduism and Christianity, a Christian form of the doctrine—if sound—would automatically issue in a new development in the Vedanta, the recognition that Vedanta is also Christian as well as Hindu. To arrive at this point is also to have found the basis of an Indian Christian theology, since what is fundamental from the Hindu point of view—Advaita/Saccidānanda—is made the foundation on which to convey the Christian experience of the mystery to India and her diverse populations.

Is Bede's method of convergence, and his attempt to "translate" the Christian mystery into Vedantic terms, an arbitrary approach? Or does it follow from the very nature of our act of faith? If the medieval definition of theology is correct—that is, "faith seeking understanding"—then Bede's method is not arbitrary but a natural extension of our desire to grasp the mystery of our faith. His method of convergence is predicated on the assumption that Hinduism can open up new levels of meaning in the Christian tradition, levels that we could not have conceived as possible. It also presupposes the organic and dynamic nature of Christianity's innate universality, ever growing and always assimilating new cells, new spiritual treasures, and always open to another way to spread the Good News of the Gospel. There are many possible ways in which the Christian experience can be formulated, and the Greco-Latin way is only one of them. Bede Griffiths believed that Hinduism's metaphysical and contemplative thought may be another.

The next chapter will consider Bede's Christology as it flows from contemplative wisdom, a contemplative understanding of Christ's place in the scheme of reality. Then we will explore Tantrism as an important element in his synthesis, and finally, we will move on to an in-depth consideration of *sannyāsa* as the basis of Christian monasticism in India, and Bede's view of the Church's future as it relates to the process of assimilating the wisdom of the Hindu tradition and the other traditions as well.

6

Christology, Tantrism, Sannyāsa, and the Future of the Church

I N CHAPTER 5, after giving considerable attention to preparatory details and the definition of terms, we saw how Bede Griffiths conceived of a Christian Advaita and how he regarded or formulated the relationship of Hinduism and Christianity from the ultimate perspective of each other's mystical intuition of the Absolute. This relationship was narrowed down to two essential terms: *Saccidānanda* and the Trinity. It was also shown, in Bede's thought, what a Christian Vedanta entails and how an Indian Christian theology is possible. Furthermore, *Saccidānanda* was found to be a possible term for the Trinity in such a theology.

It was also suggested that the relating of Advaita/ Saccidānanda and the Trinitarian intuition—if genuinely reflecting Ultimate Reality and thus valid—presupposes an ontological continuity, a continuum of realization insofar as both intuitions/ mystical doctrines arise out of the same mystery of Being and the same metaphysical reality. For both are part of the one system of being and life as it is experienced in mystical consciousness. Moreover, the meeting of Hinduism and the Christian faith, of Advaita/Saccidānanda and Trinity, on this profound level of encounter is actually an existential convergence, since there is a substantive connection between the two that goes beyond mere dialogue into the very ground of their relationship in that ultimate depth we call the Spirit. And yet we also discovered that in Bede's view, the Trinitarian intuition and doctrine represent a deeper conception of the mystery, because it recognizes as primary the personal, interpersonal, indeed *relational* dimension of the Godhead, that the divine mystery is one of *communion* at the heart of its being, and that this communion consists of knowledge and love.

In this, the penultimate chapter, I will examine the Christology of Bede Griffiths, which rounds out his doctrine of God as he understands the Divine. Clearly, his Christological insight is an absolutely indispensable element in his theological/contemplative vision. This will be the subject of the first section. The next three sections are more practical and concentrate on methodology of spiritual realization and the task of integration and assimilation as part of the Church's mission in Asia and elsewhere. More specifically, the second section deals with Bede's understanding of Tantrism and its importance for Christian spirituality, while the third considers *sannyāsa* as the way and experiential context for the encounter of Hinduism and Christianity. Here we are concerned with the possibility of a Christian form of *sannyāsa*. Finally, in the last section of the chapter, the focus is the future of the Church in relation to the process of assimilation, integration, and modifications of the spiritual insights, intuitions, and experiences of Hinduism and the other great traditions.

There is a unity to this chapter and its four sections that might not be obvious at first. The structure perhaps seems a bit arbitrary, but there is a *practical* theme that guides these issues, and so it is appropriate to situate them together in the same chapter. The practical concern of Bede's Christology ultimately centers on Christ as paradigmatic of Sonship. The concern here is not the perspective of the human potentiality for God-realization, as exemplified in the life and consciousness of Jesus, but to illustrate how Jesus became inwardly aware of His relationship with the

Father. At the same time, Jesus is the pattern or model for how the person discovers God in the depths of his or her own being. Bede's Christology also illustrates Christ's relationship with the Godhead (the Father) and the entrance into a knowledge of this ultimate level of experience. Tantrism is part of Bede's practical concerns because it is a spiritual discipline and mystical path that follows the Incarnational movement: the Divine becoming flesh and leading the Creation back to the Transcendent. *Sannyāsa* is also intimately part of this process of realizing God or the transcendent mystery because it is a living-out of this mystery in the quest for union with the Divine Reality. It is a *lived* theology. Christian *sannyāsa* realizes the Incarnation inwardly. Furthermore, the Church in India has to follow and apply the same mystery of the Incarnation in terms understandable to the Indian culture, and has a role to play beyond India. This role consists of opening up more and more to the other great religious traditions in Asia and elsewhere, an openness that allows the Church to grow into her own innate universality.

BEDEAN CHRISTOLOGY

The way in which Bede conceived of the relationship of Hinduism and the Christian faith depends in large part on his profoundly rich Christological views. Indeed the revelation of the Trinity comes through the experience of Jesus, his own inner awareness of His relationship with His Father.[1] We must remember that Bede is relating the two traditions on the basis of the quintessential mystical doctrine of each, as we have seen in chapter 5, and in order to grasp the Christian mystical doctrine we must pass through Christ. As Bede succinctly puts it: "The Christian mystical experience springs from the contemplation of the life and death of Jesus of Nazareth."[2] This statement sums up for us not only Bede's approach to the Absolute but that of Christianity generally. For Christ is the way into a knowledge of the Father in the

Spirit. I think we can isolate in Bede's method, in his approach, three essential elements as far as his Christology is concerned: the historical, the psychological-mystical, and the cosmic. His Christology is basically an elaboration of these three dimensions in their interrelation and as they relate to the overarching principle of his contemplative theology: the Trinitarian doctrine/intuition and its connection with Saccidānanda. The historical element concerns the mode of the revelation that comes through the Incarnation; the psychological-mystical element concentrates on Christ's consciousness of His inner relationship to the Father; while the cosmic dimension of Bede's Christology considers the impact of Christ on the material universe. Near the end of this section I will also take up Bede's vision of an Indian Christology.

Bede emphasizes that history is one of the elements that distinguish the Christian tradition from the Hindu.[3] Hinduism is grounded in mythological time and the contemplative doctrine that evolved out of the meditative experience of its founders. Christianity derives from the actual historical event of Jesus Christ's life in this world of space and time, in a definite period of history amid a real people. Bede expresses the importance of the historical element in this way: "It is of the essence of Christian faith that Jesus of Nazareth was 'crucified under Pontius Pilate.' This is enshrined in the earliest Christian creed and is a fact of history known to the Roman historian Tacitus. This setting in concrete historical time is of the essence of the Christian revelation."[4] This is a crucial point for Bede, one that he never tired of making whenever he compared the Christian and Hindu traditions. In an incisive essay entitled "Krishna and Christ,"[5] Bede characterizes the difference between the two traditions on the basis of this element of history. Krishna is known for the quality of ecstatic love, and for somewhat questionable behavior toward the Gopīs (the cowherding women of his village, who were his devotees), which seems to show him in an immoral light. This latter factor may indeed be symbolic. Bede asks what the difference between Krishna and Christ is, and comments that: "Krishna is a mythical character without any real base in history. There may have been an historical Krishna...but he has become a legendary character, the hero of an epic poem, the Mahabharata, and of the Puranas, which belong to the world of myth."[6]

By contrast, Christ is a real person, an actual historical figure, who can be located in a reasonably precise time frame and whose life, actions, and teachings are recorded. In this actual historical person called Jesus Christ there is no moral ambiguity, as in the case of Kriṣna. Christ represents the moral perfection of holiness, the primary characteristic of God Himself. Bede stresses the nature of Christian revelation: "The love of God was revealed in Christ not in poetry but in history. It was shown not in ecstasy but in self-giving for others, in the surrender of his life on the cross."[7] Bede asserts that this quality of moral perfection ascribed to God, or a god, is not found in any other tradition but the Judeo-Christian, and that it reaches its highest point in Christ.[8] Christ is pure holiness, the holiness of God, the very essence of which is Love. This incarnation of Divine Love entered our situation in order to bring salvation. He became subject to the historical process and the human condition. Bede again emphasizes the element of history: "The death and resurrection of Christ is a unique event. In one sense it is a mythological event, an event of supreme symbolism. It is a sign of God's salvation for the whole creation and the whole of humanity. But it is a sign which is rooted in history."[9]

The Incarnation has a meaning for all time and for all history. It was no accident that it came in the form and through the mode of historical process. Can it not be said that Christ's entrance into the human condition, into history, was meant to influence the historical life of humankind, to transform the human race forever? Bede believed so. The Incarnation communicated something essential to us, to all people and to subsequent history. It has altered the value of history, time, and life itself and reordered historical time in the direction of Christ and the Kingdom He came to establish. It has a significance for every member of the human family, for all share in the unity of the human family in God. Bede comments:

> the life and death and resurrection of Christ have not only a meaning for all, but also an effect on history. Through the death and resurrection of Christ the history of man has been changed. Mankind has been changed because mankind is ultimately one, an organic, interdependent whole extending through space and time. The death and resurrection of Christ extends to all humanity, both in the past and in the present and in the future.... It is a symbolic event and yet it is also a historic event. Here history has assumed universal meaning. The whole creation and the whole of humanity find an ultimate meaning, an ultimate purpose, in that death, resurrection, ascension, and final glorification.[10]

Bede comments how the Hindu view of life lacks this profound sense of history, the awareness of time as having a goal, working toward a concrete end, that progress is possible because of the linear nature of time recognized by Western religious tradition. The understanding of time in the Hindu and other Eastern cultures is cyclic, and the cyclic notion of time rests on the rhythms of nature: the rising and setting of the sun, the phases of the moon, the seasons of the year coming and going in regularity, in a word, the cosmic order. That is, cyclic time "is a world based on the cosmic order."[11] This approach devalues Creation in such a way that it can be dismissed as "unreal," illusory, or *māyā*. Bede maintains, furthermore, that in Hinduism there is no adequate conception of Creation, and this is a serious weakness in its philosophical worldview.[12] He says, further, that out of this system, this worldview based on the cosmic order, the notion of *karma* arises, which limits the moral perception of the Hindus, in short, does not allow them to see what in fact Christ so eloquently expressed: our essential responsibility for others, our responsibility to love them in the concrete by responding to their need. The historical awareness of the Jews and Christians is conducive to an understanding of Creation and its reality, its purpose and value. This also allows for a sensitivity to the moral order on which Jesus attempted to focus humanity's attention. This whole issue introduces a crucial difference between Hinduism and Christianity, which Bede honestly faces, and he makes this comment about the limitation of the Hindu view:

> I cannot help feeling that the present situation of India, with its masses of poor, illiterate people, of people suffering from disease and being left to die in the streets, really stems from this basic philosophy—all are caught in this wheel of samsara [cycle of births and deaths]. Your karma has brought you to this state where you are dying in the street, but when you have died you will be reborn, and, please God, you will have a better birth next time. If one can help somebody else to have a better birth, if one can help him on his way, that is good; but there is no obligation to do it. Karma is working itself out.[13]

The Judeo-Christian Revelation overcomes the exclusively mythical conception of time as cyclic and its implications for human moral and social life. In this revelation experience, God is discovered to be working in and through history, the history of Israel, and He is a Holy God who sets moral demands on His people. They are responsible for the needs of others, and as Bede says, "when they reject the orphan and the widow and the poor they reject God."[14] This is rather powerful indeed. There is an obligation to others, and there is an obligation to act. History, the sense of it in the experience of the Jews, leads to a different understanding of time. As Bede observes: "Time is no longer cyclic; time is moving towards an end, an *eschaton*. That is something completely new...."[15] It is this discovery that breaks through the cyclic notion of time and the samsaric conception of reality. Time is moving toward a definite spiritual goal. Bede comments on this and Christ's role: "Our actual human life, our deeds from day to day, belong to an eternal order, and reveal the direction in which the world is moving. All things are under the providence of God and are leading to a final fulfillment. With the coming of Christ we encounter this finality."[16]

In a very real sense, in the Christian vision, Christ is that very finality. He is the purpose of history, or the way to realize the goal of time and the historical process. The Incarnation is bound up with history, because the historical is the medium through which the Incarnation acts in and through the process and reorients it toward its proper end: the Divine Life enfleshed and conveyed in Christ, who is the way to history's fulfillment in the Kingdom of Heaven, in salvation. But this way, which Christ shows in Himself, passes through the domain of moral action, the path of love and devotion, of selfless service to others, a path that goes right through the marketplace, throughout the world, which is seen as real and valued. The historicity of Revelation and of Christ makes it possible for Jews and Christians to read the deeper lesson: that God is present in all reality and in every person.

But how did Bede understand this historical event of the Incarnation? This brings us to the second element of Bede's Christological doctrine, the psychological and mystical. This historical event/process is intimately dependent upon Christ's inner experience of His unity with God, with the Father. Such an awareness involves His own self-understanding, His psychological awareness, and this is rooted in His identity of Sonship, His mystical identity as the Son of the Living God. Because of His ontological unity with God, His Father, He is God as the Son, and so in Him, the human and the Divine meet. Bede expresses his understanding more clearly: "The Christian doctrine is expressed by saying that in Christ the divine and the human nature were united in one person. In his Person, that is in his Self, in the ultimate ground of his being, he was God. He knew himself as the Word of God, the expression of the mind of the Father. But ...

he was conscious of himself as man, having a human soul and a human body, sharing the limitations of human nature."[17]

As far as Christ's inward consciousness is concerned, Bede holds, He was aware of an "identity in relationship."[18] As we saw in chapter 5, Jesus never claims to be the Father, only to be *one* with Him. This is the identity in relationship to which Bede refers, interpreting Christ's statement in the Gospel of John (10:30). Unity-in-distinction is the basis of Christ's relationship with the Father, but this is grounded in an ontological identity. The dominant note is one of personal relationship. Bede elaborates: "It is unity in duality, by which he can say, 'I am in the Father and the Father in me' (John 14:10), which is based on an identity of being, by which he can say, 'He who sees me, sees the Father' (John 14:9). It is the experience of the Absolute in personal relationship, and that would seem to be the distinctive character of the Christian experience of God."[19]

But the reality of Christ, and what He revealed to His friends, goes beyond a simple knowledge of His ultimate identity with God, with the Source of Being, the Father. Christ not only reveals Himself as the Son of God, but He also reveals how His friends and disciples can become sons of God. He invites them into an intimacy with the Father such as He Himself enjoys as the "only begotten Son." As the one Son He expresses the exemplar of divine Sonship, the pattern in terms of which all men and women can become sons and daughters of the Father. Bede states: "For Christ communicates this experience of Sonship to his disciples—'to as many as believed in him, he gave the power to become sons of God' (John 1:12)—and this comes about through the gift of the Spirit, by which man is raised to share in the life and consciousness of God.... The significance of the incarnation is, then, that through it mankind is raised to a participation in the divine consciousness."[20]

Christ's psychological identity is founded on a deeper ontological identity that is itself a mystical relationship with the

Source of Being. But as the Son of God, as the Logos and Image of the Father's being, does this make Jesus God? Is Christ God? This is a basic question Bede raises in his provocative but quite stimulating Christology. Bede has trouble using the term *God* for Christ, the Son of God. This is because he reserves the word *God* for the transcendent Godhead, the Father, and this is again something Jesus never claimed to be. As Bede says, defining the word *God:* "God is the absolute, eternal, infinite, transcendent Being, above word and thought, the Holy Mystery beyond human conception...."[21] Christ is concrete and present to His disciples and to those others who experienced His presence to them in His life here. He is not only the remote and ineffable One, the Logos, when He is incarnated in the human situation. He is not just the transcendent Ground in His appearance before others, but also the immanent reality of the divine nature. Bede describes Christ in these terms: "Jesus is the manifestation, the self-revelation of this incomprehensible mystery, the Man who makes known what the ineffable God is like. He 'reflects the glory of God and bears the very stamp of His nature' (Hebrews 1:3). He is the Word of God, who expresses in human terms what God is.... He is not 'simply' God; he is *God in Man,* and *Man in God.*"[22] Jesus in His human nature represents archetypal Man, but Man as he has achieved perfection in God, or what man is meant to be. That is why He is often referred to as the "Second Adam," for Adam, the first man, is the archetype of man as such. This is the meaning of *adam* in Hebrew, simply "man," or all humanity. It is the generic term. Christ "is Man totally open to God, Man transparent to the Divine Reality. In him we see God as far as God can be seen."[23]

How then is Jesus God in Bede's understanding? It would seem, judging from his statements, though there is a paucity of them on this issue, that Bede conceives of Jesus' divinity primarily, though not exclusively, in a spiritual/ontological sense. That is why I have emphasized the psychological-mystical element in his Christology. He approaches this question from within the subjectivity of Christ, as evidenced by His statements to His disciples and to others, and in what He did. He considers the issue from the perspective of Christ's openness to God. This openness he calls a "capacity to receive the Spirit from God."[24] Everyone has this capacity, but in human beings it is limited by a finite personality and the tendency to sin. Jesus, however, was not subject to such limitations. He was totally open to the Spirit within the depths of His subjectivity, in the center of His being and motivation. Because of this, the Spirit led Him into a perfect knowledge of His identity and relationship with the Father. Jesus is God through an ontological identity with the divine nature, through His Sonship with the Father. Bede expresses the matter in this way: "in Jesus that capacity to receive the Spirit of God was without limit. He received the fullness of the gift of the Spirit. In this experience of the Spirit he was able to know himself as the Son of God, as sharing in the divine nature, as expressing the very Word of God.... In this knowledge of himself as Son, he was able to know the Father, not in part but in fullness. He knew himself as the 'only Son,' the One who alone knows and expresses in fullness the mind of the Father. It is in this sense that we can speak of Jesus as God."[25]

But on another occasion, in a letter clarifying the above article, Bede shifted his ground to a more theological level, stressing that rather than the mystical. Of course both are part of his doctrine. He indicates that an adequate understanding of the Person of Christ requires us to make the distinction between Christ as the incarnate Lord and Christ in His eternal being as the Logos, the Son, the Word. In the former aspect, as the incarnate Lord or Son, Bede maintains that Jesus is "less" than the Father, is not equal to the Father, for He "emptied Himself" of His divinity (Phil. 2:7).[26] As incarnate Lord, Bede says, "He is God manifested in a human nature with its inevitable limitations."[27] These limitations involve his historical, cultural, and physical attributes. He is a Jew who is subject to the social and cultural influences of the time, with a mentality of a Jew of His time. Bede's comments are made within his anthropological scheme: the human being as body, soul (psyche), and spirit. It is in Christ's body and soul that limitations arise, not in His Spirit, which is infinite and eternal. In His Spirit He is the everlasting Son of God, the Logos and Image of the Father's Glory. He is fully realized in the ultimate depth of the Spirit and knows His identity with the divine nature. Bede nuances his meaning:

> in the ground of his [Christ's] being, in the point of the Spirit, he knows himself as eternally one with the Father, as the *express Word* of the Father, perfectly reflecting the Father as his Image. In this respect the Son is altogether equal to the Father.... Each of us can also know God at this point of the Spirit, but in us there is sin and limitation of person, whereas in Jesus there is no sin, and he is a fully realized person in whom there is no limitation (on the level of the Spirit). "In him dwells the fullness of the Godhead bodily" (Col. 2:9). I would say that he only became fully realized as a man at the resurrection, but in the eternal ground of his being beyond normal human consciousness he was always one with the Father.[28]

The third element of Bede's Christology is equally subtle. This is the cosmic dimension; it bears some relation to the mystical aspect, at least in its implications. For it concerns the ultimate destiny of humanity and the universe. The Incarnation in its completion has a profound transforming effect on the material universe, just as it had on the historical process, as we saw above. In the event of the Resurrection and the Ascension, through the instrumentality of the glorified Christ, Spirit took possession of matter, and penetrates it at every level, according to Bede.[29] The goal of the cosmos is its transmutation into spirit by the Spirit who was released at the Resurrection when Christ's body and soul achieved integration with the spiritual component, when the Spirit united body and soul in Himself. The Resurrection is the point where matter was changed by the Spirit, and the destiny of humanity and the cosmos is revealed: Spirit itself. For Christ, in the Ascension this process is perfected. Bede elaborates: "at the Ascension, Jesus' subtle body passed beyond into the spiritual body in the Transcendent Reality. Matter and soul are reintegrated into the One, the Word, the Ultimate Reality ... a breakthrough took place to Ultimate Transcendence."[30] Bede maintains that the Resurrection event/process, by introducing Spirit into the cosmos, also makes the universe an interdependent system, an interdependent cosmos, the whole purpose of which is to facilitate its evolution into spirit, or spiritual reality. He says: "when the transformation of the body of Christ took place it affected the whole universe," by orienting it toward spiritual evolution.[31] When the Resurrection happened, Spirit totally penetrated matter at every level, and consciousness came to permeate it as well.[32] This is a kind of Teilhardian vision, though Bede's understanding is more mystical or contemplative and less "biological." Bede specifies the presence of Spirit in the cosmos, as a fruit of the Incarnation, as a unifying principle at work in the created order and in the lives of people. He remarks: "Whereas in the universe, as we know it, there is conflict at every level, and body and soul are in conflict with one another, in Jesus this conflict has been overcome, body and soul have been restored to unity with the Spirit, and a power of unification has been released in the world. In this sense we can say that the death of Jesus, the free surrender of his life on the Cross to his Father, was a cosmic event."[33]

Bede's cosmic Christology depends in large measure on the insight of the new physics, which interprets the universe and its processes, structures, and reality through the organic model. The cosmos is an integrated system, an interdependent whole in which what affects one part also affects every other. Temporal and historical events impact on the entire created order in some way, in Bede's view, and some of these events—the beginning of life on the earth, the dawn of consciousness in us—represent seminal stages in the world's evolutionary history. Bede felt that the Incarnation was an event of this magnitude, especially the death, Resurrection, and Ascension of Jesus. Bede reflects: "The death of Jesus...marked the point of transcendence of the human consciousness to the divine; the point where the human being was totally surrendered, body and soul, to the divine being.... The Resurrection, the transcendence of death by Jesus in body and in soul, is the historic sign of this cosmic redemption, the sign that not only the soul, the psychic being, but also the body, the physical creation, has been liberated from its present bondage and has become a 'new creation.'"[34]

The Resurrection and the Ascension inaugurate the process of cosmic transformation, a transformation that is prefigured in the event of the Transfiguration, and that includes us as pivotal players. Everything, Bede holds, is involved in this process, this cosmic transmutation in which all things are moving toward that consummation of Spirit. Bede sums up the process in this way: "To me, the vision of the future is the matter of the universe being transformed, and the human body being transformed, and through that, the human soul undergoing this transformation into the life of the Spirit. The total universe, and the total human being, is transformed by the Spirit, and enters into the Transcendent State beyond."[35]

It might be asked at this point: is Bede's Christology orthodox? I think it is, especially if all its elements are seen together, along with his deep understanding of the Trinitarian doctrine/intuition. He had controversial moments, particularly when he talked about the issue of Christ's divinity, but these "moments" are not so controversial as they may at first seem, or rather, they are more controversial only in isolation from his whole Christological view and the context in which he presents it. It has to be recalled that his context was India, or more precisely, developing an Indian Christology, as part of his (and others') desire for an Indian Christian theology and a Christian Vedanta. The question is: How does Christ fit in? I believe Bede was approaching Christ on a contemplative level, as we saw in his articulation of Christ's experience of His relationship with His Father in this and the preceding chapter, because he was trying to make the Christian mystery accessible to Indians, to make Christ intelligible to Hindus, who have a profound appreciation of contemplative interiority, of the mystical states of consciousness that arise in that depth of awareness (Advaita and Saccidānanda), and of the personal God (Bhagavan) and a loving relationship with Him. Moreover, Bede, as a mystic, was experientially aware of Christ's inner consciousness, and His understanding of His relationship to the Father as a state that contemplatives can enter into and with which they can identify.[36]

It seems to me that an Indian Christology would have to express the mystery of the Incarnation in terms that were intelligible to Hindus. And what is more intelligible to a mature Hindu than the contemplative consciousness, the deep interiority, to which the Upaniṣads refer? Not only can Hindus identify with Christ as an incarnation of God, an *avatāra,* but also as one who exemplifies spiritual wisdom, one who is a realized being, a *jīvanmukta,* who has achieved that liberation and unity with the Absolute that is the goal of all genuine religion. I think that is one reason Bede emphasizes Christ's interior life and His awareness of His relationship to the Father in the inner reality of the triune identity. It is after all from that awareness as He expressed it that we have a knowledge of the Trinitarian mystery, at least initially. For Jesus articulates His ineffable awareness of His place in the divine nature by announcing details of His intimacy with the Father, God as Source, an intimacy that is one of identity in nature, but an identity that is best expressed as distinction-in-unity. This approach is one that many Hindus can at least understand, even though they would give it a different interpretation. Bede's Christology at least reaches out to the Hindu mind, finding resonances with it. This is why he suggests the term *Puruṣa* for Christ in an Indian Christian theology, as we saw in chapter 5. A Puruṣ atic Christology would be one that does not simply equate the two terms but appropriates the word *Puruṣa* and modifies it in such a way that it is actually a new expression of an ancient insight, a Christian one, as in a Christian form of the Vedanta. Granted Puruṣa and Christ have similar functions within each tradition, but their meanings are not exactly parallel. Perhaps they do not have to be, since the term *Puruṣa* can be deliberately adopted by Christian thinkers as an Indian term for Jesus Christ. In any event, in Bede's view, India must discover Christ in order to fulfill the deepest aspirations of its own spirituality. Bede comments: "Christ alone is capable of reconciling the ancient tradition of religion in India with the demands of the modern mind. He is the fulfillment of all that the imagination of the Indian soul sought to find in its gods and heroes, in its temples and sacrifices.... His story is, if one may say so, myth become true."[37]

CHRISTIAN TANTRISM

This and the following sections are concerned with a more practical set of issues. In the present section on Tantric Yoga the question is whether or not a Christian Tantra is possible. Tantrism became an important part of Bede Griffiths's thought. We must determine precisely what he meant by the term and what role it had for him. This presents a problem for us, however, for although Bede enthusiastically espoused the Tantra as important and beneficial to Christian spirituality, it was a fairly late development in his contemplative theology, with little elaboration as yet. So I must depend on the scanty material that is available on this topic, which includes sections of two lectures, a letter he wrote to me about a possible Christian Tantrism, and the exhaustively detailed work of Thomas Matus, *Yoga and the Jesus Prayer Tradition,* which Bede highly recommends in a preface to it.[38] Bede sees the Tantra as the opposite of the Vedanta, since the latter is otherworldly, or rather seeks to transcend this world, while the former seeks an integration of all of our powers with the body, soul, and spirit. He says Tantra derives from a worship of the Mother, the Divine Feminine, and is based on a feminine image of God.[39] This image and Tantra itself are both quite archaic in origin, antedating both Hinduism and Buddhism. Thomas Matus comments on the Divine Mother: "This religion of the Mother has a great number of expressions: she is a goddess, an object of worship; she is *śakti,* the 'power' or 'energy' of the male divinity's self-manifestation in the cosmos; she is *kuṇḍalinī,* the 'potential force,' at once natural and divine, which abides within the human body and which bears the soul upward toward the realization of its own divinity...."[40]

The body, the earth, nature, and so forth are associated with the Divine Feminine, with Śakti, and the aim is to unite it, or bring it into harmony with consciousness, with Śiva, the male principle. Tantra originated from a concern for the place of the body in spiritual development, something which was disregarded in the Vedanta, and Bede pinpoints the nature of Tantra, saying: "'That by which we fall is that by which we rise.' We have to use the body, senses, appetites, feelings, etc., as a way to return to God. This is important for us [in the Christian tradition], because we have had a negative, or unbalanced view of the body and of sexuality."[41] "That by which we fall is that by which we rise" is the principle of Tantric Yoga, the implication being that we fall through the body, senses, feelings, emotions, and appetites, and the proper reintegration of these in the spiritual ascent is the way back to harmony and union with the Divine Reality. The path of Tantra emphasizes the transformation of the person, the human nature, through the right use, the creative ordering, of the powers of nature and of the body.[42] Śiva, or consciousness, and Śakti, the energy within us, have to be brought into a creative relationship. The point of Tantra is to awaken Śakti, which must be transformed by consciousness, by Śiva. This energy is also the sexual impulse, which must be transformed,[43] and this is one of the purposes of Tantra. The transformation itself occurs through a discipline that concentrates on raising the energy up from the base of the spine through the *cakras,* the energy centers (literally "wheels") located at different points of the spinal column. Bede describes the process and goal of Tantric Yoga:

> the aim in [Tantric] yoga is to gather the energy together, and to transform the person. As the energy rises, instead of going out through your physical energy, your sex energy, through your emotions, through your imagination, through your reason, you concentrate them all, you gather them all (together) until they come to a head in the *thousand-petaled lotus* (at the crown of the head). Then you are open to the Divine, the Transcendent. You are trying to turn back the energy [in order] to open it totally to God. That is the goal of this tantric yoga.[44]

The *cakras* themselves are not ends but means. They are reference points in meditation that serve to support the practice of focusing the person's concentration or awareness on the various centers of consciousness existing within the body.[45] As Matus says, "It is of little importance whether there are four, six or ten *cakras,* since the various points along the body's axis are only stages of passage on the inner fire's upward path, and *cakras* are only aids to the yogi's concentration on the dynamic movement itself."[46] And this movement itself is conceived in terms of introversion and ascension, or entering the depths of the heart and rising up above oneself. Matus says: "The yogic *sādhanā* is both a march toward the center and an upward journey."[47] This upward movement is to the apex of one's being at the crown of the head, the "thousand-petaled lotus."[48]

Unification of consciousness is the goal of Tantra, a unity that overcomes duality. The center and the apex are not reached until this unity is realized in such a way that polarities are transcended, especially that of "inner" and "outer," of *nirvāna* and *samsāra,* or profane existence.[49] This is also true of the male-female polar-

ity, which is used in the Tantra as a symbol of spiritual integration. Matus elaborates: "Realization (*sādhanā* as both process
and goal) in tantric yoga is often described in sexual terms, as
a mystical marriage of the masculine and the feminine at many
different levels: the sexual polarity of human bodies themselves,
the polarity between Nature and Spirit, the polarity between the
yogi and God."[50]

Since unity is not only the goal but the actual nature of ultimate reality, all polarities must be reconciled, and the male-female dichotomy symbolizes for Tantrism "the duality of human
existence itself, which the yogi seeks to unify."[51] Those who follow
the path of Tantric Yoga also attempt to interiorize the cosmos
through the technique of "projection," by means of which they
identify their bodily dimensions, points of reference, or *cakras*
with the dimensions of the cosmos. Here the aim is to integrate
another polarity, the larger polarity of *microcosm* (the individual
person) and *macrocosm* (the world or universe), the inner and the
outer.[52] Now, the purpose of this "projection" is not to become
totally immersed in nature but to transcend it and all other external factors, that is, to pass beyond duality. But one does not
try to escape from the world and life in Tantrism; rather one
seeks that integration with all things, that point of unity which
is their very ground and one's own ground, the point where the
transcendent and the earthly rest in their Source. Matus clarifies
this for us: "The yogi is not seeking to tie the spirit to the forces
and rhythms of the cosmos but rather to rise above the common
human enslavement to it and to the cycles of life and death, or
samsara. Both Buddhism and Vedanta, even when they use practices which assimilate parts of the yogi's body to elements of the
world, aim at liberation from the world."[53]

Various techniques are employed in Tantric Yoga to achieve
the objective of integration and unification, which means also a
unity with the Source, with the Divine Life itself. Mandalas are
significant in Tantric practice because they symbolize the goal

and the process. The *yantra,* the Hindu form of the mandala, actually captures and expresses in geometrical symbolism the essence of Tantrism.[54] Both mandala and *yantra* are tools for sparking an awareness of unity and a passing beyond dualistic consciousness. In mandala symbolism, the cosmos, the human body, and religious or ritual actions are brought together. Every Hindu temple, for instance, when seen from above, is really a mandala. Matus describes the symbolism and interior function of the mandala: "The yogi sees the whole world, or the basic polarity of the world (the male and female principles in their various manifestations), in the temple-mandala; by interiorizing the mandala, the yogi unites flesh and cosmos in the sacrificial ascent which is also the 'mystical marriage' in which all opposites coincide."[55]

Another technique of Tantrism is the mantra, which is a mental tool for altering the states of consciousness. It works by breaking down the conceptual link between speech and thought.[56] Mantras are vehicles into transcendent dimensions of consciousness. And of course their use is now widespread in meditation, though the emphasis is different from one tradition to another. In Tantrism, there is a dynamic, "energic" metaphysics that sees a bond or connection between certain words and the Source, the Ground of Being. This Ground of Being or God is *spanda,* a "vibratory energy." Matus points out: "For monistic tantric thinkers, there is no break in the continuity between 'lower' vibratory phenomena, such as words, and the highest, identified by them with the consciousness of God, whom they conceive as vibration at an infinitely high frequency."[57] The mantra is a way of entry into the highest vibratory region which is God Himself, and so is a key to integration, liberation, and perfect freedom[58] of the Spirit.

The question is: Can there be a Christian form of Tantric Yoga? Both Thomas Matus and Father Bede were inclined to believe so. Matus maintains that yoga is a means, having its own intrinsic purpose, and this purpose or end can coincide, in the concrete, living situation, with the ultimate goal of Christian faith: a union of love with the Father through the mediation of Jesus, the Son, in the Spirit.[59] Putting it another way, Matus declares that "a Christian understanding of yoga means the perception of the Christian end in all the means employed and experiences had throughout the yogic quest."[60] And then in a more theological assimilation, or appropriation of the term *yoga,* he says quite eloquently: "The Christian's yoga is the yoga of Christ, which is the yoga of cross and resurrection."[61] This is a serious comment in the way of a conclusion. Thus, we can assume that no matter how far we may take adaptation of means, for a Christian the focus is always Christ and His way.

Bede emphasizes Tantra as a balance to Vedanta, and in response to a felt need in Christian spirituality, a lack in its ascetical theology, which negates or has negated the place of the body. For the body has not been integrated into the process of ascent to God or the process of spiritual growth. But Bede does not stress adding something onto the ascetical practice of Christianity that he feels is not already implied in the tradition. He quotes several passages of the New Testament that he regards as "Tantric" by implication, if not by intention. Among these are: "And the Word became flesh" (John 1:14); "your body is the temple of God, where the Spirit of God dwells" (1 Cor. 3:16–17); "the body is not for fornication, but for the Lord" (I Cor. 5:13); and "Glorify God in your body" (1 Cor. 5:20).[62] From these passages of Scripture Bede sees the basis of a Christian Tantra. Of course it has to be developed, but the principle of the importance and sacredness of the body, which is a Tantric insight also, is clearly present in the New Testament. It is an incarnational dimension of spirituality.

CHRISTIAN *SANNYĀSA*

It would be a purely academic exercise to ask whether or not an Indian Christian *sannyāsa* is possible, since it is already a living reality; it exists and is not a matter of theological speculation, though some might question its authenticity. The work of Emmanuel Vattakuzhy[63] and others attests to the fact of a Christian tradition of *sannyāsa*, not to mention all those Christians who are ardently following the sannyasic path in their lives, as well as those who have gone before them. That of course is the real proof, that it is *lived* in the concrete. Furthermore, as I mentioned in chapter 2, the institution and state of *sannyāsa* are the context of relating Hinduism and Christianity in an ultimate way, and this was surely Bede Griffiths's position. *Sannyāsa* is the "place" of an actual existential convergence or encounter of the two great faiths, occurring within the depths of the heart of the monk, the Christian (and Hindu) *sannyāsi*. This was, I believe, Bede's experience, as it was that of Monchanin and Abhishiktananda. Both the Hindu and the Christian *sannyāsi* are engaged in the quest for the Absolute, for God, and both are committed to this quest within a life of renunciation and total dedication. There is thus a convergence of sorts on the level of monastic ideal and practice. In this section, I want to discuss the nature of *sannyāsa* in some detail, and then I will show how it has been adopted and modified by Abhishiktananda, Bede, and others, resulting in a Christian form of *sannyāsa*. It must be discerned what constitutes this Christian expression of sannyasic life.

The ultimate origin of *sannyāsa*, for Hinduism, is found in the tradition of the forest dwellers, the *rishis* of Indian antiquity. These were the Vedic seers, who after retiring to the forests discovered the reality of the Divine Mystery through a life of meditation *(dhyāna)* and asceticism *(tapas)*. They came to an experiential knowledge of the Transcendent One dwelling in the depths of the heart, in the *guhā*. The *rishis* represent the archetype of monk in the Indian tradition, the normative beginning, just as the Desert Fathers do in the Western monastic tradition.

The *rishis* are responsible not only for the genesis of monasticism in India but also for the whole mystical tradition of Hinduism, at least in its essential emphasis on Brahman, God as transcendent and immanent in the depths of the heart. They were enormously influential in the formation of Indic civilization, and their inspiration became the focus of India's religion in its epitome: contemplation. Francis Acharya, a Belgian Cistercian who with Bede Griffiths founded Kurisumala Ashram in 1958, puts it this way: "The depth of Indian culture is to a great extent the fruit of the monastic experience of India's *rishis,* or Vedic seers."[64] And even though *sannyāsa* existed in Jainism and Buddhism before it took root in Hinduism in a formal way, the *rishis* have to be regarded as the predecessors of the whole sannyasic tradition.

The derivation of the term *sannyāsa* is found in the Sanskrit *sam-ni-as,* or *sam-ny-as,* which means "to put down together," "to give up," "to abandon,"[65] but which came to connote a complete break with the world, all ties, obligations, property, and possessions; it is a total renunciation of everything except God, and a freedom from all attachments. But as Emmanuel Vattakuzhy points out, it also implies a total trust in God and a recognition that one's life and all things are in His control.[66] Technically, in the Hindu tradition, *sannyāsa* designates the fourth *āsrama,* the fourth stage of life, when a person leaves the active life and retires for prayer, penance, and meditation. Such a one who embraces this path of self-denial and prayer then becomes a *sannyāsi,* or a *sannyāsini,* the female counterpart.[67]

Sannyāsis have many names by which they are addressed, and these are descriptive of the attributes of the sannyasic observance. A *sannyāsi* may be called a *sādhu,* a virtuous or noble man, a monk; a *swami,* lord or master; a *yogi,* a person who is united with Brahman, with God, and disciplined; a *muni,* a silent one who as an ascetic seeks to realize God through meditation; a *jñāni,* a sage, an enlightened one who has awakened to the Self (the Atman, or God immanent in the heart); a *yati,* one who practices self-control; a *siddhā*, one of holiness and purity who also has special powers of a spiritual nature; a *parivārājaka*, a wandering ascetic; an *avadhūta*, a person who transcends all restrictions and is completely united with God, as much as this is possible while still having a body; a *paramahamsa*, a supreme spirit, one of the most extreme forms of *sannyāsa*; and finally, a *jīvanmukta*, one who has achieved liberation *(moksha)* while still in this life.[68] Some of these designations indicate that there are degrees to the life of renunciation, ranging from the simple self-control of the *yati* to the extreme asceticism of a *paramahamsa*, and yet in all, the goal is the same: liberation.

Renunciation is the essential characteristic of this way of life, but its implications are indeed far-reaching in a person's life. To express it another way: "The essential rule of the *sannyāsi* is to be totally free from desire. Or rather, he has but one desire—the desire for God alone."[69] Renunciation is the condition for the possibility of a life of contemplative depth, and this is true in any tradition. It frees one so that one may devote all one's energies to the quest for God in silence, solitude, and self-denial. Renunciation leads in time to an experiential awareness of God, the One who does not pass away, and a profound realization of unity with Him, or *samādhi*. The *sannyāsi*, as Abhishiktananda tells us, "penetrates to the ultimate depth of things and of the mystery of which they are signs. He has discovered 'the further shore,' the Reality of which everything 'on this side' is simply a sign, like foot prints which lead one 'to find this all' (Br. Up., 1.4.7)."[70] But the deepest, most radical form of renunciation is of the false self, or what we call the ego or self-will. This radical renunciation goes to the root of sin, conflict, and spiritual stagnation, and is the real or great renunciation. Bede puts it well: "the essence of *sannyāsa* ... is renunciation of the self [the egocentric identity]. It is not a renouncing of action or external things; it is a matter of inner renunciation. The man [or woman] who works without attachment, free from any self love, is a true *sannyāsi....*"[71]

The *sannyāsi*, however, does not just renounce the world and his false self; he also renounces the appearances, or the "signs," the whole system by which we represent the sacred to ourselves. He or she is not satisfied with the sign but desires what is signified, or that which is ultimately inexpressible. Bede elaborates: "the *Sannyāsi* is called to go beyond all religion, beyond every human institution, beyond every scripture and creed, till he comes to that which every religion and scripture and ritual signifies but can never name. In every religion, whether Christian or Hindu or Buddhist or Muslim, it has been recognized that the ultimate Reality cannot be named and the *Sannyāsi* is one who is called to go beyond all religion and seek that ultimate goal."[72]

But the *sannyāsi* never rejects religion as such, nor does he reject the signs, for he has a deep appreciation of their meaning, and that is also why he cannot stop there. He must go beyond to their source. Again, Bede says: "To go beyond the sign is not to reject the sign, but to reach the thing signified. In the language of St. Thomas Aquinas, it is to pass from the *sacramentum* to the *res.*"[73] The *sannyāsi* knows that the whole cosmos is a symbol, is theophanic because it manifests the mystery of the Divine Reality. Creation, being, and life reveal as through a symbolic "story" the whole mystery of existence. *Sannyāsis* have discovered this truth in their own way and so proceed to find the source of the symbol. They are not satisfied with the appearance when they can have Reality itself.

The life and ideal of the *sannyāsi* is basically *acosmic.* This was also true of the Desert Fathers. The acosmic element means that a *sannyāsi* has no ties, no obligations or family commitments, no social or political functions. He is dead to society.[74] A *sannyāsi* is "beyond all *dharma* (religious/social norms and duties), including all ethical ... duties whatever."[75] He is totally free *to be.* This call to *sannyāsa* comes usually through a profound inner, experiential illumination, and the experience makes it imperative for the one who receives it to leave all else behind in order to dwell in those depths of the Spirit, for "the inner awakening frees him from all duties, and for him the life of *sannyāsa* has become a necessity, whether or not he passes through a *dīkṣā*,"[76] a ceremony of initiation into the sannyasic state. The call is so deep, so urgent and compelling, that he cannot ignore it. The response to the call, to the mystical awakening, is the ultimate sacrifice of one's own being and former life. For "*Sannyāsa* is an inner revolution exploding in a total liberation from the past."[77]

The sannyasic life is one of pure contemplation, of active seeking after an experiential awareness of Ultimate Reality through meditation, austerity, and discipline, with few books and usually no companions. As Bede remarks, the *sannyāsi* seeks perfect transcendence, and "the perfect man is one who has simply gone beyond this world. He has no further concern with the world at all."[78] Ideally, the life of a *sannyāsi* is one of wandering from place to place, staying no more than two nights in any one place. At times, *sannyāsis* will settle in groups for a while or live in solitude, perhaps in caves or little huts. Their diet is simple, and they often engage in long fasts. Everything in the sannyasic state is oriented toward spiritual realization of the Divine Reality. For the *sannyāsi* is the one who has "reached the highest light," in the words of the *Chandogya Upaniṣad*.[79] In the Indian tradition, *sannyāsa* is considered the quickest way to achieve the fullness of spiritual life, and as Abhishiktananda says, it "is certainly a man's most direct route for becoming a jñāni and finding liberation ... when genuinely lived with all its implications...."[80] It is a totalization of mystical consciousness that permeates all aspects of one's existence.

Indian tradition recognizes two forms of *sannyāsa*, or two essential ways in which the call to *sannyāsa* can come to a person. These are *vidvat-* and *vividiṣā-sannyāsa*. The former kind is based on an overpowering mystical realization which compels one to take the path of renunciation in search of the Divine Reality and liberation. The inner experience calls one to the state of *sanny-āsa*. The latter case is different since it is not based on mystical experience but on the desire for it, the desire for *jñāna*, or wisdom, and liberation, or *moksha*. Taking *sannyāsa* thus becomes a means to acquire wisdom and liberation.[81] Moreover, a Christian *sannyāsa* would be of the *vividiṣā* type, because Christian monks normally do not begin their vocation by a dramatic kind of mystical illumination. That might come later, though in the earlier stages it just is not there, in most cases, as Westerners are a bit more undeveloped in this area than some Indians.

The *sannyāsi* cultivates the inner vision and mystical life in the depths of the Spirit. He has acquired self-realization in God. Abhishiktananda characterizes sannyasic consciousness: "The *sannyāsi* has discovered that unique Brahman, and has discovered himself in that unique Brahman beside which there is no other.... He has no further desire, for he has reached the fullness...."[82] He has achieved knowledge of the Supreme, knowledge of Brahman, or God, what is called *brahmavidyā*. *Brahmavidyā* is a transcendent gnosis; it is *jñāna*, or spiritual wisdom arising from mystical experience. It is a direct intuition into the nature of God and of oneself.

Usually *brahmavidyā* or mystical wisdom, which is a living realization, is imparted through a spiritual master, a guru who has himself experienced the Divine Reality directly. Every *sannyāsi*, when he is initiated, is expected to receive this experience, this *brahmavidyā*, this knowledge of God, from the guru who awakens it in the disciple with a word, a touch, or a look; these are ways it is communicated from guru to disciple. This experience has been handed down from the beginning in the guru-disciple relationship. And "this idea of an experience of God is the essential thing of Hindu *sannyāsa*."[83] The guru will not initiate his disciple until he feels he is ready to receive the illumination. The guru instructs the disciple in the art and science of meditation and the process of quieting the mind. The disciple must withdraw his mind from sense objects and the stirrings of the imagination by focusing his attention in deep concentration on a single point, and by repetition of God's name, or the practice of *nāmajapa*. It is only when the disciple is sufficiently selfless, free from desire, and quite proficient at inner silence that the master will finally initiate his disciple in the experiential knowledge of God, of Brahman,[84] or *brahmavidyā*. Of this crucial relationship, Abhishiktananda says: "The guru is one who has himself first attained the Real and who knows from personal experience the way that leads there; he is capable of initiating the disciple and of making well up from within the heart of his disciple, the immediate ineffable experience which is his own—the utterly transparent knowledge, so limpid and pure, that quite simply he is."[85]

The *sannyāsi* does have an extraordinarily important function in the spiritual order, indeed, an indispensable one. He is a living symbol of the transcendent goal of human life, the purpose of our very existence. He has been set apart by his vocation in order "to witness to the one unique Absolute."[86] He has the role of witnessing to the Ultimate Reality, the One who is beyond all signs, and to be himself "a sign of that which is beyond signs."[87] The *sannyāsi* by his example calls others to that same depth of being, that life in the Spirit that he concretizes so well in himself. He "is the outward expression of our ultimate freedom in our innermost being; his existence and his witness are vitally necessary for human society, whether secular or religious."[88] It is no exaggeration to say that a civilization cannot long survive without such generous and inspired souls, that is to say, contemplatives of whatever tradition.

The Hindu ideal of the monk actually unites two important elements in the notion of the acosmic ascetic: the virtuous man, the highest expression of which is the saint—the moral dimension—and a total transcendence of the human condition in such a way that the *sannyāsi* is not subject to its demands;

he has completely overcome it in himself, in his own acosmic life of contemplation. Thus, a *sannyāsi* or *sannyāsini* is a holy man or woman who is acosmically related to the world and the human condition,[89] so that they live in the world but transcend its structures in order that they may *be*, in the deepest sense of the term. They have passed over, or are passing over, to the "further shore" of eternity, beyond Being, if by Being we understand the first determination of the Absolute, the realm of manifestation and multiplicity, the ontological domain proper. The *sannyāsi* lives at the level of the Source of Being, immersed in its depths. Abhishiktananda, who embraced the sannyasic path whole-heartedly, or more completely than any other Christian up to our time, and who was certainly equal to any Hindu *sannyāsi* in his dedication and in his spiritual wisdom, describes his mystical consciousness in the act of union with Ultimate Reality in the transcendent state beyond: "I am so deeply immersed in the mystery of God himself that it is within the very act by which God calls himself into being that I myself am."[90] This gives us some indication of how ultimate is the state to which *sannyāsa* calls a person, and how profoundly noble is the sannyasic ideal.

There has been a long interest on the part of Christians in *sannyāsa*, and this interest really starts in the sixteenth century with de Nobili, who assumed it in his own life, while it was cultivated further by Upadhyay in the latter half of the nineteenth century. But it was not until the mid-twentieth century that a Christian form of sannyasic observance was developed in India. There were many attempts, but two in particular are worthy of note here. These are Shantivanam and Kurisumala ashrams, both of which exist today and are flourishing. In both of these instances there was a conscious attempt to relate and integrate the Benedictine tradition of monastic life with that of Hindu *sannyāsa*. Neither of these "experiments" can be considered syncretistic, as a potential critic might assume, since both were and are serious and careful attempts at adaptation and synthesis. Panikkar distinguishes for us the difference between syncretism and synthesis: "Syncretism... is external juxtaposition; synthesis is a living assimilation. Syncretism is amassment; synthesis is a living organism."[91] The development of sannyasic monasticism, or Christian *sannyāsa*, at both Shantivanam and Kurisumala exhibits the nature of synthesis. This synthetic quality of Christian *sannyāsa*, as it has unfolded, is characterized by its existentiality, its concreteness, its *living* reality. Syncretism, it would seem, is almost always an exercise of abstract reason. It does not arise—usually—out of careful deliberation and assimilation.

Shantivanam, or Saccidananda Ashram, which is dedicated to the Holy Trinity, was established in 1950 by Father Jules Monchanin, who adopted the Hindu name of Parama Arupi Ananda, "Bliss of the Supreme Spirit," and by Dom Henri Le Saux, O.S.B., who assumed the name of Abhishiktananda, the name by which he has been known ever since, a name that means "Bliss of Christ," or "Bliss of the Anointed One."[92] The ashram itself was founded on the banks of a sacred river, the Kavery, near Tiruchirapalli. Bede tells us the significance of changing their names and of calling the ashram Saccidananda: "By taking these names and calling the ashram by the name of Saccidānanda, the Hindu name for the Godhead, as a symbol of the Christian Trinity, they intended ... to show that they sought to identify themselves with the Hindu 'search for God,' the quest of the Absolute, which has inspired monastic life in India from the earliest times, and to relate this quest to their own experience of God in Christ in the mystery of the Holy Trinity."[93] In other words, they identified themselves with the state of *sannyāsa* by embracing it, assimilating its incomparable values, and related these with those of the Christian faith, especially in its very epitome: the Trinitarian mystery. Their intention all along was to live as Christian *sannyāsis* open to the spiritual wisdom of the Hindu tradition, particularly Advaita/Saccidānanda. They recognized from the start not simply the antiquity of *sannyāsa* but also its extraordinary value for Christian spirituality, as well as its profound authenticity. Bede describes their life in Shantivanam: "Here they lived in the utmost simplicity, wearing the kavi dress of the Hindu *sannyāsi,* going barefoot, sleeping on a mat on the floor, and adapting themselves in all their habits of food and behavior to Hindu customs."[94] Their ideal of a Christian *sannyāsa* was based on nearly total acceptance of the Hindu ideal in its essential practices, but they also sought to incorporate in their model the Christian personalism of the Trinitarian mystery, that is, they did not completely embrace the Advaitic doctrine but tried to modify it with the insight of the personal and interpersonal nature of the Godhead, which they expressed in the notion of Father. This is especially true of Monchanin, although somewhat altered by Abhishiktananda later in his life, after Monchanin's departure. But summing up their ideal, they say:

> all the traditions of Indian "monasticism," when well weighed and purified of their unnecessary dross, have to be taken into account and compared with our Christian monastic traditions; and, as far as possible, our anxiety should be, with the help of God, to harmonize them both—so that the Indian soul, which down the ages has expressed itself best in vanaprastha and *sannyāsa,* may keep on seeking God through the same vanaprastha and *sannyāsa* chastened and christianized and then find Him no more only as "the Absolute" but also as the "Father."[95]

Thus, there is the vision of Christianizing *sannyāsa,* and presumably this amounts to a Christian form of sannyasic life. They also stress the importance not only of concentrating on the Trinity as the focus of contemplation, but that the Christian *sannyāsi* can perceive in the notion of Saccidānanda a symbol of the life-giving Trinity itself, and they are better able to understand the ultimate meaning of Saccidānanda as a hidden expression of the Trinitarian intuition. They tell us:

And, more fervently and with greater appreciation than any of his fellow *sannyāsis* can the Christian monk utter: SAT, when thinking of the Father, the "Principleless" Principle, the very source and end of the expansion and "recollection" of the divine life—CIT, when remembering the eternal Son, the *Logos,* the intellectual consubstantial Image of the Existent— ANANDA when meditating on the Paraclete, unifying together the Father and the Son.[96]

Both Monchanin and Abhishiktananda saw that Hindu *sannyāsa* could enrich and reform Christian monasticism as well as Christianity itself through monasticism, and a Christian *sannyāsa.* For the sannyasic values of renunciation, total dedication to the quest, mendicancy, realization of God experientially as the goal of life, solitude, self-denial, inner freedom, the transcendent state as a way of achieving mystical enlightenment, meditation and unity, poverty and asceticism, and so on, all make *sannyāsa* such a vital monastic institution, vital to humankind's education in the depth dimension of life. Emmanuel Vattakuzhy conveys the importance of *sannyāsa* so eloquently when he says: "Indian *sannyāsa* proclaims to the world in terms unequivocal that God is the ultimate goal of man in a manner human eyes have never seen in the religious history of mankind. Without exaggeration, *sannyāsa* is India's greatest contribution to the spiritual heritage of mankind."[97] And this value also exists in Christian *sannyāsa,* which has the same intensity of commitment, expressed in a life of renunciation and a total dedication to the quest for God in contemplation, in the practice of meditation.

The other significant attempt to develop a Christian form of *sannyāsa* occurred at Kurisumala Ashram, which was founded in 1958 in Kottayam, Kerala State, in South India. It was established by Bede Griffiths, who was then an English Benedictine monk, and by Father Francis Mahieu, also known as Francis Acharya, a Belgian Cistercian from Caldey Abbey off the coast of Wales. Like Monchanin and Abhishiktananda, their intention was a blend

of Western monasticism—the Cistercian variety—and sannyasic practice. They also introduced elements from ancient Syrian
and Egyptian monasticism, and followed the Syrian rite in the
liturgy. Their plan was to develop a synthesis between Eastern
and Western monasticism, but they identified closely with the
sannyasic ideal. Bede characterized their hope in these words: "It
was our desire to enter into this tradition of Indian *sannyāsa* and
to establish a Christian ashram, in which the life of prayer and
asceticism could be followed along Christian lines, yet keeping
always in touch with the traditions of India."[98]

The Christian *sannyāsi* lives fully as a renunciate, but his
focus is Christ. Christ is his approach to the triune Godhead, to
the state of unity with it. The Christian *sannyāsi* pursues his quest
for the Absolute through the incarnate Son. His is an experience
of communion, not of identity. Christ leads him into communion
with the Persons of the Trinity, and with others in the mystical
body. It is this emphasis on Christ as the center of spiritual life
that distinguishes the Christian from the Hindu *sannyāsi*. Bede
elaborates on the importance of this focus for the Christian *sannyāsi*: "It is this witness to Christ, through a life lived in intimate
union with Him, which we believe to be the work of the monk
in India, and perhaps there is no more important work in India
today. Ultimately a Hindu will not be convinced by arguments,
but by a life lived in the closest intimacy with God."[99]

A Christian *sannyāsi* takes the contemplative consciousness
of Hindu sages with utmost seriousness and respect. He does
not try to reduce it to his own faith system but tries rather to
understand it in its own right. Respect implies recognition of its
authenticity, or at least the possibility of its authenticity. Bede
and others in the movement maintain that Christians must enter
into the Hindu experience of the Ultimate Mystery and make it
part of their own interior life. And again, he poses the challenge:
"We have to live this Hindu experience of God, and we must
live it from the depth of our experience of God's revelation in

Christ and in the Church."[100] That is essentially the task of the Christian *sannyāsi* and other interested parties. The Christian *sannyāsi*, and the ordinary Christian open to the Hindu faith, appreciates and appropriates the Advaitic/Saccidanandan experience but then passes beyond into the warmth, depth, and love of communion that is the inner life and nature of the Trinitarian identity. It is this Trinitarian vision at the heart of the Real as focus and goal that constitutes Christian *sannyāsa*, at least ultimately. And this requires a sensitivity to the mystery of Christ who is the way into the fullness of the Divine Reality. Vattakuzhy remarks: "Christian *sannyāsa* is not to be an intellectual concept, but an actual experience of Jesus in the fullness of the Spirit. Therefore a Christian *sannyāsi* has to be filled with Christ, the incarnate plentitude of God with the highest degree of interiority. The appropriation or personalization of the interiority of Jesus in 'the cave of the heart' or at the depth of one's being is the essence of Christian *sannyāsa*. The identity of a Christian *sannyāsi* is nothing but this deep interiority."[101]

As we saw above in the section on Christology and in chapter 5, the interiority of Christ's experience, His inner consciousness, is one of an intense existential realization of His unity with the Father, and this is an awareness in the Spirit. This is very clear in Bede Griffiths's writings and lectures. To have the interior experience of Christ is to have an intimate communion with the Father, to know their unity in the abyss of the Spirit. The Hindu *sannyāsi* gives the Christian one a profound sense of the interior orientation to the transcendent mystery, and a deep experiential "bathing" in pure unity, or Advaita. But the Christian *sannyāsi* pushes behind and deeper into that unity, that Advaita of the Spirit, and discovers the Word in the bosom of the Father, welling up eternally from the infinite depth and inwardness of the Spirit, the very abyss of God Himself. Thus, in Bede's view and in that of others, Christian *sannyāsa* is the product of a synthesis, one can say, of an existential convergence between Hindu *sannyāsa* and Christian faith expressed in the refinement of consciousness of a Christian monk; it is the uniting of the Hindu ideal of the monk with that of the Christian, resulting in a magnified, enriched form of sannyasic monasticism. As Bede points out, the goal is the same in both traditions: to bring the body and soul in harmony with the Spirit.[102] And this means to allow that mystical consciousness—Advaita/Saccidānanda and Trinity—to penetrate all aspects of the person's life and being, so that he or she is thus totally transformed and transfigured by the Light of eternal Glory.

There is one problem I do see, however, or think I see in Bede's notion of Christian *sannyāsa*—and that of others, notably Abhishiktananda—and that concerns the inner freedom and acosmic element of the sannyasic observance. By definition a *sannyāsi* is beyond all, including all religion. How then can a Christian be a *sannyāsi,* since he or she presumably cannot as such transcend the demands of the Gospel, which are religious and moral in essence? I wonder if it is sufficient simply to speak in terms of modifying the Hindu interpretation of *sannyāsa*. At any rate, I find this issue quite unclear in Bede as well as in Abhishiktananda. I do not think, for example, that the Desert Fathers can be characterized as "beyond religion," and they are the nearest in the early Christian tradition to *sannyāsa*. If by "beyond religion" is meant formal religion or the externals, then perhaps the problem is not so great as one might assume. For many of the Desert Fathers probably did not have the sacraments too often. This area needs more study.

Since Bede Griffiths's move to Shantivanam in 1968 when he assumed spiritual headship of the community and became its *acarya,* its spiritual teacher, he steadily and progressively developed the Christian sannyasic life there,[103] and it can be said with certainty that it is well established in India and in the Church there. It is now more than just another experiment, for it is now an existential fact that an Indian Christian monasticism has emerged and taken form in the Church.

THE FUTURE OF THE CHURCH

The understanding that Bede Griffiths had of the Church, of her nature and role in humanity's destiny, was a vision emanating from what he regarded as her essential attribute of universality, which by definition requires of her an assimilation of all the spiritual treasures of humankind. In other words, for Bede, the Church is universal in her scope and extent around the world, but she has yet to realize that ultimate universality whereby she becomes the repository of all humanity's spiritual wisdom, which she has then translated into the terms of Christian faith, and becomes the focus of the human family, of nations, cultures, and religions. His view of the Church is profoundly noble and subtle, and it is the fruit of his understanding of her nature.

He perceives in the nature of the Church the Divine Feminine as the archetype of her all-encompassing universality. She is the Mother of all people and nations. In this, he has recourse to an early Christian treatise, *The Shepherd of Hermas,* in which the Church is portrayed as an old woman. Someone asks why this is so, and the answer is that she was created before all else. The world was created for her. This is how she gets her ancient quality.[104] Bede believed it is necessary to understand the Church in this cosmic dimension. Indeed, the Church has always existed in the Spirit as a manifestation of His or Her creativity in time and history. Bede reflects: "The Church as a historical institution has a very recent origin and occupies a very small part of the world. But the Church in herself is the eternal Mother; she is the created aspect of the uncreated Spirit."[105] The Providence of God assumes concrete form in her. Furthermore, she "is Man become conscious of his destiny as a son of God."[106]

Adam is Man, or represents all human beings. He was created in God's image and likeness and so was destined to be a son of God, and we with him. He was the medium through which evolution was moving toward eternal life through life and consciousness to Spirit. When he sinned, this evolutionary process, in Bede's view, was halted. And yet this is also providential, because it inaugurates the great mystery of redemption. It is in this way that the Church is born. Bede elaborates: "A new power of the Spirit, the *Śakti*, enters the creation and begins to draw man back into the life of the Spirit. This is the beginning of the Church, humanity drawn out of sin by the power of the Spirit and responding to the Word of God. In this sense, the Church is pres-ent in humanity from the beginning of history."[107]

The Church is the voice of the Spirit calling every person to salvation. And this voice of the Spirit, this presence of the Church, is inviting us in all the religious traditions, in their prayer and sacrifice, ritual, doctrine, and sacrament. This is the Church in her true function of universality, a universality that also includes the entire cosmic order. Bede clarifies this point:

> It is not only the whole of humanity but the whole creation which constitutes the body of the Church. Matter was created from the beginning with an innate tendency towards life and consciousness. Human consciousness was created from the beginning with an innate tendency towards the final and perfect consciousness of the Spirit. The same Spirit was present in matter, in life and in man, from the beginning drawing him towards itself. In Jesus this movement of matter and consciousness towards the life of the Spirit reached its culmination.[108]

Moreover, the Church is the fullness, the Pleroma, the point at which all things are consummated in the Spirit, the goal of evolution itself. Nature and humankind have been penetrated by consciousness and have been united to the Spirit, the eternal Spirit of God. And it is in the event of the Resurrection that the destiny of the entire creation is revealed and symbolized, according to Bede. Bede declares: "What was accomplished in Jesus through his sacrificial death and his rebirth to eternal life, is what is destined to happen to all of us, and in all creation."[109] And because of this supernatural dignity and destiny of the human and cosmos, because both are united in God's plan and called to salvation, to life in His eternal Spirit with Him, both are part of the Church's being. The Church thus reveals this mystery and is herself part of His self-revelation, manifestation, indeed His "becoming" in the finite realm of temporality. She is consequently, because of God's presence in her, a spiritual power at work in the world, in time and history, a "dynamic power, changing the course of history and transforming the world."[110]

If the Church is ever to actualize her inherent universal function, then she must open herself to all the other religious traditions in their contemplative or mystical dimension. She must adapt to the needs of other cultures and assume new forms and structures. By assimilating the wisdom of other traditions in the light of her own, her universality is discovered and actualized, and her hidden relationship to the other religious traditions is made explicit and operative, valuable and effective. Her relevance to the contemporary world is then clearly seen.[111] This is part of humankind's task in the future, as Bede saw it, for all the members of the human family are invited to become involved in the expansion of the Church into her larger identity. Bede says: "The building of the Church as the manifestation in history of the presence of God in man ... is the work of all mankind."[112] This includes every religion, culture, and movement, including humanists, scientists, poets and philosophers, workers and teachers, doctors and students.

But this requires of the Church and her leaders a far-reaching generosity and a new attitude of openness and trust. For Bede was convinced that God is calling the Church to open herself to what He is saying and expressing to her in the wisdom of the Eastern traditions. He regarded this as her essential task in the future: to embrace the other traditions and to assimilate their wisdom, making it her own by relating it to the mystery of Christ. He believed that this would be the primary work of the Church for the next two centuries, and that this work should be guided by the principle of *growth-in-continuity,* in which the Church appropriates the wisdom of other cultures and makes use of their metaphysical and spiritual resources in the formation of a Christian theology in their terms, but modified by the essential nature of the Christian faith. The model for this kind of growth is the experience of the Early Church assimilating the Greco-Roman culture, its philosophy, law, and structure. The Eastern tradition is more profound, in his view, because of its mystical orientation. Bede Griffiths was quite clear that the Church must do the same in relation to the other traditions, particularly those of Asia, the same kind of appropriation and modification that she once did with the Greco-Roman civilization. This is an aspect of actualizing her universal nature, and she "may be called to recover and renew the fundamental tradition of India, China and the East."[113]

In all the religions God has been at work since the inception of each; they are all related to Christ in the interdependent cosmic scheme. These different revelation systems will eventually converge in Christ, in the spiritual understanding of His place in the cosmic drama. But furthermore, Bede felt that these religious systems will find their way into the Church, that the Church will become for them the "place" of convergence and reconciliation. This he expressed as a hope and a conviction, and certainly this is consistent with his cosmic vision of the Church's nature and role. He expressed this hope and conviction in a number of ways and contexts. In speaking to a community of Camaldolese monks in September 1983, he said: "more and more I think we have to see the Church as a point of *convergence* ... of these different religious traditions, but which means we have to be totally open to whatever those traditions can give us."[114] That is the task of the Church in the future as she encounters the other spiritual traditions, entering into the depths of the heart, where the definitive encounter occurs in the Spirit. This means that she has to meet them on the contemplative or mystical level of religion, not on the level of dogma, doctrine, and belief. Bede formulates the task of the Church in a universal sense: "there is need now of an ecumenical movement in religion, by which we seek to discover what is the common ground in the different religious traditions of mankind and then in the light of this understanding to comprehend all these different religious traditions in their vital relationship to the living Christ. This is the great task of the future."[115]

In the next chapter, which is the conclusion, I will at some point take up this issue of the Church's role and introduce, in the way of a model, what seems to me a possibility in the relationship of the various traditions to the Universal Church, a model of how the Church can actualize her intrinsic though hidden universality. I will also evaluate Bede Griffiths's attempt to formulate in his contemplative theology—with the aid of others—a Christian form of the Vedanta, and I will also try to draw some significant conclusions.

Before going on to chapter 7, I would like to raise a few questions that arise out of the concerns of this chapter. Is Bede's criticism of the lack of an adequate understanding of Creation and history in Hinduism a bit exaggerated, especially in the light of his emphasis on the centrality of myth in religion? How far is the experiential approach to the divinity and the divine personality of Christ valid? How far can Tantric Yoga be Christianized? I do not think that Bede's criticism of Hinduism's lack in the area of an adequate concept of Creation and history is overstated. The reason is that although myth is indeed central to all religion—as all religions do in fact have a mythical dimension—Christianity also has historical awareness, something essentially absent in the Hindu tradition. And, as we saw above, this lack has important consequences for how the world and human responsibility are regarded. These consequences are not small matters.

The question concerning the validity of the experiential approach to the divinity and to Christ is difficult to answer. I believe it is quite valid—as far as it can go—if we adhere to the New Testament texts, especially with the aid of biblical scholarship, and if we have a fully formed contemplative understanding of the Gospel. This means really we must have an inner appreciation of Christ's experience because we have a point of reference in our own inner life and awareness.

The question of how far Tantric Yoga can be Christianized is again not an easy issue to resolve. Surely, much of Tantrism can be brought into the Church's contemplative tradition and can become a means to the ultimate end of the Christian life, as Matus has suggested. At the same time, there are aspects of Tantric Yoga that probably would not be appropriate in the Christian tradition. There might, for example, be a serious problem with the element of the free use of sex in Tantric practice. I doubt that it could be Christianized, particularly in view of the fact that the Church regards sex as an exclusive property of marriage and conjugal love. This issue is very new to Christianity and needs considerable study.

7

Conclusion and Implications

In this chapter, after summarizing the key elements of Bede Griffiths's contemplative theology—taking this term in the broadest sense as encompassing his entire "system" of thought and articulated experience—and after a critical evaluation, I would like to reflect on and unfold three essential and interrelated insights that have gradually become clear to me as I have worked in this fascinating area. These three insights or intuitions have organically emerged as metaphysical and contemplative implications of the attempt and positive result of relating Hinduism and Christianity on the deepest possible level of encounter: the mystical realization/consciousness of Advaita/Saccidānanda and Trinity, the fruit of which is a Christian Vedanta.

SUMMARY AND EVALUATION

In chapter 2, the historical context was presented for a substantive relating of the two traditions around Advaita/Saccidānanda and the Trinity, and this context was found to be sannyasic monasticism, or Christian *sannyāsa*. The development of this movement was traced from Roberto de Nobili in the sixteenth century, through Brahmabandhab Upadhyay in the latter half of the nineteenth century, to Jules Monchanin, Abhishiktananda, and Bede

Griffiths in the twentieth century. It is of course to this movement, as a monastic attempt at adaptation, that Bede belongs,
and it is within its cross-cultural spirituality that the attempt at
relating the two traditions has occurred. Christian *sannyāsa* is
thus the lifestyle in which explorations of Hinduism's mystical
doctrine have been pursued, and then related to Christian faith,
especially the central doctrine/intuition of the Trinity.

But in order to acquire a knowledge of Bede's contemplative
understanding, which embraces Christianity and Hinduism, it
was necessary to present his critique of what he regarded as the
rationalism of Western culture and thought, and of the "old" science, both of which he believed interpret the world too narrowly
by recourse to reason and analysis based on empirical observa-
tion. This critique we found is part of his epistemology, which
also includes the "new" science, that is, new developments in
physics, for instance, quantum mechanics and relativity theory,
in which there has been a move away from the old Newtonian
model of the universe as composed of discrete particles (atoms) to
the *organic* model, a model that reintroduces a sense of the cosmic
whole. The new science also includes discoveries in cosmology,
biology, and psychology, which indicate a broader view required
in our notions of reality, knowledge, and life. Essentially, Bede
saw the new science as an indication of the truth of the *perennial*
philosophy, the primordial metaphysics, which he adopted as
his own and which he considered to be eloquently formulated
in our time by Seyyed Hossein Nasr. The perennial philosophy
rests on an intuitive—rather than exclusively rational—approach
to and experience of the Divine Reality. And this metaphysical
tradition, updated with the aid of the new science, is a profound
opening to the experience of pure mystical contemplation, and
the basis of Bede's contemplative theology. The perennial metaphysics is actually the fruit of an intuitive capacity of the intellect
to be illumined by the divine Intellect, and so to be led into an
inner understanding of the mysteries. It is *scientia sacra,* and the

plenitude of it is mystical realization.

Bede's contemplative theology depends on the perennial philosophy and the notion of the intuitive faculty of the mind, for that is what receives the Divine Light. We explored his contemplative theology because this is the medium through which he articulates his understanding of the relationship of Christianity and Hinduism. For the relationship of these two traditions is in the subtle realm of mystical experience and contemplation, and Bede's contemplative theology is through and through a mystical theology. It is also a monastic and *spiritual* theology, the latter term uniting the ascetic and mystical aspects. His contemplative theology was also found to emphasize the place of meditation, or *dhyāna*, as the way to inner realization of the Divine. This mystical realization is *jñāna* in the Hindu tradition, especially as expressed in the doctrine of Advaita/Saccidānanda, which is *brahmavidyā*, and *gnosis* in the Christian tradition, particularly as expressed in the notion of mystical union with God, with the Trinity. Bede's contemplative theology was discovered to have five essential characteristics: It is practical, experiential, existential, reflective, and synthetic.

Bede's theological scheme was presented with its emphasis on the doctrines of God, Creation, Incarnation, contemplation, the Church, myth, and the Cosmic Revelation, the aim of which was to give a sense of his "system" and overarching vision. The notion of myth as intuitive thought and experience, a kind of symbolic theology that draws on the imagination, was presented, since it is a central category of Bede's understanding and is the basis of what he calls the Cosmic Revelation, the revelation of God in the cosmic order, nature, and the depths of the self. Myth, in his vision, is often the recording of mystical experience, but in the story genre. It is through the mythical notion of the Cosmic Revelation, the primordial revelation, that Bede unites or sees the first link between Judeo-Christian faith and Hinduism, for they are bound together in this pristine revelation experience that is universal. It was also shown that the Vedic revelation is an integral part of this primordial revelation, though it is deeper because its experience of unity, especially as an inner awareness of oneness with Brahman or Atman, is more subtle. We saw that this Cosmic Revelation is also a Covenant in which all share, and that this principle allows Bede to connect all the religions. The important point here is the recognition by him of an original link between the Hindu and Christian faiths, and evidence that they share in the same essential mystery, the same basic reality. This discussion prepared the way for the treatment of Advaita/Saccidānanda and the Trinitarian mystery, and this within the context of inquiring whether or not a Christian Vedanta was possible.

Before we delved into that issue and these essential categories, we examined a number of Hindu principles, for instance, Brahman, Ātman, Puruṣa, the *ekam sat* (the one being), the four *mahāvākyas* (great sayings), the structure of the hierarchy of being (the cosmic hierarchy), the feminine dimension of the Godhead, and so forth; and we looked for a correspondence between Brahman, Ātman, Puruṣa, and the Christian understanding, or whether or not these terms could be incorporated into an Indian Christian theology. The conclusion was a tentative yes but with reservations and with the recognition that these terms are being given a different meaning in the Christian context. We studied the Hindu notions of Advaita and Saccidānanda very carefully and determined that Advaita is the state of unity, while Saccidānanda is the content: absolute being in absolute consciousness, resulting in absolute bliss.

It was asked whether or not a Christian Advaita is possible, and the answer was in the affirmative. The basis of a Christian Advaita was found to be in Jesus' experience of unity with His Father, as recorded in the Gospel of John. We then examined Bede's notion of the Trinity, and it was acknowledged that the Trinity is a mystery of unity, or of *distinction-in-unity*, a mystery of interpersonal relationship based on knowledge and love. The deepest reality of the Trinity, however, in Bede's understanding, is that of *communion* or pure Love itself, what is called *koinonia*. It was shown how real distinctions in the Godhead make a real world possible, since these distinctions are the model for multiplicity being actual, and not illusion. Indeed, the principle of multiplicity in the Godhead is the Logos, for He is the ground of all distinction. Then we came to the heart of the book: how Saccidānanda and Trinity relate in Bede's understanding of the issue from his own experience and reflection. On this relation depends a Christian Vedanta.

Bede, it has been shown, realized that if Hinduism and Christianity are indeed relatable, then they are so by grasping a connection between the Hindu and Christian mystical principles, that is, finding the point of encounter in the depths of interior experience, as both traditions conceive it, and that is to relate Saccidānanda and the Trinity. This relatability of the two mystical/theological doctrines presupposes a unity of being in our experience, and that is what the point of discussing the Cosmic Revelation was, to show an underlying ground of unity to humanity's experience of the Ultimate Reality. But though Bede assents to their relatability, he does not identify them, that is, he does not reduce the Trinity to Saccidānanda or vice versa. What he does allow—and this in view of his desire to witness the emergence of an Indian Christian theology—is the possibility of adopting the term *Saccidānanda* as an Indian or Sanskrit equivalent for the *Trinity,* a term with which to express the Trinitarian mystery in a way intelligible to Hindus. Furthermore, as we also discovered, Bede accepts the validity and authenticity of the Saccidanandan intuition, but he sees the Trinitarian intuition as essentially deeper and more ultimate. At the same time, he regards the two approaches as the product of a mystical dimension of experience in which both share. They are both connected in the same unity of metaphysical reality, though the Trinitarian intuition goes farther.

This dimension in which they share—and in which all religions do—is called a *continuum of realization,* and the way in which Bede and others are engaged in the encounter of Hinduism and Christianity has been identified as an *existential convergence.* These are insights that have emerged organically from this study, and in the second section of this chapter I will consider more deeply the implications of these insights for the various religions in their interrelationship, and for the Church in her relationship to them and they to her. I think that from the consideration of Saccidānanda and Trinity, when the connection was grasped, a new principle was also seen of how the various traditions relate.

Furthermore, I examined in detail Bede's very rich and subtle Christology, which is important, as it is through Jesus' experience of His oneness with the Father that we have our initial knowledge of the great mystery that we call the Trinity. Christ was seen to be *God in man* and *man in God,* and I discussed the historical, psychological/mystical, and cosmic dimensions of Bede's Christology. Then I considered at some length the nature of Tantrism and sought to answer the question of whether a Christian Tantrism was a possibility and found that it was, because Tantra is a means, and it has only to be Christianized in order to have a Christian form in our spiritual tradition, just as there exists a Christian form of ordinary yoga.

I went on to examine the idea of a Christian *sannyāsa,* and it was shown that its existence is an actual fact, so that to ask whether or not it is possible would be purely academic. Tantra, or Christian Tantrism, and *sannyāsa* belong to the practical implications of a Christian Vedanta and spirituality. The nature of *sannyāsa* was discussed in some detail, as well as the modifications to *sannyāsa* by Christian monks in order to create a Christian form of sannyasic monasticism. In both Hindu and Christian *sannyāsa* we saw that the goal is essentially the same: the quest of the Absolute, or God. It was indicated what a Christian *sanny-*

āsa entails, and this centers on Christ. For the Christian sannyāsi seeks the Absolute, the Triune Godhead, through a cultivation of the interiority of Christ; he seeks to enter into His experience of the Father in the depths of the heart. Both the Hindu and Christian sannyāsi strive after brahmavidyā, or knowledge of God through interior encounter with Him, and both embrace the way of total renunciation, as far as this is possible in this life. Furthermore, both are completely dedicated to the cultivation of spiritual wisdom, which is the fruit of mystical or contemplative realization. And it is in and through the sannyasic life that the attempt to find the point of depth encounter has occurred and is occurring. The authenticity of Christian sannyāsa has been clearly demonstrated by de Nobili, Upadhyay, Monchanin, Abhishiktananda, Francis Acharya, and Bede Griffiths. This Christian sannyāsa, particularly as lived by the latter four, is the product of a synthesis between Benedictine/Cistercian monasticism and Hindu sannyāsa. So, even on the monastic level we found an example of existential convergence.

Finally, I considered briefly the role of the Church in the future in relation to the other religious traditions. We saw that role in terms of her innate but unrealized universality as far as they are concerned, that though her scope is universal, indeed cosmic, as the whole Creation and humanity are part of the Church's body, she has yet to assimilate the spiritual wisdom of the other traditions and make it her own or bring it to Christ. Bede felt that this task of assimilation is the work of the Church for the future, and he believed that she is the "place" of convergence for all the religions and movements of humankind. In her, all humanity will be reconciled, in Bede's wonderful vision. I want to turn now to a brief evaluation of Bede's contribution before going on to a presentation of my own insights and how they are related to his.

I think the essential contribution of Bede Griffiths was in the area of a contemplative, spiritual, or mystical theology that is global in scope, dialogical in commitment, and unitive in its goal. It is through this experiential theology, a theology on the frontier between the Hindu and Christian faiths, that a fruitful relationship may emerge in India and beyond. This of course will have implications for the other traditions as well. The aim of his contemplative theology, insofar as Hinduism and Christianity are concerned, is to locate the "place" of their encounter in the inner, experiential realization of the Divine Consciousness and a union with it. Bede's is a theology of inner exploration which has found the focus of relating these two ancient faith systems in the awareness of Advaita/Saccidānanda and the Trinitarian identity. On this relationship rests a Christian Vedanta, and ultimately also, an Indian Christian theology.

Bede's contemplative theology has illustrated how Advaita and the Trinity are related. Here there has been obscurity in his various presentations in writings and lectures, and so I have introduced the notion of an *ontological continuum* to describe how it is that they can be relatable. Through a participation in the same metaphysical mystery, the ontological continuum—though the Trinity is a more ultimate plunge into the Godhead, which is evident in its personal nature as a communion of love in a triune identity—the two mystical doctrines meet in their living origin. This is the inner reality: their mutual discovery in the depths of Divine Consciousness in the experience of Christian and Hindu *sannyāsis* and nonmonastic pilgrims. Here they encounter the reality and truth of each faith in its ultimate value on the continuum of realization. But when this relationship is grasped in a living situation and an open commitment to mutual discovery, that relationship can be described as an existential convergence. This kind of depth relationship, in the case of the Hindu and Christian traditions, is permitting a more flexible, dynamic, and fluid understanding to emerge, a new vision of the intimate bond that unites the two traditions in their common quest for Ultimate Reality, the Absolute, or God. That is how I would describe Bede Griffiths's achievement.

Now I want to move into a consideration of a few insights of mine that are directly related to Bede's enterprise and hopefully will clarify it still further. This will also include more on existential convergence, the ontological continuum, and the future of the Church.

CREATIVE IMPLICATIONS

A number of questions have continually come to me during the two years that I have worked on this volume. If indeed these two religions are relatable, as Bede, Abhishiktananda, and others say—and this is an intrinsic relationship, an interior one—then what constitutes that relation? What is the medium through which they are in fact relatable? What is the structure of reality that permits them to be participants in the same ontological mystery? Are they in the same ontological reality? As I pondered what Bede had done—along with Monchanin, Abhishiktananda, and others—I began to understand that what in fact was happening in these few decades since the Second World War, in the relationship of the Christian faith and Hinduism as they were encountering each other in the experience and commitment of these great pioneers of the Spirit, these Christian monks, was what I have called an *existential convergence.*

It is important, however, to distinguish this convergence from mere dialogue, or even *existential dialogue,* which though profound is not as ultimate. Mere dialogue can be and often is a casual matter, but the deeper, more substantial type is governed by an intrinsic commitment to finding the point of unity between the two traditions, finding the common ground that permits them to be related in a direct way. Bede Griffiths describes this profounder sort of dialogue, what I call existential dialogue: "The primary purpose of inter-religious dialogue is mutual understanding, but this means understanding the other religion from *within,* that is, by sharing the other person's experience of his religion. This comes about not only through shared conversation but also through sharing in religious rituals and prayer together."[1] Existential dialogue is this inner openness to the other in mutual trust, respect, and sympathy. But existential convergence goes even deeper.

It presupposes an intimate knowledge of both traditions in their mature teachings, their fully formed spirituality or mystical/contemplative doctrine. Existential convergence occurs between and among religions, between and among representatives of different faith systems, and most especially within the depths of interiority of a person who has achieved a genuine assimilation of the spiritual values and insights of another tradition and integrates them with his own or finds the point of complementarity between the ultimate teachings of both systems. This certainly was Bede Griffiths's experience in his depth encounter with Hinduism. In that same letter quoted above, he continues: "From this shared experience of religion a kind of osmosis takes place, so that each person begins to see his own religion in a new light. A Christian, for instance, by sharing with a Hindu or a Buddhist begins to see Christ in a new light."[2] This osmotic quality is what I mean by existential convergence, and it points up the double tendency of this osmotic or assimilative process to absorb and integrate new insights, while relating them to the core truth of one's own faith in such a way that they actually shed light on it, allowing one to appreciate the truth more profoundly. Christ, for example, stands out more clearly when seen through the spiritual sensitivity of the Hindu.

The osmotic, assimilative activity characteristic of the relationship of Christianity and Hinduism in the sannyasic context is the groundwork of a new spiritual and cultural identity that is at once both Hindu and Christian in a very real sense. Furthermore, as Bede's letter reveals, there is a natural progression in dialogical relations, as they shift from simple inner openness to the other tradition to actual fruitful and genuine appropriation. There is an inner dynamism working in the encounter of the two traditions—and other traditions as well—that leads them to discover the metaphysical ground of their relationship in the Source of Being itself. For in the existentiality of interreligious dialogue and convergence there is a deeper call of Being itself, and this call invites us to that authenticity that proceeds from the truth of both, and the hope of finding the further truth that unites them. It is this truth as goal that propels interreligious relations and allows for actual existential confluence.

Now in this work we saw an instance of existential convergence take place in the relating of Advaita/Saccidānanda and the Trinitarian intuition, although the latter was seen to be more ultimate than the former. At the same time, they were found to be participating in the same ontological mystery and reality. That is precisely why they are relatable. So, to the question of how an existential convergence is possible, how it is constituted, the answer suggests itself: in the structure of reality itself; but this is reality taken in its ultimate degree and state, in the realm of the Godhead itself. There is a deeper unity of Being underlying all reality, a subtle unity that is not immediately evident to the senses. This unity, when regarded from the vantage point of the highest mystical consciousness of which the human being is capable, becomes the matrix of an actual existential convergence, particularly when the artificial barriers dissolve and the ultimate mystical states, as articulated by both traditions, face each other in their open, eternal truth, in their pure facticity in the depths of contemplative consciousness. They discover the truth of each other's intuition in the living, vibrant, and dynamically actual continuum of realization, which is an *ontological continuum* that is also a spiral of ever expanding depth and awareness, a spiral of ultimate consciousness of the Divine Essence, the Godhead. Thus, existential convergence is possible and is based on an ontological continuum that is also a spiral of realization, a deeper and deeper penetration of the divine mystery. To express it another way, existential convergence implies an ontological continuum, and this continuum is the way into a knowledge and experience of the ultimate mystery at its Center, its ultimate point, where the spiral becomes the generating "heart" of reality.

The ontological continuum is ultimately a spiral, and with each turn of this spiral closer to the center, a deeper penetration of the divine mystery occurs. The ontological continuum is the spiral of mystical knowledge, of experiential wisdom deriving from a direct contact with the Absolute, the transcendent Reality. The ontological continuum is an ultimate transcendent state of consciousness, a state in which all the genuine mystical traditions have their origin. One tradition, in my view, differs from another by reason of its position on the continuum, and more specifically, by its position on the spiral of transcendent realization. This is certainly suggested in Bede Griffiths's understanding of the relationship of Saccidānanda to the Trinity. Far along on the spiral is pure unity, or Advaita, but more ultimate still is distinction-in-unity characteristic of the triune identity, a mystery of interpersonal relationship, of communion in knowledge and love. The relational element of the Divine Unity is the essence of the Godhead, a relationalness that is eternally established on pure *care*, pure affirmation and self-giving, that which we call love. This attribute of relationship, of communion, is at the heart of the mystic spiral; it is the goal of the ontological continuum. For relationship, which is the actuality we attempt to name in the term *Trinity*, is the ground of divine identity and creativity. Unity knows itself in Trinity, and the act by which it knows is also the act by which it creates. In more theological language, the Father knows Himself in the Son, and the act by which He knows the Son, and the Son knows the Father, is the Holy Spirit, who is communicated in the relationship. The fruit of knowledge is self-communication, which is partially what Creation is. In the formula Bede is fond of, the Father knows Himself in the Son and communicates Himself in the Spirit.

The Trinitarian mystery is the ultimate point of the mystic

spiral, and that is why Advaita can never be the last word in these matters. A particular spiritual tradition has a position on the spiral relative to the Center, which is the triune identity, and Christ, as Logos, as the Eternal Son, is at the heart of this identity. He is the term mediating between unity and Trinity, between undifferentiation and inner comprehension of unity's infinite capacity to be, and its unlimited possibilities. He is the portal of manifestation. A tradition like Buddhism will see one aspect, one kind of transcendent consciousness, that which stresses the undifferentiated and the ineffable, while Islam and Judaism will see another, that which emphasizes distance from the One, or God's total transcendence and otherness to us. These latter traditions would seem the farthest from the Center, and the nearest to manifestation and Creation. Hinduism, however, goes beyond difference or distinction into the nonduality of the Spirit, the Advaita or pure unity of the Godhead, but it stops short of the personalism of the Center, although it has a sense of what dwells in the depths of the unity through the intuition of Saccidānanda. It stands at the threshold of final enlightenment, the discovery of personalism and communion as emanating from the hidden well-springs of Being, and Being's source.[3] Perhaps it is Christ who will lead Hindus "to the further shore" beyond mere Advaita, lead them into the incomparable love of the Trinitarian nature, the fontal source of all life, being, and manifestation.

In the Eastern tradition's various doctrines of the ultimate state of reality, there does not seem to be a reasonable accounting for the human dimension and for Creation. This defect insofar as Creation is concerned was mentioned in chapter 6. These doctrines do not make sense of human life, for the relational characteristic is totally lacking. The personalism is absent, with notable exceptions. And yet, in this life, in this consciousness, every flower, every tree and bird, and every individual person eloquently proclaims, just by being, the *personal* nature of the Absolute, and Being itself. And that somehow has got to be part

of Ultimate Reality itself, as we see it is in the Christian doc-
trine/intuition of the Trinity. This is why I regard the Eastern
traditions, and others, as at a greater distance from the Center
of the mystic spiral, at a point on the ontological continuum
that is not yet aware of the plenitude of Divine Life as a communion of Being.[4] This awareness is the singular achievement
and contribution of the Christian theological and contemplative
tradition and is part of the permanent landscape of interreligious dialogue, especially as regards the issue of the nature of
ultimate consciousness.

My third point flows directly from the second, and it involves
an ecclesial implication of the ontological continuum and the
mystic spiral of realization. This concerns a new model of the
Church in relation to and for the other religious traditions, a new
model that is also consistent with Bede Griffiths's cosmic vision
of the Church and her role, which was developed briefly in the
preceding chapter. This new model would also allow the Church
to actualize her innate though as yet unrealized universality. In
this model of the Church, the spiral is transmuted into a series
of concentric circles. Each circle represents a different degree of
participation in the inner life of the Church. Thus, Christianity,
particularly Catholicism, Orthodoxy, the Anglican and Lutheran
communions, are symbolized by the innermost circle, since the
Christian faith is nearest to the vision of the interpersonal triune
identity, the community of Being at the heart of the Godhead.[5]
The other traditions would be represented by different circles
depending on their relative proximity to the Center. Judaism,
Islam, and Hinduism in its Bhakti tradition would be on the circle
adjacent to Christianity, while Buddhism, Taoism, and Hinduism
in its Advaitic tradition would be on one of the outer circles,
because of the lack of the relational element in their respective
doctrines of the ultimate state of consciousness.

In this model of the Church there are two essential forms of
participation, which are determined by how a particular tradition

or person regards Christ: the Church's tradition and the Gospel in its fullness. If, for example, Buddhism has difficulty with the doctrine of Christ's divinity and the authority He has invested in His Church, then there is no point in permitting Buddhists into full communion with the Church in her sacramental life. If a Hindu adherent to Advaita cannot accept transubstantiation, what point is there in offering him or her the Eucharist? If a Jew can only see Jesus as a good man or a teacher, and a Muslim considers Him only a prophet, then it is meaningless, from their point of view, to admit them into complete participation in the ecclesial sacramental economy. To do so is to reduce the significance of the sacraments, to degrade them in the eyes of those who do not accept them or who comprehend them as mere symbols, with little sense of their supernatural meaning. So, to open the Church to the other traditions, to invite them into her life as a medium of universal convergence and encounter, and to become a "place" of reconciliation among nations and peoples does not mean or require that she change the nature that has been given to her. It means, rather, that the Church assumes a new and vital mission in the interest of all humankind, a mission that pursues the long-term aims of building up the unity, solidarity, and community of humankind. In this way she becomes the sacrament of unity and reconciliation.

The participation of other traditions in the Church—if their view of her nature and of Christ's is limited—has to be confined to a general kind of relationship, one that emphasizes goodwill, cooperation, reconciliation, dialogue, and mutual understanding. It means also, on the part of the Church and those traditions and people who enter into this existential relationship with her, an attitude of openness and truth, of trust and a continual probing attempt to grow in understanding, mutual understanding. Furthermore, it demands a cooperation on all the human issues that divide the planet into hostile camps: peace; economic, social, political, and spiritual justice; human rights; ecology; redistribution of wealth; sharing of resources; hunger and famine; ignorance; and disease, to mention some of the more pressing areas of concern where cooperation is not only possible but quite crucial. If the Church and the various other religious traditions can work together on saving the planet from nuclear and conventional war and terrorism, and can cooperate in the task of bringing genuine justice, freedom, and lasting peace, with a true respect for the ecology of the earth, then perhaps at a later point in history a more intimate relationship will emerge between the Church and the other systems of faith, an intimate relationship within her own inner life and depth.

Of course the other degree of participation is based on faith in Jesus Christ and the authority of the Church He established through Peter and the other Apostles. This form of participation is the fullest possible and is accessible to all Christians who find their way into union with the Church in her total nature as the Mystical Body and who embrace those doctrinal insights that symbolize her faith, a faith expressed and concretized in her children, especially in her saints. But this is a faith and a holiness that can be realized in any and every culture and nation, any and every genuine philosophy and religious structure. For the Gospel is capable of infinite variation in form and articulation and can utilize all symbols that arise from a deep experience of faith and encounter with Divine Reality, no matter the language and the cultural configuration.

And yet the Church is a *Mystical Body,* and like all bodies she grows and evolves by acquiring new cells, new members destined for salvation, and new treasures of the Spirit that she acquires through assimilation and organic development. All the traditions have a vital contribution to make to this essential, indeed quintessential growth of the Church in her mystical reality. This is one of the ultimate implications of interreligious dialogue, of existential encounter and convergence. She has something precious to give to them and all the members of humankind, but equally, they have something to add to her universal tradition. Their spiritual wisdom also belongs to her, because it belongs to Christ. This is not a proposal for a form of religious imperialism, nor a tactic to advance Catholicism from within the other traditions by drawing them into a closer relationship with the Church. It is not a new and hidden triumphalism, neither is it the old triumphalism and religious imperialism under a different, more modern guise. It is rather the vision of humankind finding in the Church a universal form and vehicle in and through which it will achieve its ultimate potentiality for divinity, the medium in which humanity will be divinized by realizing or actualizing its destiny. In the long run, as humanity matures, and as the various spiritual traditions grow in mutual understanding within the universal structure of the Church, as integration of the various traditions occurs within the one, all-embracing *catholic* tradition, the concentric circles will link up with each other and merge into the Center. The differences will not be lost or transcended, just comprehended in a larger unity of faith. We will have found that point of identity where we are one, where we have always been one. Then the various traditions will be seen to be part of the same fabric, like patches in the one quilt. This will not be a syncretism but the final realization of the overarching reality to which we all belong. It will be the achievement of a true synthesis.

The model for how the religious traditions will relate at that point, and perhaps even now, is again *distinction-in-unity* and *unity-in-distinction*, taking their new form of relationship from that of the Trinitarian identity. The distinctions express and enrich the unity, while the unity gives being and identity to the distinctions. In this new relationship, the Church will have assimilated the other religions in their essential wisdom, and they will have assimilated her; she will indwell in them, and they in her, while all will actualize a heightened identity. The Church will then be equally Hindu, Buddhist, Jewish, Islamic, Sikh, Taoist, as well as quintessentially Christian, and she will be *catholic* and Christian in all of these expressions. Her nature as Christian will manifest itself in these, as so many elements of her actualized universality. The Christian mystery will express itself in the terms and categories of all the other faith systems. At the Center will be Christ, perfect man because He is God and the one who reveals us as we can and *will* be. He leads humankind to the Father in the Spirit. He is the way, because He is humanity perfected and divinized, for we must be like God in order to be eternally one with Him. Christ is the way to that likeness. In that mystical union with the Trinity of Persons, all substance, accidents, form and structure, and relations and distinctions are assumed into the form of the Logos. Everything is taken up into unity, while retaining distinction, but everything enters into the ultimate intelligibility of the divine nature and reality.

I think Bede Griffiths contributed substantially to the advancement of the ideal of universal unity and solidarity. This is especially evident in his subtle attempt to formulate, along with others, a Christian Vedanta and more generally in his very profound contemplative theology. It is also evident in his synthetic genius. Bede's attempt is, I believe, a model of how the various traditions can and should discover one another's depth, beauty, and richness. Most important, it is a prophetic indication of the future. He has made a beginning, as have Abhishiktananda and countless others in India and elsewhere, and from this beginning an evolution will take place. The seed will grow and become a worthy edifice for the Spirit, and these experiments will inspire others all around the planet, until the whole world is renewed in the enlarged identity of the Kingdom of Heaven.

Epilogue

Sage of a New Age: The Prophetic Significance of Bede Griffiths

❧

As I look back now some ten years after Father Bede's death, a number of characteristic marks stand out in prominence to define the extraordinary uniqueness of this remarkable Benedictine monk, interspiritual visionary, and eloquent prophetic figure, who was "a Western prophet shining in the East," as Sister Marie Louise puts it in a 1993 documentary on his life entitled *A Human Search*.[1] Bedeji, as those of us close to this spiritual teacher called him (the suffix *-ji* being an Indian expression of respect), was a living miracle of grace for us all. In these pages are unfolded the chief distinguishing features of his witness to humankind, to the Church, and to the world. You will notice, no doubt, that these characteristics of his life are in continuity with the body of his thought in the book.

BEDE AS SAGE AND PROPHET

Bedeji's spiritual teaching is indeed multifaceted, as can easily be gleaned above from the various dimensions of his rich experience and thought unfolded in these pages. Nearly all of his teaching has a prophetic character to it, often indicating parallels and connections between East and West; between the great world religions and indigenous wisdom; between cosmic, historical, and mystical revelation; between the earth and humankind; and finally between science, mysticism, and faith. These numerous dimensions of his experience and wisdom are outlined here.

A prophet is one who speaks, teaches, guides from, and models a wisdom inspired of the Divine. A prophet is thus often a sage, one in intimate union with God, the Source, the Ultimate Mystery. Bedeji was such a sage, a mystic seer formed and informed by a constant awareness of the Divine Presence that shaped his understanding, prompted his words, compelled his actions, and was the substance of his relationships and interactions with others.

Bede's inner life was molded by a mysticism of love, or rather it was divine love that animated his spiritual journey. His mysticism was inwardly dynamic and personally relational. In this—his constant focus and consciousness—Bedeji was thoroughly a Christian contemplative seer. No one can doubt this view who knew him, since it came through everything he said, did, and wrote. He experienced the whole of the Christian mystery in terms of this dynamic relational quality, this emphasis on divine love: the union of the human person with God, the personal though transcendent Source. Even in his profound and subtle assimilation of Advaitic awareness in Vedantic mysticism, he always maintained the relational identity and its fullness in agapic, selfless, unconditional divine love.

Near the end of his life, after two debilitating strokes, when his intellect was gone, he continued to emphasize love in every conscious moment, and every breath he took reflected his intense awareness of love. As Russill Paul wrote in a circular letter at the time to Bedeji's many friends: "Love is all he ever talks about, whether awake or asleep. It is the one, all encompassing category of his experience."[2] His mysticism of love came full circle and was the leitmotif of his *mahāsamādhi* (his passing over into the Eternal).

BEDE AS A VOICE IN THE CHURCH

There can be no doubt that Bedeji was a powerful prophetic figure in the Catholic Church itself and in Christianity more generally. He loved the Church but never spared his criticism of its leaders, particularly where he identified instances of abuse of authority by Rome. Anyone who has ever read his seemingly endless letters to the editor of *The Tablet*, the London Catholic weekly, knows what I mean. I remember once visiting John Wilkinson, the editor of this important publication, and he told me how he often had to tone down Father Bede's letters when they were too critical of some Vatican official, perhaps the Pope, or Cardinal Ratzinger of the Congregation for the Doctrine of the Faith. Bede often voiced his views publicly in homilies and in conversations. At other times he sided with controversial theologians, such as Hans Küng, Matthew Fox, and Leonardo Boff, or peace activists such as Daniel and Joseph Berrigan. His critical remarks were always constructive and relevant.

Bede continually stressed the task of the Church as one of careful assimilation of the mystical, psychological, theological, moral, and ritual treasures of the other traditions. Only in this way can the Church realize her nature and mission as genuinely universal. Bedeji never tired of calling the Church to this path and reminding her of this vitally important work. Otherwise, the Church would remain universal simply in a geographic sense.

AN INTERSPIRITUAL PIONEER

Like his eminent predecessors de Nobili, Upadhyay, Monchanin, and Abhishiktananda, Bedeji showed a passion for an interspiritual vision. Like these others, he was way ahead of his time. His passion for intermystical exploration had begun in England when he was a young monk reading some of the sacred texts of the East. His study awakened him to the conviction of the authenticity of spirituality in other traditions, notably the Asian forms. This conviction only deepened as he cultivated an experiential knowledge of Hindu and Buddhist mysticism in his nearly forty years in India, especially those at Shantivanam.

Father Bede's interspiritual bridge between Hinduism and Christianity became, first of all, his very disciplined meditation practice, and meditation is a contemplative activity that is capable of bringing all the religions together in their common depth dimension.

At Shantivanam, Bede integrated sacred readings, prayers, poems, and songs from other traditions in the spiritual life of his community. Sanskrit and Tamil were part of the daily worship in the ashram. Readings from the Upaniṣads, the Bhagavad Gita, the Tao Te Ching, the poets Kabir and Rumi, and the Dhammapada, and other Buddhist *suttas* would be celebrated along with Christian readings, prayers, and hymns. Bede was naturally interspiritual in a vision of prayer and contemplative experience that drew on a discerned universal tradition underlying spiritual life and practice. This tradition is neither intentional nor systematic, but includes all manifestations of spirituality that arise from the dimension of depth in human experience that is found everywhere. As an interspiritual visionary, Father Bede found nourishment in this universal tradition of mysticism.

A WITNESS FOR THE EARTH

Bedeji was eloquent and persistent in his advocacy of the natural world, an advocacy formed by his early nature mysticism and his great love of the simple pastoral existence of preindustrial society. His youthful idealism for this simplicity of life pursued with his friends at Eastington in a Cotswold cottage after his graduation from Oxford, where they lived a community rhythm close to the earth, matured into a permanent commitment to an enlightened ecology. Such an ecological understanding was inspired by a deep knowledge of the spirituality of nature and cosmos, in a mysticism or religion of nature that knows the spiritual and aesthetic values of the natural world, in the midst of the sanity and peace of the countryside and the wilderness. He preferred this more meaningful simplicity to the noise, confusion, fragmentation, poverty, and complexity of the modern industrial world. Bedeji was a prophet of natural living, close to the earth, where needs are basic and the leisure required for contemplation is maximal. Along with Thomas Berry and others, he would see this approach as the way to planetary healing and a more balanced life conducive to spiritual realization and maturity. With Mother Teresa, he emphasized an evangelical poverty that shaped his commitment to simplicity of lifestyle and harmony with the natural world, which he and his community lived in a spirit of great generosity and dedication. Bede realized so well that the spiritual life is an uncluttered life in which inner freedom makes space for a relationship with God, with others, especially the most vulnerable, and with the cosmos and nature.

HIS INTEGRATIVE WISDOM

Bede was an integral thinker and mystic who was far ahead of other theologians and spiritual writers of his time. Although his view of integral knowing and synthesis falls short of Ken Wilber's more comprehensive and sophisticated articulation, nevertheless he had the spirit of the larger perspective required. He was always seeking the common ground, the bridge that unites all ways of knowing in an overarching unified knowledge, a kind of new species of wisdom. His wide-ranging concerns made him a complex figure intellectually, since he addressed virtually everything of importance to the age: the partnership of science, religion, and mysticism; ecological responsibility; justice; war and peace; the weaknesses of capitalism; the failure of communism; the role of the Church and the need for reform; relating the traditions in the interreligious sphere; the value of community life to humankind's future; and the reform of society globally, to mention the most prominent areas that preoccupied his fertile reflections.

BEDE AS TEACHER OF HARMONY

Bedeji always radiated a genuine warmth toward and acceptance of everyone. Not just an abstract openness to other religions, or an intellectual or theoretical acceptance, but an authentic human openness and availability in the concreteness of his numerous encounters with persons from all traditions, cultures, and ethnic backgrounds that characterized his life and presence. He always made himself available quite spontaneously to those who arrived at the door of his austerely simple hut at Shantivanam. He was equally available to all those who wrote to him, and it was not uncommon for Bedeji to write some twenty or so letters by hand every day!

He had an enormous capacity for love, and it touched all those who came into contact with him. India profoundly changed him in a cultural, spiritual, and psychological sense, opening him to a larger understanding of his identity. It greatly increased his ability to love others, far beyond his own English culture. It is a well-known fact that the British—not all of them, of course—had fairly blatant racist views of Indians and other dark-skinned colonial subjects. E. M. Forster's *A Passage to India* and Paul Scott's *The Jewel in the Crown* have graphically portrayed the depth and ugliness of British colonial racial attitudes so tragically affecting India's countless millions. Bede never shared in these destructive prejudices and in his psychological and moral being became actually an icon of reversal,[3] a brilliant example of compassion and of healing in deep humility. He reversed in his life, his attitudes, his actions, and his words this terrible past of Britain, born out of ignorance, blind ambition, and greed. In a very real sense, Bedeji became an Indian psychologically, spiritually, and culturally, and wedded this expanded identity with his Christian faith and English personality. He became truly a son of the rich soil of the subcontinent. His Indian identity was subtly embedded in his heart. In this profoundly prophetic behavior he modeled the essence of harmony in his healing acceptance and presence.

His expression of harmony was cultivated by his heartfelt commitment to Gandhi's compassionate teaching on *ahimsā,* or nonviolence, and *satyagraha,* soul power, the power of truth itself. He always witnessed to these methods of compassion, of subtle communication, advocating them in his writings and talks. He was preeminently a "prophet of dialogue," as Judson Trapnell calls him,[4] and his emphasis on nonviolence, love, and the power of truth all served to underscore this overarching commitment to dialogue in his observance and relations with others.

Bedeji was also a voice for the Divine Feminine and the role of women in the Church and society. India greatly sensitized him to the feminine dimension of the Divine, where God is regarded equally as Mother and Father. Bede's own mystical process that he went through after a stroke in 1990 opened him up to the feminine both in God and in himself, and this significantly changed his view, making him far more receptive to this important part of life. He made much of the impact of the Divine Feminine on his life, how it altered his experience of spiritual life and marked his vital immersion into India's understanding of relationship with God in its feminine aspect, and his transformation in this powerful inner reality affected all aspects of his being.

HIS TEACHING ON COMMUNITY

Bedeji was an inspiring advocate of small communities; he saw them as the salvation of the world, especially as old structures collapse or change. In traditional societies around the planet a great deal of emphasis is still placed on community and extended family ties, but this communal option hasn't existed much in America and the West in general. There is a longing for that special quality of belonging that community makes possible. Bede understood so well not simply the need for communal life, but also how nurturing it is to us all psychologically, morally, spiritually, and even materially.

I remember with great fondness the fascinating and compelling experiments in small contemplative community that Bede, Russill Paul, Asha Paul, and I enjoyed during many months in 1991 and 1992 in both Vermont and California. These times together were precious for us; we had really become a community at Shantivanam, a community within the larger monastic ashram. These periods were quite revealing of the value that small-scale community has for individuals and societies.

Our life together, in the Vermont phases, was intimate and memorable. We followed a fairly informal horarium. We would rise around 5:00 A.M. and have tea or coffee before morning prayer and meditation, while sharing some reflection. Looking out at the surrounding mountains in Waitsfield, on the beautiful, solitary eighty acres of our hosts, Harrison and Olivia Hobletzelle, we would drink in the extraordinary natural splendor that irradiated the landscape as dawn approached. Then we would have our morning prayer consisting of Sanskrit chants from the Upaniṣ ads, readings from the Bhagavad Gita and the New Testament, and an hour of contemplative meditation. After morning prayer, we would have a simple breakfast, following a strict vegetarian diet. At the time, Bede's health was a bit delicate, and so he was put on a macrobiotic diet arranged by Asha, who so patiently cooked his meals and nursed him in so many ways, along with us. Bede wasn't terribly fond of this unimaginative diet but accepted it quietly. Asha's patience paid off because Bede's health improved dramatically. Russill, Asha, and I would take turns cooking the regular meals, and Bede would assist with cleanup. He wanted to be part of all our activities.

Following breakfast, there would be free time until 9:00 A.M., which might be spent doing *lectio divina* or some private prayer. From 9:00 to 10:00 we would meet for *satsang*, time with the teacher and sharing with him, with Bedeji. These sessions were often profoundly stimulating. After *satsang* we would attend to our personal work. Normally Russill would be absorbed in his music, Bede and I in our writing, and Asha in her studying. One of us would prepare lunch, which might consist of brown rice, greens, and tofu. There was usually time for a nap after lunch. Around 2:30 we would all take an hour-long walk together, rather leisurely, given Father Bede's age and health.

We would return for afternoon tea, followed by more time for *lectio divina*, with evening prayer and meditation at 6:00 P.M. Around 7:00 we would have a simple dinner, wash the dishes, and then have an hour or so of recreation. We retired around 8:30, but Bede often read until he fell asleep, by 9:30 or 10:00, while Russill, Asha, and I would talk till around 11:00. Such was the simple, joyous life we shared, a deeply nourishing, balanced contemplative experience, saturated with humor, laughter, incredible conversations, and endless insights.

Often others joined us for brief periods, notably Sister Pascaline Coff, a Benedictine from Osage Monastery in Sand Springs, Oklahoma; Father Thomas Keating, the Trappist spiritual teacher and writer from St. Benedict's Monastery in Snowmass, Colorado; and the entire community of monks from Weston Priory in Weston, Vermont. All came and drank from the well of spiritual joy in the matrix of a loving community.

On so many occasions in his long and fruitful life, Bede

Griffiths had announced the dawning of a new age, which was not the popular notion of the New Age movement but really the opening to an integral humanism that brought together all the religions/spiritualities, science, and mysticism with the concern for the earth and the indigenous wisdom traditions, in a new vision of a reconciled humanity, where community and its gifts of sharing are the focus. Bedeji, as the sage of this new age, granted us, like Gandhi before him, an example of a concrete embodiment of engaged holiness and spirituality, heralding in the Interspiritual Age, in the sense above, and becoming in the process an intermystical as well as Christian saint. The impact of this gentle prophetic figure will be felt throughout the course of the third millennium and far beyond.

Notes

Preface

1. Bede Griffiths, *A New Vision of Reality: Western Science, Eastern Mysticism, and Christian Faith*, ed. Felicity Edwards (Springfield, Ill.: Templegate, 1990).

2. Wayne Teasdale, *The Mystic Heart: Discovering a Universal Spirituality in the World's Religions* (Novato, Calif.: New World Library, 1999).

Introduction

1. There were some articles here and there of a popular nature, and he was mentioned in more serious works on occasion, but little else. Some of these articles include: Pier Gheddo, "Bede Griffiths: Un 'guru' cristiano in India," *Mondoe Missione*, no. 7 (1978); A. K. Saran, "Further towards a Hindu-Christian Dialogue," *The Clergy Monthly* 32, no. 5 (May 1968), which discusses Father Bede's approach to dialogue; and Thomas Emprayil, *The Emerging Theology of Religions* (Rewa, India: Vincentian Publications, 1980), pp. 118–20. There was also a title article entitled "Bede Griffiths and Our Small Earth," in Mark Gibbard, *Guides to Hidden Springs: A History of Christian Spirituality through the Lives of Some of Its Witnesses* (London: SCM Press, 1980), pp. 82–88, and he was discussed in some detail in an article on him by Judith M. Brown in *A Dictionary of Christian*

Spirituality, ed. Gordon S. Wakefield (London: SCM Press, 1983), pp. 183–84. A lot of material has come into print since the original publication of this book in 1987. See "Works in English by Bede Griffiths," page 236, for a more complete and updated list of publications.

2. Harrison Hoblitzelle, "A Visit with Father Bede Griffiths: India's Christian Guru," *New Age,* August 1983.

3. Tantra is a system of yoga that unites the body, senses, feelings, imagination, and sexuality with the mind in the journey to Ultimate Reality. It is concerned with transforming the energy by raising it to higher levels of consciousness.

4. As a general principle, this is also an issue for the Church and Christian theology in other cultures. Can there be a Christian Taoism and Confucianism in China? Can there be a Christian Buddhism and Zen? Can primitive societies evolve a Christian theology that expresses their particular gifts, their language, myths, and customs?

5. *In Quest of the Absolute: The Life and Works of Jules Monchanin,* ed. and trans. J. G. Weber (Kalamazoo: Cistercian Publications, 1977), Bede's preface, p. 1.

6. *Advaita,* or nonduality (unity), refers to the ninth-century Indian philosopher Śankara's system of Vedanta.

7. This term goes back to the time of the Vedas and permeates most of the tradition with various connotations. Sanskrit is a very fluid language, and words can have a variety of meanings that depend on the context in question. This is especially true of the term *Puruṣa.*

8. The *guhā,* the "cave" or secret place of the heart, is a metaphor that Bede, along with Abhishiktananda and others, frequently used to express the deepest dimension of interiority or introversion where we meet God, the Ultimate Reality. It is an image taken from the Upaniṣads.

9. A. K. Saran, in his article on Father Bede's method mentioned in note 1 above, "Further towards a Hindu-Christian Dialogue," uses the term "actual dialogue" (p. 213) to describe what Bede was doing

in India, but I do not think that this term captures the radical nature of the Bedean approach to interreligious communication, which is open to mutual assimilation, sharing, and enrichment but not to syncretism. Consequently, I prefer the term "existential convergence" because it conveys better the nature, value, and uniqueness of Bede's dialogical activities and his life of depth in India.

10. In a certain sense he could be said to be engaged in experimentation insofar as this was a relatively new situation for a Christian monk to be in, and as a consequence, he must feel his way along. But it was not an experiment in the classic sense, since he was really *being* what he was doing. He was not just "trying it out," so to speak.

11. First published in 1954 by Harvil Press, London, and by Kenedy Publishers, New York. I prefer to use the Templegate edition because it is more up to date.

12. First published under the title *Christian Ashram* (London: Darton, Longman and Todd, 1966).

13. First published privately in India in 1968. This book was initially a collection of lectures delivered at Madras University in 1968.

14. First published in Britain with a similar title, *Return to the Centre* (London: Collins, Fount Paperbacks, 1976). I will study and quote from the American edition.

15. Published by Collins, London, in 1982.

16. Under this title are six lectures originally given at Conception Abbey, Conception, Missouri, in August 1979.

17. In this work, Bede presents an in-depth study of the Gita.

18. I will use the term *spiritual theology* interchangeably with *contemplative theology* since it has the same connotations insofar as it unites mystical theology and asceticism.

19. It is very important for the sake of clarity to point out that I am not relating Hinduism and Christianity, but studying Bede's attempt to do so. And because of this—because I am trying to comprehend his experience and to elucidate his own inner awareness—my method is partially phenomenological.

20. I must caution, however, that these assumptions, which underlie his thought, were inwardly certain for him.

21. See *Christ in India*, p. 96.

CHAPTER 2. THE HISTORICAL CONTEXT AS SANNYASIC MONASTICISM

1. The principles and some of the history are discussed in the following: Abbe J. Monchanin, S.A.M., and Dom Henri Le Saux, O.S.B., *A Benedictine Ashram* (Douglas, Isle of Man: Times Press, 1964); Bede Griffiths, *Christ in India: Essays towards a Hindu-Christian Dialogue* (New York: Scribner's, 1966); and Emmanuel Vattakuzhy, *Indian Christian Sannyāsa and Swami Abhishiktananda* (Bangalore: Theological Publications in India, 1981).

2. Abhishiktananda, *The Further Shore* (Delhi: ISPCK, 1975), pp. 28–29.

3. Bede Griffiths, "Saint Benedict: His Significance for India Today," *Vidyajyoti* 44 (October 1980): 433.

4. This is true of the Buddhist and Jain *sannyāsis* as well.

5. Or *monotropos*, the monk, the one who is "alone with the Alone," a "unified being," which comes through a life of holiness and contemplation, in the writings of Greco-Christian literature.

6. See *Indian Christian Sannyāsa*, pp. 14–18.

7. This information came to me in a letter from my mentor, Rev. Dr. John B. Chethimattam, dated February 23, 1985, from Trivandrum, Kerala, India.

8. There were other, earlier attempts as well.

9. Weber, *In Quest of the Absolute*, p. 73.

10. See Vincent Cronin, *A Pearl to India: The Life of Roberto de Nobili* (New York: Dutton, 1959), p. 11.

11. Ibid., pp. 18–27.

12. Ibid., pp. 40–48.

13. Ibid., p. 48.

14. Ibid., pp. 70–71.

15. Ibid., pp. 74–87.

16. Ibid., pp. 87–89.

17. Ibid., pp. 90, 95, and 117.
18. D. Ferroli, S.J., *The Jesuits of Malabar*, 2 vols. (Bangalore: Bangalore Press, 1939), vol. 1, p. 354.
19. Joseph Thekkedath, *History of Christianity in India: From the Middle of the Sixteenth to the End of the Seventeenth Century (1542–1700)*, 2 vols. (Bangalore: Theological Publications in India, 1982), vol. 2, p. 224.
20. *Christ in India*, p. 60.
21. From John Chethimattam's letter.
22. Ibid. Father Kuriakos Elias has written at length on the history of this serious attempt. His works are published in Malayam in four volumes, entitled *Chavara* (Mannanam: St. Joseph Press, 1981–1982). The history of the community is sketched in volume 1 in a section entitled "The Chronicles," pp. 1–121.
23. B. Animananda, *The Blade: The Life and Work of Brahmabandhab Upadhyay* (Calcutta: Roy & Son, 1945), p. viii.
24. Martin Jarrett-Kerr, C.R., *Patterns of Christian Acceptance* (London: Oxford University Press, 1972), p. 211.
25. *The Blade*, p. 58.
26. Ibid., p. 59.
27. Ibid., p. 46.
28. *Patterns*, p. 211.
29. *Indian Christian Sannyāsa*, p. 42. Vattakuzhy's study has a brief account of modern Hindu *sannyāsa* that includes sketches of Mohan Roy; Rabindranath Tagore (1817–1905), the poet's father; Keshab Chandrasen; Swami Dayananda Sarasvati (1824–1883); Ramakrishna; Vivekananda; Gandhi (1869–1948); and Gandhi's disciple whom Bede Griffiths knew, Acharya Vinoba Bhave. See pp. 42–50.
30. *The Blade*, p. 59.
31. Ibid., p. 71.
32. Ibid.
33. Quoted ibid., p. 75.
34. Ibid., p. 77.
35. Ibid., pp. 78–79.

36. Abhishiktananda, "Le Monachisme chrétien aux Indes," *Vie Spirituelle Supplémént* 96 (1956): 284.

37. *The Blade*, p. 67.

38. Ibid., p. 185.

39. Brahmabandhab Upadhyay, "Christianity in India" (I), *The Tablet* 69 (January 3, 1903): 8.

40. *The Blade*, p. 121.

41. Upadhyay composed a beautiful hymn to the Trinity under the name of Saccidānanda.

42. *Indian Christian Sannyasa*, p. 68.

43. It is true that two Christian ashrams were founded in the 1920s by Anglicans: Christukula Ashram, established by J. Jesudasan and Dr. Forrester, and Christa Prema Seva Ashram, opened by Jack Winslow in 1927 at Shivajinagar, Pune. Both were attempts at indigenization. See *Indian Christian Sannyāsa*, p. 196.

44. Jules Monchanin, *Ecrits spirituels*, introduction by Edouard Duperray (Paris: Centurion, 1965), p. 6.

45. Ibid., p. 7.

46. *In Quest of the Absolute*, p. 25, from his notes.

47. See Henri de Lubac, *Images de l'abbé Monchanin* (Paris: Aubier, 1967), p. 15. This is one of the best and most intimate portraits of Monchanin. Another important study is *Jules Monchanin, mystique de l'Inde, mystère chrétien*, ed. Suzanne Siauve (Paris: Fayard, 1974).

48. *In Quest of the Absolute*, p. 71.

49. Ibid., p. 1, Bede's preface.

50. *Indian Christian Sannyāsa*, pp. 62–63.

51. Ibid., p. 63.

52. Ibid.

53. *A Benedictine Ashram*, p. 27.

54. Ibid.

55. Ibid., p. 29.

56. *In Quest of the Absolute*, p. 105. The Trinity was even the main theme of all his retreats to religious (ibid., p. 84). Monchanin says: "It is because of the mystery of the Trinity—Alpha and Omega—that I

am a Christian" (ibid., p. 106).

57. "In Quest of the Absolute," in *Indian Culture and the Fullness of Christ*, Proceedings of the All India Study Week, December 6–13, 1956, (Madras: The Catholic Centre, 1957), pp. 50–51. It was this lecture that became the title of Weber's edition of Monchanin's life and writings. For a similar emphasis, see his essay entitled, "Panchristism," in Weber, *In Quest of the Absolute*, pp. 153–55.

58. *In Quest of the Absolute*, p. 73 (Weber).

59. "In Quest of the Absolute," p. 49 (All India Study etc.).

60. Ibid., p. 50.

61. *Swami Parama Arubi Anandam (Fr. Jules Monchanin), 1895–1957: A Memorial* (Tiruchirapalli: Saccidananda Ashram, 1959), p. v.

62. M. M. Davy, *Swami Abhishiktananda: Le Passeur deux rives* (Paris: Cerf., 1981), p. 195.

63. Ibid., pp. 195–96.

64. Ibid., pp. 197–200.

65. *Indian Christian Sannyāsa*, p. 60.

66. Ibid., p. 74. Abhishiktananda relates the story of Ramana Maharshi's own awakening in *Saccidānanda: A Christian Approach to Advaitic Experience* (Delhi: ISPCK, 1974), pp. 19–29, and he speaks of Ramana's effect on his own being. There are further indications of Ramana's influence in his work in *The Secret of Arunāchala* (Delhi: ISPCK, 1979), pp. 1–18. See also *Ascent to the Depth of the Heart: The Spiritual Diary (1948–1973) of Swami Abhishiktananda (Dom H. Le Saux)* (Delhi: ISPCK, 1998).

67. Abhishiktananda, *Guru and Disciple* (London: SPCK, 1974), p. 87.

68. Ibid., p. 29.

69. *The Further Shore* (Delhi: ISPCK, 1975), from the essay *"Sannyāsa,"* p. 14.

70. Ibid., p. 26.

71. Ibid., pp. 28–29.

72. And that of Monchanin, Bede, and others as well.

73. *The Further Shore*, p. 102.

74. *Hindu-Christian Meeting Point* (Delhi: ISPCK, 1969), p. 48.

75. Swami Abhishiktananda, "The Upanishads and the Advaitic Experience," *Clergy Monthly* 38 (1984): 474.

76. Abhishiktananda, "Experience of God in Eastern Religions," *Cistercian Studies* 9, nos. 2 and 3 (1974): 151–52.

77. Ibid., p. 156.

78. *Abhishiktananda, Saccidananda: A Christian Approach to Advaitic Experience* (Delhi: ISPCK, 1974), p. 135.

79. Ibid., p. 178.

80. *Indian Christian Sannyāsa*, p. 94.

81. Ibid., p. 207.

82. Bede Griffiths, *The Golden String: An Autobiography*, rev. ed. (Springfield, Ill.: Templegate, 1980), pp. 18–24.

83. Ibid., p. 10.

84. Ibid., p. 16.

85. Ibid., pp. 30–32.

86. Ibid., p. 48.

87. Ibid., p. 64.

88. Ibid., pp. 132–40.

89. Ibid., p. 168.

90. Ibid., pp. 170–72.

91. Ibid., p. 174.

92. Ibid., p. 190.

93. *Christ in India*, p. 42. For a detailed account of life at Kurisumala Ashram, see pp. 41–47.

94. The preceding chapter also contains a list of his books, but that is strictly in relation to methodology. Here the purpose is simply to present their chronology of appearance.

CHAPTER 3. EPISTEMOLOGY, METAPHYSICS, AND CONTEMPLATIVE THEOLOGY

1. Seyyed Hossein Nasr, *Knowledge and the Sacred* (New York: Crossroad, 1981). The contents of this work were the Gifford Lectures in 1981.

2. Jean Leclercq, O.S.B., *The Love of Learning and the Desire for God:*

A Study of Monastic Culture, trans. Catherine Misrahi (New York: Fordham University Press, 1961).

3. *The Golden String,* p. 28.

4. Ibid., p. 181.

5. Bede Griffiths, *The Marriage of East and West* (Springfield, Ill.: Templegate, 1982), p. 15.

6. Ibid., p. 164.

7. Ibid., p. 30.

8. He had not used this term in his published works as yet, but he had in many of his talks around the world. It was not a precise term, however, as is clear from the way he used it.

9. Bede Griffiths, "Self-Realization: Return to the Center," from a talk given to the Ojai Community, Ojai, Calif., September 1993, cassette, side 1.

10. *The Marriage of East and West,* p. 72.

11. Ibid., p. 159.

12. Ibid., p. 31.

13. Bede Griffiths, *Return to the Center* (Springfield, Ill.: Templegate, 1976), p. 41.

14. Ibid.

15. *The Marriage of East and West,* p. 29.

16. *Return to the Center,* p. 19.

17. *The Marriage of East and West,* p. 165.

18. Ibid., p. 166.

19. Ibid., p. 199.

20. "Transcending Dualism: An Eastern Approach to the Semitic Religions," *Cistercian Studies* 20, no. 2 (1985): 78.

21. Bede Griffiths, "Convergence of Religions and the Biblical Tradition," a lecture given at the Esalen Institute, September 9, 1983, tape 2, side 1.

22. Bede Griffiths, "Emerging Consciousness for a New Humankind: Emerging Consciousness and the Mystical Traditions of Asia," lecture presented to a conference in Madras, January 1985, pp. 1–2. The metaphor of the "web" is Fritjof Capra's, from *The Tao*

of Physics: An Exploration of the Parallels between Modern Physics and Eastern Mysticism (Berkeley: Shambhala, 1975).

23. Bede Griffiths, "The Church and the New Science and the New Theology," in *Riches from the East* (Kansas City, Mo.: Credence Cassettes), tape 5, side 1.

24. *The Tao of Physics*, p. 142.

25. "Emerging Consciousness," p. 2.

26. Ibid.

27. Bede Griffiths, "Christianity, Science and Eastern Mysticism," lecture given at the Esalen Institute, September 7, 1983, tape 1, side 1.

28. "Emerging Consciousness," p. 2.

29. David Bohm, *Wholeness and the Implicate Order* (London: Routledge & Kegan Paul, 1980), p. 147.

30. "Emerging Consciousness," p. 2.

31. Rupert Sheldrake, *A New Science of Life: The Hypothesis of Formative Causation* (Los Angeles: J. P. Tarcher, 1981).

32. "Christianity, Science and Eastern Mysticism" (Esalen lecture), tape 1, side 1.

33. Ibid.

34. Ibid.

35. *A New Science of Life*, pp. 115–16.

36. "Christianity, Science and Eastern Mysticism," tape 1, side 1.

37. See Ken Wilber, *The Spectrum of Consciousness* (Wheaton, Ill.: Quest, 1977); *The Atman Project: A Transpersonal View of Human Development* (Wheaton, Ill.: Quest, 1980); and *Up from Eden: A Transpersonal View of Human Evolution* (Boulder: Shambhala, 1981).

38. "Emerging Consciousness," p. 3.

39. Ibid.

40. "Christianity, Science and Eastern Mysticism," tape 1, side 1.

41. *The Tao of Physics*, p. 143, and Lama Anagarika Govinda, *Foundations of Tibetan Mysticism* (New York: Weiser, 1960), p. 93.

42. *The Tao of Physics*, p. 306.

43. See *The Atman Project*, especially pp. 71 ff.

44. "Emerging Consciousness," p. 1.

45. Ibid., p. 3.

46. Letter to the author, March 18, 1985.

47. Seyyed Hossein Nasr, *Knowledge and the Sacred*, p. 130.

48. *The Marriage of East and West*, p. 31.

49. *Knowledge and the Sacred*, pp. 130–31.

50. Letter to the author, March 18, 1985.

51. *Knowledge and the Sacred*, p. 132.

52. Ibid., p. 136.

53. Ibid., p. 133.

54. Ibid., p. 134.

55. Ibid., pp. 134–35.

56. Ibid., p. 139.

57. Ibid., 151.

58. *The Marriage of East and West*, p. 157.

59. Ibid., pp. 168–69.

60. Ibid., p. 170.

61. Bede Griffiths, *The Cosmic Revelation: The Hindu Way to God* (Springfield, Ill.: Templegate, 1983), p. 65.

62. Ibid., p. 85.

63. Jordan Aumann, O.P., *Spiritual Theology* (Huntington, Ind.: Our Sunday Visitor, 1980).

64. Ibid., cf. pp. 14–24.

65. "Transcending Dualism," p. 80.

66. "Christianity, Science and Eastern Mysticism," side 1.

67. *The Cosmic Revelation*, p. 67.

68. Bede Griffiths, "Hindu and Christian Experience of God," talk given at the Esalen Institute, September 1983, cassette, side 2.

69. *Summa Theologiae*, I, 1, 6, ad 3: "*spiritualis homo judicat omnia*, etc. et Dionysius dicit, 2 cap. *De divinis nominibus* (II, 9, PG 3,648) *Hierotheus doctus est non solum discens, sed patiens divina.*"

70. Jacques Maritain, *The Range of Reason* (New York: Scribner's, 1942), p. 24.

71. Jean Leclercq, O.S.B., *The Love of Learning and the Desire for God: A Study of Monastic Culture* (New York: Fordham University Press,

1961), pp. 251–52.

72. Ibid., p. 254.

73. Ibid., p. 263.

74. Ibid., p. 266.

75. Ibid., p. 277.

76. Ibid., p. 279.

77. Ibid., pp. 279–80.

78. "Contemplative Theology and the Experience of God," *Riches from the East* (Kansas City, Mo.: Credence Cassettes), tape 2, side 1.

79. *The Cosmic Revelation*, p. 76.

80. "Contemplative Theology and the Experience of God," tape 2, side 2.

81. *The Marriage of East and West*, pp. 79–80, 183–84.

CHAPTER 4. BEDE'S THEOLOGICAL SCHEME, MYTH, AND THE COSMIC REVELATION

1. But he did have his systematic moments. *The Marriage of East and West*, for instance, is distinguished by its disciplined treatment of myth as intuitive thought, its clarity, and its originality.

2. See *In Quest of the Absolute*, p. 25.

3. It is a common assumption of many in the monastic movement or among people interested in it in America and abroad.

4. "Reflections and Prospects," in *Emerging Consciousness for a New Humankind*, ed. Michael von Bruck (Bangalore: Asian Trading Corp., 1985), pp. 123–24.

5. For an important source of this history and a valuable bibliography, see Thomas Emprayil, *The Emerging Theology of Religions* (Rewa, India: Vincentian Publications, 1980).

6. In a letter to me dated September 1978, Father Bede and R. Panikkar corrected me for implying a distinction between Godhead and Trinity, and Bede explicitly identified the Godhead with the Father, on that occasion.

7. Plotinus, Pseudo-Dionysius, and Eckhart, to name a few.

8. *The Marriage of East and West*, pp. 96–99.

9. Ibid., pp. 84–85.

10. Ibid., pp. 116–17.

11. Ibid., pp. 187–88, 195.

12. To my knowledge he did not write anything extensive on his profound theory of transmigration. I have heard him talk about it, but his view is too complex for this brief theological summary. He discussed his view of transmigration in a talk at the Esalen Institute in September 1983 entitled "Convergence of Religions and the Biblical Tradition," tape 2, side 1.

13. *The Marriage of East and West*, pp. 192 ff.

14. Ibid., p. 197.

15. It is worthy of note that Bede Griffiths always stressed meditation in his books, articles, lectures, and personal conversations. It is the way into true spiritual life and another bond uniting Christians and Hindus as well as Buddhists. See *Return to the Center*, pp. 136–46, for a good summary.

16. There has already been one very significant study done in this area, and it was originally a Fordham doctoral dissertation. I am referring to Thomas Matus, *Yoga and the Jesus Prayer Tradition: An Experiment in Faith* (Ramsey, N.J.: Paulist Press, 1984). Bede endorsed it with a preface. It is a valuable work, and I will have occasion to refer to it in chapter 6.

17. "The Church and the New Science and the New Theology," in *Riches from the East*, lecture given at the East-West Monastic Conference on Formation, 1983. Kansas City, Kansas (NCR-Credence Cassettes, 1983), tape 5, side 1.

18. Bede's thought was very dynamic, always growing, ever expanding and adding new elements, but always in light of his basic principles, which did not change, though they did become more refined.

19. *In Quest of the Absolute*. pp. 2–3.

20. Ibid., p. 3.

21. Ibid.

22. "Contemplative Theology and the Experience of God," in *Riches from the East*, tape 2, side 1.

23. *Return to the Center*, p. 76.

24. Ibid.
25. *The Marriage of East and West*, p. 47.
26. Ibid., p. 29.
27. Ibid., p. 30.
28. Ibid., p. 104.
29. *Return to the Center*, pp. 80–81.
30. Ibid., p. 81.
31. Ibid., pp. 79–80.
32. Ibid., p. 78.
33. Ibid.
34. *The Marriage of East and West*, p. 174.
35. *The Cosmic Revelation: The Hindu Way to God* (Springfield, Ill.: Templegate, 1983), p. 35.
36. *Return to the Center*, p. 21.
37. *The Marriage of East and West*, p. 88.
38. Ibid.
39. Ibid.
40. Ibid., p. 89.
41. Ibid.
42. Ibid.
43. *The Cosmic Revelation*, p. 27.
44. *The Marriage of East and West*, p. 51.
45. *The Cosmic Revelation*, p. 41.

CHAPTER 5. CHRISTIAN VEDANTA

1. *The Marriage of East and West*, p. 89.
2. *In Quest of the Absolute*, p. 73.
3. It is a fair statement to make that such a theology already exists in India, to a large extent, though a number of elements have yet to be worked out. There is a vast literature on various aspects of the issue in India today. This fact is alluded to in chapter 4.
4. This could represent a polytheistic phase or simply the recognition of the Divine Presence under innumerable forms.
5. *Rig Veda* 1.164.46.

6. Bede Griffiths, "Transcending Dualism: An Eastern Approach to the Semitic Religions," *Cistercian Studies* 20, no. 2 (1985): 75. This was a lecture given at the Ecumenical Institute, Tantur, Jerusalem, on May 3, 1984.

7. Ibid., and *The Marriage of East and West*, pp. 62–63.

8. "Transcending Dualism," p. 75; cf. also *Taittiriya Upaniṣad* 3.1.

9. *The Marriage of East and West*, p. 63.

10. Ibid., pp. 63–64.

11. "Transcending Dualism," p. 76.

12. Ibid.

13. Ibid.

14. St. Elmo Nauman, Jr., *Dictionary of Asian Philosophies* (Secaucus. N.J.: Citadel Press, 1978), p. 7.

15. *The Principal Upaniṣads*, ed. and trans. S. Radhakrishnan (London: George Allen & Unwin, 1953), p. 74.

16. *Aitareya Upaniṣad*, 5.3.

17. *Māṇḍākya Upaniṣad*, 2.

18. *Chandogya Upaniṣad*, 6.8.7.

19. *The Principal Upaniṣads*, p. 458.

20. *Bṛihadāranyaka Upaniṣad*, 1.4.10.

21. Ibid. This statement is similar to that of Eckhart when he says: "I am God, but God is not me." When I realize myself in God, I am God, or a realized potentiality, but God is not me, because He is infinite, and I am only one of His infinite possibilities. This seems to be Eckhart's meaning, and I think the fourth *mahāvākya* is suggesting the same kind of insight.

22. "Transcending Dualism," p. 81.

23. *Katha Upaniṣad*, 2. 12; *The Marriage of East and West*, p. 69.

24. Ibid., p. 76.

25. Ibid., p. 77.

26. Ibid.

27. Ibid., p. 70.

28. Cf. *Chandogya Upaniṣad*, 8.12.3.

29. Raimundo Panikkar, *The Vedic Experience (Mantramanjari): An*

Anthology of the Vedas for Modern Man and Contemporary Celebration (Pondicherry: All India Books, 1983), p. 729.

30. "Transcending Dualism," p. 76.
31. *The Marriage of East and West,* pp. 70–71.
32. Ibid., p. 71. Cf. also *Katha Upaniṣad,* 3.10–11.
33. *The Cosmic Revelation,* p. 75.
34. *The Vedic Experience,* p. 380.
35. *Śvetāśvatara Upaniṣad,* 3.7.
36. Ibid., 3.8 (Panikkar translation).
37. *The Marriage of East and West,* p. 74.
38. *Katha Upaniṣad,* 3.13; *The Marriage of East and West,* pp. 74–75.
39. Ibid., p. 75.
40. Ibid.
41. Ibid., p. 80.
42. Ibid.
43. Ibid., 81.
44. Ibid.
45. Ibid., cf. also *Śvetāśvatara Upaniṣad,* 3.9.11.
46. "Transcending Dualism," p. 75.
47. *The Marriage of East and West,* p. 55.
48. Ibid.
49. The emphasis on the feminine is a contribution of the Tantric tradition, which profoundly influenced later Hinduism.
50. *The Cosmic Revelation,* p. 75.
51. Ibid., p. 76.
52. "Transcending Dualism," p. 83.
53. Ibid. Bede also found Ramanuja's conception defective; see *Vedanta and Christian Faith,* p. 25. His criticism of Śankara is actually a rejection of an interpretation of Śankara's doctrine, not of a more subtle understanding of it, which he would accept.
54. *The Marriage of East and West,* p. 89.
55. Ibid.
56. "Advaita and Trinity," lecture given to the Camaldolese Community, Big Sur, Calif., Sept. 3, 1983, cassette, side 1.

57. Ibid.

58. *The Vedic Experience*, p. 867.

59. *Bṛihadāraṇyaka Upaniṣad*, 3.7.23; *The Marriage of East and West*, p. 90.

60. Ibid., p. 91.

61. Ibid.

62. "The Experience of God in Eastern Religions," *Cistercian Studies* 9, nos. 2 & 3 (1974). This was a paper to be read at the Second Asian Monastic Congress, Bangalore, October 1973, but Abhishiktananda never gave it. It was one of the last things he wrote.

63. Bede claimed this. He said it exists in virtually every tradition: in Buddhism; in Islam; in Christianity in such figures as Eckhart, Ruysbroeck, and John of the Cross; and, he believed, also in Kabbalah, the Jewish mystical tradition. See "Transcending Dualism," pp. 84–85.

64. "Indian Christian Spirituality," a lecture given to the monks of St. Joseph's Abbey, Spencer, Mass., July 4, 1979, cassette, side 1.

65. *The Vedic Experience*, p. 891.

66. *Saccidānanda*, pp. 167–68.

67. Ibid., pp. 168–69.

68. Ibid., p. 169.

69. Ibid.

70. Ibid.

71. *The Vedic Experience*, p. 869.

72. *Saccidānanda*, p. 170.

73. Ibid., pp. 170–71.

74. Ibid., p. 171.

75. Ibid.

76. *The Marriage of East and West*, p. 27.

77. "Declaration of the Relationship of the Church to Non-Christian Religions," in *The Documents of Vatican II*, ed. Walter M. Abbott, S.J. (New York: America Press, 1966), p. 663.

78. "Advaita and Trinity" (Big Sur), cassette, side 1.

79. John 10:30.

80. John 17:21.

81. John 17:22–23.

82. "The Personal God: The Trinity," lecture given to the Ojai Community, September 17, 1983, cassette, side 1. This process is carried further when Bede suggests the possibility of interpreting Jesus' experience in the light of the Hindu intuition of the Godhead, of Saccidānanda. See *The Marriage of East and West*, p. 190, and the section "Saccidānanda and Trinity" in the present chapter.

83. Abhishiktananda, *Hindu-Christian Meeting Point: Within the Cave of the Heart* (Delhi: ISPCK, 1969), p. 77.

84. Ibid., p. 84.

85. Consider some of the recent examples of Trinitarian theology; they all seem to lack this dynamic, experiential element. They appear to be products of dry scholarship, but this does not detract from the writer's faith. Some of these include Karl Raher, *The Trinity*, trans. Joseph Donceel (New York: Herder & Herder, 1970); Raimundo Panikkar, *The Trinity and the Religious Experience of Man* (New York: Orbis, 1973); William Hill, *The Three-Personed God: The Trinity as a Mystery of Salvation* (Washington, D.C.: Catholic University, 1982); Robert Jenson, *The Triune Identity* (Philadelphia: Fortress, 1982); Bertrand de Margerie, *The Christian Trinity in History*, trans. Edmund Fortman (Still River, Mass.: St. Bede's Publications, 1982), and James Mackey, *The Christian Experience of God as Trinity* (London: SCM, 1983). These are just some examples. Of these, Panikkar's is the most global, de Margerie's the most historical (a fine work), Rahner's and Hill's the most reformist, and Mackey's the most superficial.

86. "Advaita and Trinity," cassette, side 1.

87. "The Personal God: The Trinity," cassette, side 1.

88. Ibid.

89. Ibid.

90. Ibid.

91. Ibid.

92. "Hindu and Christian Experience of God," a talk given at the Esalen Institute, Big Sur, Calif., September 1983, tape 1, side 2.

93. "Indian Christian Spirituality: Vedanta," a lecture given to the community of St. Joseph's Abbey, Spencer, Mass., July 4, 1979, cassette, side 1.

94. *Saccidānanda*, p. 135. Also see pp. 133–47.

95. "The Personal God: The Trinity" (Ojai), cassette, side 2. The Godhead is both with and without attributes, that is, is both totally transcendent and personal. The personal dimension allows for attributes. This distinction is like that of Saguna Brahman, Brahman with attributes, and Nirguna Brahman, Brahman without attributes.

96. "Advaita and Trinity," side 1.

97. Ibid.

98. "Hindu and Christian Experience of God" (Esalen), tape 1, side 2.

99. *The Marriage of East and West*, p. 99.

100. Ibid., p. 97.

101. "Hindu and Christian Experience of God" (Esalen), tape 1, side 2.

102. "The Personal God and the Absolute Godhead," from *Riches from the East*, tape 3, side 2.

103. *The Marriage of East and West*, p. 99.

104. *Return to the Center*, p. 113.

105. *The Blade*, p. 75.

106. Ibid., p. 78.

107. Ibid., p. 121.

108. *Christ in India*, p. 63.

109. *In Quest of the Absolute*, p. 73.

110. Ibid.

111. Abhishiktananda with Jules Monchanin, *Ermites du Saccidānanda: Sagesse hindoue mystique chretienne* (Paris: Casterman, 1956).

112. *Saccidānanda*, appendix 3, p. 228.

113. Ibid., p. 178.

114. Ibid.

115. *The Marriage of East and West*, pp. 189–90.

116. Ibid., p. 190.
117. See *Saccidānanda*, appendix 1, pp. 203–14.
118. *The Marriage of East and West*, p. 202.
119. Ibid.

CHAPTER 6. CHRISTOLOGY, TANTRISM, SANNYĀSA, AND THE FUTURE OF THE CHURCH

1. *The Marriage of East and West*, p. 189.
2. Ibid., pp. 178–79.
3. Ibid., p. 175. This is of course the traditional Catholic position, but it is also one verified by biblical scholarship.
4. Ibid., p. 177.
5. *Return to the Center*, pp. 82–85.
6. Ibid., p. 82.
7. Ibid., p. 83.
8. Ibid., pp. 84–85.
9. *The Cosmic Revelation*, p. 125.
10. Ibid., p. 128.
11. Ibid., p. 118.
12. *Return to the Center*, p. 84.
13. *The Cosmic Revelation*, p. 118. Of course Gandhi, among others, tried to modify this doctrine, and his reform was somewhat influenced by the Gospel.
14. Ibid., p. 122.
15. Ibid.
16. Ibid., pp. 122–23.
17. *Vedanta and Christian Faith*, p. 54.
18. Ibid., p. 55.
19. Ibid.
20. Ibid.
21. "In What Sense Is Jesus Called God?," unpublished article, p. 12.
22. Ibid.
23. Ibid.
24. Ibid., p. 13.

25. Ibid.

26. Letter to the author, dated January 31, 1984, from Shantivanam.

27. Ibid.

28. Ibid.

29. "Self-Realization: Return to the Center," a talk given to the Ojai Community, Ojai, Calif., September 1983, cassette, side 1.

30. Ibid.

31. "Christianity, Science and Eastern Mysticism," a talk given at the Esalen Institute, Big Sur, Calif., September 1983, cassette, side 2.

32. Ibid., side 1.

33. *The Marriage of East and West*, pp. 187–88.

34. Ibid., p. 188.

35. "Christianity, Science and Eastern Mysticism," cassette, side 2.

36. We must also bear in mind the great contemporary interest in Christ's psychological understanding, and the issue of how much Christ really knew about Himself and His mission.

37. *Christ in India*, p. 111.

38. *Yoga and the Jesus Prayer Tradition: An Experiment in Faith* (Ramsey, N.J.: Paulist Press, 1984).

39. "This World and the Absolute Reality," in *Riches from the East* (NCR Credence Cassettes), tape 4, side 1.

40. *Yoga and the Jesus Prayer Tradition*, pp. 21–22.

41. "This World and the Absolute Reality," side 1.

42. Ibid.

43. Ibid., sides 1–2.

44. "Yoga and Asceticism," a lecture given to the Camaldolese Community, Big Sur, Calif., September 1983, cassette, side 1.

45. *Yoga and the Jesus Prayer Tradition*, p. 30.

46. Ibid., p. 31.

47. Ibid.

48. Ibid.

49. Ibid., pp. 31–32.

50. Ibid., p. 32.

51. Ibid.

52. Ibid., pp. 32–33.

53. Ibid., p. 35.

54. Ibid., p. 39.

55. Ibid., p. 40.

56. Ibid., p. 44.

57. Ibid.

58. Ibid., p. 46.

59. Ibid., p. 26.

60. Ibid.

61. Ibid., p. 153.

62. The discussion occurred in a letter from Bede Griffiths to the author dated March 8, 1984.

63. *Indian Christian Sannyāsa and Swami Abhishiktananda* (Bangalore: Theological Publications in India, 1981).

64. "Reorientation of Monastic Life in an Asian Context," in *A New Charter for Monasticism,* ed. John Moffitt (Notre Dame: University of Notre Dame Press, 1970), p. 109. This volume contains the Proceedings of the Meeting of the Monastic Superiors, Bangkok, December 9–15, 1968, the meeting at which Thomas Merton died.

65. Panikkar, *The Vedic Experience,* p. 890.

66. *Indian Christian Sannyāsa,* p. 11.

67. Ibid. The three other *āśramas* are *brahmacarya,* the first, which is that of a student; *grihastha,* the second *āśrama,* the stage of householder; and the third *āśrama, vānaprastha,* the stage of being a hermit or forest dweller.

68. Ibid., pp. 13–14.

69. Abhishiktananda, *The Further Shore* (Delhi: ISPCK, 1975), p. 5.

70. Ibid.

71. *The Bhagavad Gita: A Christian Reading* (Warwick, N.Y.: Amity House, 1987), p. 105.

72. *The Marriage of East and West,* pp. 42–43.

73. Ibid., p. 43.

74. *The Further Shore,* p. 13.

75. Ibid., p. 18.

76. Ibid., p. 22.
77. Francis Acharya, "Reorientation of Monastic Life," p. 120.
78. *The Bhagavad Gita: A Christian Reading,* chap. 5, verse 29, commentary.
79. *Chandogya Upaniṣad* 8, 12, 3.
80. *The Further Shore,* p. 11.
81. Ibid.
82. Ibid., p. 19.
83. Bede Griffiths, "Indian Christian Spirituality: *Sannyāsa,*" lecture given at St. Joseph's Abbey, Spencer, Mass., July 3,1979, cassette, side 1.
84. *The Further Shore,* p. 13.
85. *Guru and Disciple,* trans. Heather Sandeman (London: SPCK, 1974), p. 29.
86. *The Further Shore,* p. 13.
87. *The Marriage of East and West,* p. 43.
88. *The Further Shore,* p. 14.
89. Panikkar, *The Vedic Experience,* p. 437.
90. *Hindu-Christian Meeting Point: Within the Cave of the Heart* (Delhi: ISPCK, 1969), p. 91.
91. Raimundo Panikkar, *Blessed Simplicity: The Monk as Universal Archetype* (New York: Seabury Press, 1982), p. 99. This volume represents the proceedings of the East/West Monastic Symposium of November 1980, Holyoke, Mass.
92. Bede Griffiths, *Saccidananda Ashram: Shantivanam* (Tannirpalli: Saccidānanda Ashram, n.d.), p. 3. This is essentially a pamphlet. These facts have been mentioned in chapter 2.
93. Ibid.
94. *Christ in India,* p. 63.
95. Abbe J. Monchanin, S.A.M., and Dom Henri Le Saux, O.S.B., *A Benedictine Ashram* (Douglas, Isle of Man: Times Press, 1964), p. 49.
96. Ibid., pp. 77–78.
97. *Indian Christian Sannyāsa,* p. 55.
98. *Christ in India,* p. 42.

99. Ibid., p. 47.

100. *The Cosmic Revelation*, p. 16.

101. *Indian Christian Sannyāsa*, p. 215.

102. "Eastern Religious Experience," *Monastic Studies* 9 (Autumn 1982): 160.

103. For a good study of Christian ashrams and their relationship to Hindu ashrams and spiritual leaders, see Sister Vandana's work, *Gurus, Ashrams and Christians* (Madras: Christian Literature Society, 1980), and for a concentrated examination of the Christian ashram itself, see also her "The Ashram Movement and the Development of Contemplative Life," *Vidyajoti* 47 (May 1983).

104. *The Marriage of East and West*, p. 192; cf. *The Shepherd of Hermas*, 2:24.

105. Ibid.

106. Ibid., p. 193.

107. Ibid., pp. 193–94.

108. Ibid., p. 194.

109. Ibid., p. 195.

110. Ibid.

111. Ibid., p. 197.

112. Ibid., pp. 202–3.

113. "Indian Christian Spirituality: *Sannyāsa*," (Spencer), cassette, side 2.

114. "Indian Monasticism Today and Contemplation," cassette, side 1.

115. *Christ in India*, pp. 164–65.

CHAPTER 7. CONCLUSION AND IMPLICATIONS

1. From a letter to the author dated August 22, 1985, from Shantivanam.

2. Ibid.

3. It is not so much that personalism is absent from Hindu thought as that it has not effected an evolution in the understanding of Saccidānanda. The philosophies of Ramanuja, Madhva, and the Bhakti tradition represent the personalist insight, but it is not pres-

ent in the more ancient Hindu notion of the Godhead as represented in Saccidānanda.

4. Of course we need desperately a hermeneutics of ultimate mystical
consciousness that can adequately interpret the experience of each
tradition in relation to an overarching absolute standpoint that can
be said to represent the highest or deepest level of consciousness.
Panikkar has made a good start in this direction.

5. Of course this is from a Christian perspective.

EPILOGUE

1. *A Human Search: The Life of Father Bede Griffiths,* produced by John
Swindells, More than Illusion Films, Sydney, Australia, 1993.

2. Russill Paul, unpublished circular letter, March 1993.

3. See Wayne Teasdale, "Bede Griffiths as Mystic and Icon of
Reversal," *America* 173, no. 9 (September 30, 1995) for an in-depth
discussion of this insight.

4. Judson B. Trapnell, *Bede Griffiths: A Life in Dialogue* (Albany: State
University of New York Press, 2001), see pp. 114–27.

Glossary

acharya: A spiritual teacher.

Advaita: The doctrine and experience of nonduality or unity.

advaita: Nonduality.

advaitic: Pertaining to the doctrine of advaita.

aham brahmasmiti: One of the four *mahāvākyas,* or great utterances; it means, "I am Brahman." It is a mystical utterance.

ahankara: The ego, or concept of the person as separate.

ananda: Bliss, one of the characteristics of the Godhead.

āśramas: The four stages of life: student *(brahmacarya),* householder *(grihasthā),* forest dweller *(vanaprastha),* and renunciate *(sannyāsi).*

Ātman: The person's innermost principle, the true self, the supreme Self, God immanent in the human self.

atmavidyā: The mystical knowledge of the Ātman.

avatāra(s): A descent of God.

avidyā: Ignorance.

avyakta: The Unmanifest in the cosmic hierarchy.

bhakti: Devotion.

Brahma: The Creator, but can also be used for the Brahman.

brahmacarya: The student stage *(āśrama)* of life.

Brahman: God, the Absolute, the supreme principle, the Godhead.

brahmavidyā: The mystical knowledge of Brahman, of God.

buddhi: The intellect in the cosmic hierarchy; that which is illumined.

cakras (alternatively, *chakras*): The energy centers of the body in Tantric Yoga.

cit: Consciousness, knowledge; one of the characteristics of the Godhead.

circuminsession: The way the Persons of the Trinity indwell or are in one another. It is also called *perichoresis.*

co-esse: The inner being of the Trinity as *koinonia,* communion, a being-with.

darśan: Vision, sight, the presence of God, or a saint, also an image of either.

devas: The cosmic powers, the powers of nature, the angels.

dharma: Religious and social norms and duties.

dhyāna: Meditation.

diksa: Ceremony of initiation into the sannyasic life.

ekam sat: "The one being," the Brahman.

eschaton: The end toward which time moves; the coming of Christ at the end of time.

existential convergence: The relating of two traditions internally through their mystical intuitions. In the case of this book, the relating of Hinduism and Christianity.

gnosis: To know, transcendent knowledge, mystical knowing.

grihasthā: The householder stage (*āśrama*) of life.

guhā: The cave of the heart; it symbolizes interiority.

jīva: The individual ego.

jīvanmukta: One who has achieved liberation and union with the Absolute.

jīvātman: The human spirit.

jñāna: Wisdom, transcendent knowledge.

jñānī: One who has awoken to reality, who has mystical knowledge, a sage.

karma: Action, work, the consequences of acts done in a previous life.

koinonia: Communion of love in the Trinity.

lectio divina: Spiritual reading.

Mahat: The Great Self or cosmic consciousness.

mahāvākyas: The four "great utterances, sayings, or sentences."

manas: The mind or reason.

mantra: Prayer word, or formula.

māyā: The condition or state of the world as being neither being *(sat)* or nonbeing *(asat);* sometimes called illusion.

moksha: Liberation, final liberation and salvation.

nāmajapa: Repetition of God's name(s).

nāmarūpa: The "names and forms" of the Divine Unity.

Nirguna Brahman: Brahman without attributes, the Godhead, which is totally undetermined.

nirvāna: The mystical state of the Void as one of blissful omni-science.

Paramātman: The absolute or supreme Spirit.

perichoresis: The way the Persons of the Trinity are present or indwell in one another; also called *circuminsession.*

philosophia perennis: The perennial philosophy, the primordial metaphysics.

photismos: Illumination.

Puruṣa or Purusha: The cosmic Man or Lord; archetypal man.

Purushottama: The supreme Person.

rishis: The forest dwellers of Indian antiquity.

Saccidānanda: The Godhead as Being *(sat),* knowledge *(cit),* and bliss *(ananda).*

sādhanā: Spiritual exercises.

Saguna Brahman: Brahman or the Godhead with attributes, God.

śakti: The power or energy of God, the divine feminine.

samādhi: Enlightenment or the final awakening; union with Ultimate Reality.

samsara: The wheel of life; ceaseless flux; the cycle of births and deaths.

sannyāsa: Monkhood, the life of total renunciation.

sannyāsi: One who has embraced renunciation to seek God-realization.

sannyasic monasticism: The Christian form of *sannyāsa.*

sapience: A "tasting" knowledge; it is mystical illumination.

sat: The Real, being, real, true.

scientia sacra: Sacred knowledge; it is the perennial philosophy.

spanda: Ground of being, God as a "vibrating energy."

śūnyatā: The Void in Buddhism, or Emptiness.

Tantrism: A system of yoga that incorporates the energies of the body in the ascent to the Divine.

tapas: Austerity or asceticism.

tat tvam asi: One of the four *mahāvākyas;* it means "That art that."

theophany: Manifesting or revealing God; it is said of all creation and being; the *theophanic* is this capacity of reality to reveal.

vanaprastha: Period of retirement to the forest; the third stage (*āśrama*) of life.

Select Bibliography

Primary Sources

The following list of primary sources by Bede Griffiths does not include audio cassettes, which are cited in the notes. See also "Works in English by Bede Griffiths," page 236, for a more complete and updated list of publications.

Griffiths, Bede. *The Bhagavad Gita: A Christian Reading.* Warwick, N.Y.: Amity House, 1987.

———. *Christ in India: Essays towards a Hindu-Christian Dialogue.* New York: Scribner's, 1966.

———. *The Cosmic Revelation: The Hindu Way to God.* Springfield, Ill.: Templegate, 1983.

———. *The Golden String: An Autobiography.* Rev. ed. Springfield, Ill.: Templegate, 1980.

———. *The Marriage of East and West: A Sequel to "The Golden String."* Springfield, Ill.: Templegate, 1982.

———. *Return to the Center.* Springfield, Ill.: Templegate, 1982.

———. *Vedanta and Christian Faith.* Los Angeles: Dawn Horse, 1973.

——. "Eastern Religious Experience." *Monastic Studies* 9 (1979).

——. "Experience of God and External World in Asian Religions." *Cistercian Studies* 9, nos. 2 and 3 (1974).

——. "Indian Christian Contemplation." *The Clergy Monthly* 35, no. 7 (1971).

——. "In What Sense Is Jesus Called God?" Unpublished article.

——. "The Monastic Order and the Ashram." *The American Benedictine Review* 30, no. 2 (1979).

——. "The Mystical Dimension in Theology." *Indian Theological Studies* 14, no. 3 (1977).

——. "Mystical Theology in the Indian Tradition." *Jeevadhara* 9 (1979).

——. "Reflections and Prospects." In *Emerging Consciousness for a New Humankind*. Edited by Michael von Bruck. Bangalore: Asian Trading Corp., 1985.

——. "Saint Benedict: His Significance for India Today." *Vidyajyoti* 44 (1980).

——. "Transcending Dualism: An Eastern Approach to the Semitic Religions." *Cistercian Studies* 20, no. 2 (1985).

Other Works

Abhishiktananda. "The Experience of God in Eastern Religions." *Cistercian Studies* 9, nos. 2 and 3 (1974).

——. *The Further Shore*. Delhi: ISPCK, 1975.

——. *Guru and Disciple*. Translated by Heather Sandeman. London: SPCK, 1974.

——. *Hindu-Christian Meeting Point: Within the Cave of the Heart*. Delhi: ISPCK, 1976.

——. *Saccidānanda: A Christian Approach to Advaitic Experience*. Delhi: ISPCK, 1974.

Animananda, B. *The Blade: The Life and Work of Brahmabandhab Upadhyay*. Calcutta: Roy & Roy, 1945.

Cronin, Vincent. *A Pearl to India: The Life of Roberto de Nobili*. New

York: Dutton, 1959.

Goel, Sita Ram, ed. *Catholic Ashrams: Adopting and Adapting Hindu Dharma*. New Delhi: Voice of India Publications, 1988, 1994.

Leclercq, Jean. *The Love of Learning and the Desire for God: A Study of Monastic Culture*. Translated by Catherine Misrahi. New York: Fordham University Press, 1961.

Matus, Thomas. *Yoga and the Jesus Prayer Tradition: An Experiment in Faith*. Ramsey, N.J.: Paulist Press, 1984.

Monchanin, Jules. *Ecrits Spirituels*. Introduction by Edouard Duperray. Paris: Centurion, 1965.

———. "In Quest of the Absolute." *Indian Culture and the Fullness of Christ*. Madras: The Catholic Centre, 1957.

Nasr, Seyyed Hossein. *Knowledge and the Sacred*. New York: Crossroads, 1981.

Panikkar, Raimundo. *The Vedic Experience: An Anthology of the Vedas for Modern Man and Contemporary Celebration*. Pondicherry: All India Books, 1983.

Upadhyay, Brahmabandhab. "Christianity in India" (1). *The Tablet* 69 (London, January 3, 1903).

Vattakuzhy, Emmanuel. *Indian Christian Sannyāsa and Swami Abhishiktananda*. Bangalore: Theological Publications in India, 1981.

Weber, J. G., ed. *In Quest of the Absolute: The Life and Works of Jules Monchanin*. Kalamazoo: Cistercian Publications, 1977.

Works in English by Bede Griffiths

BOOKS

1954, 1980. *The Golden String: An Autobiography*. Rev. ed. Springfield, Ill.: Templegate.

1964. *India and the Eucharist*, edited by Bede Griffiths. Ernakulam, India: Lumen Institute.

1966, 1984. *Christ in India: Essays towards a Hindu-Christian*

Dialogue. Springfield, Ill.: Templegate. Published in England as *Christian Ashram*.

1973, 1991. *Vedanta and Christian Faith*. Clearlake, Calif.: Dawn Horse Press.

1976. *Return to the Center*. Springfield, Ill.: Templegate.

1982. *The Marriage of East and West: A Sequel to "The Golden String."* Springfield, Ill.: Templegate Publishers.

1983. *The Cosmic Revelation: The Hindu Way to God*. Springfield, Ill.: Templegate.

1987. *River of Compassion: A Christian Commentary on the Bhagavad Gita*. Warwick, N.Y.: Amity House. Reissue: New York: Continuum, 1995.

1990. *A New Vision of Reality: Western Science, Eastern Mysticism and Christian Faith*. Edited by Felicity Edwards. Springfield, Ill.: Templegate.

1992. *The New Creation in Christ: Christian Meditation and Community*. Edited by Robert Kiely and Laurence Freeman. Springfield, Ill.: Templegate.

1995. *Pathways to the Supreme: The Personal Notebook of Bede Griffiths*. Edited by Roland Ropers. London: HarperCollins.

1997. *The Mystery Beyond: On Retreat with Bede Griffiths*. London: Medio Media.

2001. *The One Light: Bede Griffiths's Principal Writings*. Edited by Bruno Barnhart. Springfield, Ill.: Templegate.

ARTICLES AND LECTURES

1935. "The Poetry of St. Benedict." *Pax* 25 (August): 101–106.

1937. "St. Justin's Apology." *Pax* 27 (March): 289–93.

1938. "A Pilgrimage to Jerusalem." *Pax* 28: 7–11, 30–35.

1938. "The Mysticism of Mary Webb." *Pax* 28 (October): 161–65.

1938. "Integration." *Pax* 28 (November): 185–89.

1939. "The Church of England and Reunion." *Pax* 29: 36–46.

1939. "The Poetry of the Bible." *Pax* 29: 124–28.

1939. "Christian Democracy." *Pax* 29: 255–62.

1940. "The Platonic Tradition and the Liturgy." *Eastern Churches Quarterly* 4, no. 1 (January): 5–8.

1946. "The New Creation." *Pax* 36: 15–23.

1946. "Pluscarden: September 8th." *Pax*: 111–13.

1948. "The City of God." *Catholic Mind* 46 (1948): 410–13.

1949. "The Mystery of Sex and Marriage." *Pax* 39: 77–80.

1950. "Catholicism To-day." *Pax*: 11–16.

1951. "The Divine Office as a Method of Prayer." *The Life of the Spirit* 6, nos. 62–63 (August–September): 77–85.

1952. "Liturgical Formation in the Spiritual Life." *The Life of the Spirit* 6, no. 69 (March): 361–68.

1952. "The Mystery of the Scriptures." *The Life of the Spirit* 7, nos. 74–75 (August–September): 67–75.

1952. "The Divine Office as a Method of Prayer." *Theology Digest* 1 (1952): 42–44.

1952. "Swiss Monasteries." *Pax* 42: 166–72.

1953. "A Catholic Commentary on Holy Scripture." *Pax* 43: 76–78.

1953. "Christian Existentialism." *Pax* 43: 141–45.

1953. "The Cloud on the Tabernacle." *The Life of the Spirit* 7, no. 83 (May): 478–86.

1953. "The Enigma of Simone Weil." *Blackfriars* 34, no. 398 (May): 232–36.

1953. "Monks and the World." *Blackfriars* 34, no. 404 (November): 496–501.

1954. "On Reading Novels." *Pax* 44: 124–28.

1954. "The Transcendent Unity of Religions." Review of *The Transcendent Unity of Religions* by M. Frithjof Schuon. *Downside Review* 72, no. 229 (July): 264–75.

1954. "Our Lady and the Church in the Scriptures." *Liturgy* 23: 87–92.

1955. "The Meaning of the Monastic Life." *Pax* 45: 132–37.

1955. "For a Hindu Catholicism." *The Tablet* 205, no. 6000 (May 21): 494–95.

1956. "The Taena Community." *Pax* 46: 112–15.

1957. "Vinoba Bhave." *Blackfriars* 38: 66–71.

1957. "Symbolism and Cult." In *Indian Culture and the Fullness of Christ*. Madras: Madras Cultural Academy, 52–61.

1958. "Experiment in Monastic Life." *The Commonweal* 68, no. 26 (September 26): 634–36.

1958. "Kurisumala Ashram." *Pax* 48: 128–33.

1959. "John Cassian." *The Month* 21, no. 6 (June): 346–62. Reprinted in *Spirituality through the Centuries: Ascetics and Mystics of the Western Church*, edited by James Walsh. New York: P. J. Kennedy, 1964, 25–41.

1959. "The People of India." *The Commonweal* 71, no. 4 (October 23): 95–98. Reprinted in *Christ in India*, 115–25.

1959. "Role of the Layman." *The Commonweal* 71, no. 5 (October 30): 119–21.

1959. "Eastern and Western Traditions in the Liturgy." *The Clergy Monthly Supplement* 4 (1959): 223–28.

1960. "An Ecumenical Movement in Kerala." *The Star of the East* 21: 10–12.

1960. "An Ecumenical Movement in Kerala." *Arunodayam* 16: 18–19.

1960. "The Church Universal: Efforts toward Reunion." *The Commonweal* 71, no. 14 (January 1): 387–90. Reprinted with slight changes in *Christ in India*, 235–42.

1960. "The Language of a Mission." *Blackfriars* 41, no. 478 (January–February): 20–27.

1960. "Liturgy and the Missions." *Asia* 12: 148–54.

1960. "The Kerala Story." *The Commonweal* 71, no. 26 (March 25): 692–94.

1960. "A Letter from India." *The Life of the Spirit* 15, no. 172 (October): 178–82.

1960. "The Seed and the Soil." *Good Work* 23: 59–64.

1960. "The New Creation." *Sponsa Regis* 31: 223–30.

1960. "The Ideal of an Indian Catholicism." *The Examiner* 111: 425.

1960. "Indian Catholicism and Hindu Culture." *The Examiner* 111 (1960): 633–34.

1961. "Three Roads to Unity." *The Commonweal* 73, no. 26 (March 24): 651–53.

1961. "Non-violence and Nuclear War." *Blackfriars* 42, no. 490 (April): 157–62. Reprinted in *Christ in India*, 143–50.

1961. "Non-violence and Nuclear War." *Bhoodan* 6: 6–7.

1961. "Non-violence and Nuclear War." *Pax Bulletin* 86: 1–3.

1961. "The Ecumenical Approach to Non-Christian Religions." *The Catholic World* 193, no. 1157 (August): 304–10.

1961. "The Contemplative Life in India." *Pax* 51: 105–11.

1961. "The Goal of Evolution." *Sponsa Regis* 32: 125–34.

1961. "Paradise Lost." *Sponsa Regis* 32: 210–19.

1961. "The Promised Land and Paradise Regained." *Sponsa Regis* 32: 278–88.

1961. "The World Council and the Syrian Church." *The Star of the East* 22: 55–59.

1961. "The Church Universal." *The Star of the East* 22: 16–22.

1961. "The Ecumenical Movement in the Roman Catholic Church." *Arunodayam* 17: 17–18.

1961. "The Birth of Christ in India." *The Examiner* 112: 783.

1961, 1964. "A Christian Approach to Hindu Mysticism." In *Occasional Papers*, Series II. New York: World Council of Churches (Office of the Division of World Mission and Evangelization).

1962. "God and the Life of the World: A Christian View." *Religion and Society* 9 (September): 50–58.

1962. "Gandhi's India, Mao's China." *The Commonweal* 77, no. 12 (December 14): 309–12.

1962. "The Challenge of India." *Good Work* 25: 82–87.

1963. "Placing Indian Religion." *Blackfriars* 44, no. 521 (November): 477–81.

1964. "Liturgy and Culture." *The Tablet* 218, no. 6471 (May 30): 602–603.

1964. "Background to Bombay." *The Month* 32, no. 6 (December): 313–18.

1964. "The Vatican Council." *The Star of the East* 25: 9–12.

1964. "Dialogue with Hinduism." *The Clergy Monthly* Supplement 7: 144–49.

1964. "The Ecumenical Approach to the Missions." *India* 15: 64–67.

1964. Review of *Why Christianity of All Religions?* by Hendrik Kraemer. *Journal of Ecumenical Studies* 1 (Spring): 327–30.

1965. "India after the Pope." *The Commonweal* 81, no. 20 (February 12): 641–42.

1965. "The Dialogue with Hinduism." *New Blackfriars* 46, no. 538 (April): 404–10. Reprinted in *The Catholic Mind* 63 (1965): 36–42.

1965. "The Church and Non-Christian Religions." *The Tablet* 219, no. 6552 (December 18): 1409–10.

1965. "The Ecumenical Approach to Hinduism." *The Examiner* 116: 505.

1966. "Light on C. S. Lewis." *The Month* 35, no. 6 (June): 337–41.

1966. "Monastic Life in India Today." *Monastic Studies* 4 (Advent): 117–35.

1966. "The Declaration on the Church and Non-Christian Religions." *The Examiner* 117 (December 17): 117, 122.

1966. "The Dialogue with Hindus." *The Examiner* 117 (December 17): 821–22.

1967. "The Christian Doctrine of Grace and Freewill." *The Mountain Path* (April): 124–28.

1968. "Further Towards a Hindu-Christian Dialogue," by Bede Griffiths and A. K. Saran. *The Clergy Monthly* 32, no. 5 (May): 213–20. A response by A. K. Saran to *Christ in India*, followed by Griffiths's reply.

1968. Reply to review by S. Svenkatesananda of *Christian Ashram*. *Journal of Ecumenical Studies* 5 (Winter): 148–51. Review precedes Griffiths's response, 144–48.

1969. Review of *L'Esprit de l'homme: Etude sur l'anthropologie religieuse d'Origene* by Jacques Dupuis. *Indian Journal of Theology* 18 (October–December): 264–65.

1969. "St. Benedict in the Modern World." *Pax* 59: 77–79.

1970. "The Ecumenical Situation in Kerala Today." In *The Malabar Church: Symposium in Honour of Rev. Placid Podipara, C.M.I.*, edited by J. Vellian. Rome: Pont. Institutum Orientalium Studiorum, 307–10.

1971. "Indian Christian Contemplation." *The Clergy Monthly* 7, no. 35 (August): 277–81.

1972. "Eastern Religious Experience." *Monastic Studies* 9 (Autumn): 153–60.

1972. "Salvation in India." *The Tablet* 226, nos. 6912–13 (December 23, 30): 1221.

1972. Review of *Concordant Discord*, by R. C. Zaehner. *Journal of Ecumenical Studies* 9: 644–66.

1973. "Erroneous Beliefs and Unauthorised Rites." *The Tablet* 227, no. 6928 (April 14): 356, 521.

1973. "The Sources of Indian Spirituality." In *Indian Spirituality in Action*, edited by R. B. Pinto. Bangalore: Asian Trading Corp., 63–67.

1974. "The One Mystery." *The Tablet* 228, no. 6975 (March 9): 223.

1974. "Experience of God and External World in Asian Religions." *Cistercian Studies* 9: 273–76.

1974. "Kurisumala and Indian Monasticism." In *Kurisumala: A Symposium on Ashram Life*, edited by M. F. Acharya. Bangalore: Asian Trading Corp., 37–42.

1974. "Swami Parama Arubi Ananda." In *Kurisumala: A Symposium on Ashram Life*, edited by M. F. Acharya. Bangalore: Asian Trading Corp., 65–67.

1974. "Shantivanam: A New Beginning." In *Kurisumala: A Symposium on Ashram Life*, edited by M. F. Acharya. Bangalore: Asian Trading Corp., 75–76.

1974. "The Future of Christian Monasticism in India." In *Kurisumala: A Symposium on Ashram Life,* edited by M. F. Acharya. Bangalore: Asian Trading Corp., 110–13.

1975. "The Universal Truth." *The Tablet* 229, no. 7022 (February 1): 101–2, 347.

1975. "Revelation and Experience." *The Tablet* 229, no. 7023 (February 8): 136–37, 1167–68.

1975. "Indianisation." *The Examiner* 126, no. 19 (May 10): 233.

1975. "Shantivanam." *The Spirit and Life* 70: 24–27.

1976. "Dialogue with Hinduism." *Impact* 11 (May): 152–57.

1976. "Village Religion in India." *The Tablet* 230, no. 7098 (July 24): 726–27.

1976. "The Indian Spiritual Tradition and the Church in India." *Outlook* 15, no. 4 (Winter): 98–104

1976. "A Christian Ashram." *Vaidikamitram* 9: 14–20.

1976. "Shantivanam: An Explanation." *Vaidikamitram* 9: 44–48.

1976. "An Open Letter to Father Anastasius Gomes." *Vaidikamitram* 9: 67–70.

1977. "The Vedic Revelation." *The Tablet* 231, no. 7165 (November 5): 1053–54.

1977. "The Mystical Dimension in Theology." *Indian Theological Studies* 14: 229–46.

1978. "Christian Monastic Life in India." *Journal of Dharma* 3, no. 2 (April–June): 123–35. Reprint, with revisions, of "Monastic Life in India Today." *Monastic Studies* 4 (Advent 1966): 117–35.

1978. "Intercommunion Now." *The Tablet* 232, no. 7200 (July 8): 660–61.

1978. "In Filial Disobedience." *New Blackfriars* 59, no. 701 (October): 463–66.

1978. "The Advaitic Experience and the Personal God in the Upanishads and the Bhagavad Gita." *Indian Theological Studies* 15: 71–86.

1978. "Moksha in Christianity." In *Interfaith Dialogue in Tiruchirapalli,* edited by X. Irudayaraj and L. Sundaram.

Madras: Siga, 15–18.

1979. "The Monastic Order and the Ashram." *American Benedictine Review* 30, no. 2 (June): 134–45.

1979. "The Search for God." *The Tablet* 233, no. 7251 (June 30): 620–21.

1979. "Mystical Theology in the Indian Tradition." *Jeevadhara* 9, no. 53 (September–October): 262–77.

1979. "The Birth in a Cave." *The Tablet* 233, nos. 7276–77 (December 22, 29): 1252.

1979. "The Adventure of Faith." In *C. S. Lewis at the Breakfast Table, and Other Reminiscences*, edited by James T. Como. New York: Macmillan, 11–24.

1980. "The Benedictines in India." *The Examiner* 131, no. 12 (March 22): 178–79.

1980. "Death into Life." *The Tablet* 234, nos. 7291–92 (April 5, 12): 336–38.

1980. "The Two Theologies." *The Tablet* 234, no. 7299 (May 31): 520–21, 677.

1980. "Saint Benedict: His Significance for India Today." *Vidyajyoti* 44, no. 9 (October): 432–36.

1980. "Dialogue between Faiths." *The Tablet* 234, no. 7324 (November 22): 1145–46.

1980. "Quest for Truth and Authentic Living." *Akasavani* 45: 13–14.

1980. Foreword to *The Child and the Serpent: Reflections on Popular Indian Symbols* by Jyoti Sahi. London: Routledge and Kegan Paul.

1980. "Towards an Indian Christian Spirituality." In *Prayer and Contemplation*. Studies in Christian and Hindu Spirituality, vol. 1. Bangalore: Asirvanam Benedictine Monastery, 383–88.

1981. "Death and Resurrection." *The Tablet* 235, nos. 7345–46 (April 18, 25): 386–87.

1981. "The Benedictines in India." *Indian Theological Studies* 18: 346–53.

1982. "The Church of the Future." *The Tablet* 236, nos. 7396–97 (April 10, 17): 364–66.

1982. "The Mystical Tradition in Indian Theology." *Monastic Studies* 13 (Autumn): 159–73. Same article as printed in *Jeevadhara*, September 1979.

1982. "Indigenisation of Religious Life in India from a Benedictine Point of View." *Word and Worship* 15: 149–53.

1983. "Science Today and the New Creation." *The American Theosophist* 71: 412–17. A slightly revised version of Griffiths's talk at the February 1982 conference in Bombay titled "East and West: Ancient Wisdom and Modern Science," printed in *Ancient Wisdom and Modern Science,* edited by Stanislav Grof. Albany: State University of New York Press, 1984.

1983. "The Trinity and the Hologram." Unpublished talk concluding a conference entitled "Religion in the Light of the New Scientific View," Shantivanam, 1983.

1984. "Science Today and the New Creation." In *Ancient Wisdom and Modern Science,* edited by Stanislav Grof. Albany: State University of New York Press, 50–58.

1984. "Inner Disarmament and the Spiritual Warrior." Contemplative Review 17: 17–21.

1984. "The Ashram and Monastic Life." *Monastic Studies* 15 (Advent): 117–23.

1984. "The Ashram and Monastic Life." *Christo* 22: 217–22. Same article as in *Monastic Studies* (1984).

1984. Preface to *Yoga and the Jesus Prayer Tradition: An Experiment in Faith* by Thomas Matus. Ramsey, N.J.: Paulist Press.

1984. "Christian Ashrams." *Word and Worship* 17: 150–52. Institute for Theological Studies, 1983–84 (*Tantur Year Book*).

1984. "A New Vision of Reality: Western Science and Eastern Mysticism." In *G. R. Bhaktal Memorial Lecture.* Bangalore: Indian Institute of World Culture, 1–16.

1985. "Emerging Consciousness for a New Humankind." *The Examiner* 136 (February 9): 125, 128.

1985. "The Church of Rome and Reunion." *New Blackfriars* 66, no. 783 (September): 389–92.

1985. "Emerging Consciousness and the Mystical Traditions of Asia." In *Emerging Consciousness for a New Humankind: Asian Interreligious Concern*, edited by Michael von Bruck. Bangalore: Asian Trading Corp., 48–64.

1985. "Reflections and Prospects." In *Emerging Consciousness for a New Humankind: Asian Interreligious Concern*, edited by Michael von Bruck. Bangalore: Asian Trading Corp., 122–25. With slight revision, this is the same summary of a January 1985 conference in Madras published in *The Examiner* (February 1985).

1985. "Avatara and Incarnation." *The Examiner* 136: 161, 233, 403. Three responses by Griffiths to letters reacting to his article of this title in *The Examiner* (1984).

1985. "Transcending Dualism: An Eastern Approach to the Semitic Religions." Edited by Wayne Teasdale. *Cistercian Studies* 20, no. 2: 73–87. Reprinted in Griffiths, *Vedanta and Christian Faith* (1991 ed.), 73–93, an edited version of talk printed in the *Tantur Year Book* (1983–1984) cited above.

1985. "Love and Community in the Ultimate State." In *Freedom, Love, Community: Festschrift in Honor of Metropolitan Paulos Mar Gregarios,* edited by K. M. George. Madras: Christian Literature Society, 1–6.

1986. "Dialogue and Inculturation." *The Examiner* 137, no. 33 (August 16): 777–78.

1986. "A Meditation on the Mystery of the Trinity." *Monastic Studies* 17 (Christmas): 69–79.

1986. "Transformation in Christ in the Mystical Theology of Gregory of Nyssa." *The American Theosophist* 74: 156–60.

1988. "A Symbolic Theology." *New Blackfriars* 69, no. 817 (June): 289–94.

1988. "The Meaning and Purpose of an Ashram." In *Saccidananda Ashram: A Garland of Letters.* Tiruchirapalli: Saccidananda

Ashram, 4–9.

1989. "The Significance of India for Camaldolese Monasticism." *American Benedictine Review* 40, no. 2 (June).

1989. "Christianity in the Light of the East." The Hibbert Lecture, 1989. London: The Hibbert Trust.

1989. "A Benedictine Ashram." In *Saccidananda Ashram: A Garland of Letters*, 3–5. Tiruchirapalli: Saccidananda Ashram.

1990. "Vatican Letter Disguises Wisdom of Eastern Religions." *National Catholic Reporter* 26, no. 29 (May 11): 12.

1990. "The M-word." *The Tablet* 244, no. 7830 (August 11): 1002.

1990. "Monk's Response to the Document on Christian Prayer from the Congregation for the Doctrine of the Faith." *N.A.B.E.W.D. Bulletin* 11 (Trappist, Ky.: Abbey of Gethsemani).

1990. Foreword to *Christ as Common Ground: A Study of Christianity and Hinduism* by Katherine Healy. Pittsburgh: Duquesne University Press.

1991. "Religious Truth and the Relationship between Religions." In *Inter-faith Dialogue and World Community*, edited by G. S. S. Sreenivasa Rao. Madras: Christian Literature Society, 3–10. Lecture originally given in January 1986.

1991. "Swamy Amaldas" and "Renewal of Monastic Life." In *Saccidananda Ashram: A Garland of Letters*. Tiruchirapalli: Saccidananda Ashram, 1–2 and 3–6.

1991. "The Silence and Solitude of the Heart: Communion with God." Edited by Roland Ropers. Unpublished talk at Shantivanam.

1992. "In Jesus' Name." *The Tablet* 246, nos. 7915–16 (April 18, 25): 498–99.

1992. "For Those without Sin." *National Catholic Reporter* 28, no. 36 (August 14): 20.

1992. "The Human Condition." *Monos* 4, no. 8 (September): 1–4.

1992. Afterword to *Sheer Joy: Conversations with Thomas Aquinas on Creation Spirituality* by Matthew Fox. San Francisco: HarperCollins.

1992. "A Center of Contemplative Living." Unpublished description of a lay contemplative community of oblates of Shantivanam.

1993. "The New Consciousness." Acceptance speech for the John Harriott Memorial Award. *The Tablet* 247, no. 7954 (January 16): 70.

INTERVIEWS

"The Silent Guide." Interview by Marvin Barrett. *Parabola* 11, no. 1 (February 1986): 36–47. Reprinted in *Gathering Sparks: Interviews from* Parabola *Magazine*, edited by Marvin Barrett. New York: Parabola Books, 2001.

"Interview with a Spiritual Master: The Trinity." Interview by Wayne Teasdale, Shantivanam, India, December 1986. *Living Prayer* 21, no. 3 (May–June 1988): 24–31.

Books and Dissertations on Bede Griffiths

Book reviews are not included.

Anandam, Lourdu. *The Western Lover of the East: A Theological Inquiry into Bede Griffiths's Contribution to Christology*. Kodaikanal, India: Salette Publications, 1998. Originally a Ph.D. dissertation for Albert-Ludwigs Universität, Freiburg, Germany.

Bruteau, Beatrice, ed. *The Other Half of My Soul: Bede Griffiths and the Hindu-Christian Dialogue*. Wheaton, Ill.: Quest Books, 1996. Expanded edition of *As We Are One: Essays and Poems in Honor of Bede Griffiths*, edited by Beatrice Bruteau. Pfafftown, N.C.: Philosophers' Exchange, 1991.

Conlan, Douglas. "Journey to the Cave of the Heart: Spiritual Direction and the Unfolding of the Self in Mid-Life." M.A. thesis, Fordham University, 1996. Forthcoming from the University of South Australia Press.

Consiglio, Cyprian. "The Space in the Heart of the Lotus: Spirit as an Anthropological Element Based on the Writings of Bede

Griffiths." M.A. thesis, St. John's Seminary, Camarillo, Calif., 1997.

Devaraj, Soosai Adaikalam. "The Uniqueness of Jesus Christ in the Current Indian Theological Discussion: An Analytico-critical Study of the Contributions Made by M. M. Thomas, Stanley Samartha, Bede Griffiths, and Raimundo Panikkar." Ph.D. dissertation, Pontificia Universitas Urbaniana, 1993.

Du Boulay, Shirley. *Beyond the Darkness: A Biography of Bede Griffiths*. New York: Doubleday, 1998.

———. "Bede Griffiths and the One Universal Reality." In *Contemporary Spiritualities: Social and Religious Contexts*, edited by Clive Erricker and Jane Erricker. New York: Continuum, 2001, 32–47.

Fernandes, Albano. "The Hindu Mystical Experience according to R. C. Zaehner and Bede Griffiths: A Philosophical Study." Ph.D. dissertation, Gregorian Pontifical University, 1993.

Flanagan, Finbarr. *Bede Griffiths Quo Vadis*. Dynamedia, 1991.

Forster, Dion. "Aspects of the Cosmic Christ in the Spirituality of Bede Griffiths." M.A. thesis, Rhodes University, Grahamstown, South Africa.

The Golden String, Bulletin of the Bede Griffiths Trust, vols. 1– , Spring 1994–present).

Kaiser, Patricia A. "Spirituality and Interreligious Dialogue in the Life and Writings of Father Bede Griffiths." M.A. thesis, University of Denver, 1995.

Kalliath, Antony. "Inward Transcendence: A Study on the Encounter of Western Consciousness with Indian Interiority Based on the Works of Fr. Bede Griffiths." Master's thesis, Dharmaram Pontifical Institute, 1986.

Kuvaranu, John Martin, O.S.B. Cam. "The Primacy of Seeking God: St. Romuald and the Indian Christian Ashram Ideal of Bede Griffiths." Licentiate degree thesis, Gregorian University, Rome, 1996–1997.

———. "Christian Approaches to Truth." *Horizons* 25, no. 2 (Fall

1998): 217–37.

Maloney, Stephen R. "Tongues of Flame: A Study of Five Modern Spiritual Autobiographies" (G. Stein, T. Merton, B. Griffiths, C. S. Lewis, and J. Muir). Ph.D. dissertation, University of Rochester, N.Y., 1971.

Moffitt, John. *Papers of John Moffitt*, 1967 and 1971–1982. Archives of University of Virginia. Includes letters from Griffiths.

Pandikattu, Kuruvila. *Religious Dialogue as Hermeneutics: Bede Griffiths' Advaitic Approach to Religions*. Washington, D.C.: Council for Research in Values and Philosophy, 2001.

Rajan, Jesu. *Bede Griffiths and Sannyasa*. Bangalore: Asian Trading Corp., 1989. Originally a Ph.D. dissertation submitted to the Pontifical University of St. Thomas Aquinas, Rome, 1988.

———. *Bede's Journey to the Beyond*. Bangalore: Asian Trading Corp., 1997.

Saccidanandaya Namah: A Commemorative Volume, 1950–2000. Shantivanam: Saccidananda Ashram, 2002.

Savio, Samuel. "The Principle of Relatedness in the Ecological Ethic of Bede Griffiths." Ph.D. dissertation, Catholic University of America, Washington, D.C., 2000.

Schulein, Sunelei. "The Life and Work of Dom Bede Griffiths." M.A. thesis, California State University, Long Beach, 1981.

Spink, Kathryn. *A Sense of the Sacred: A Biography of Bede Griffiths*. Maryknoll, N.Y.: Orbis Books, 1989.

———. *Towards a Christian Vedanta: The Encounter of Hinduism and Christianity According to Bede Griffiths*. Bangalore: Asian Trading Corp., 1987. Originally a Ph.D. dissertation submitted to Fordham University, Bronx, N.Y., 1986.

Swami Bede Dayananda: Testimonies and Tributes. India: Shantivanam Publications, 1994.

Trapnell, Judson B. "Bede Griffiths's Theory of Religious Symbol and Practice of Dialogue: Towards Interreligious Understanding." Ph.D. dissertation, Catholic University of America, Washington, D.C., 1993.

————. "Bede Griffiths, Mystical Knowing and the Unity of Religions." *Philosophy and Theology* 7, no. 4 (Summer 1993): 355–79. Reprinted in revised form as "Multireligious Experience and the Study of Mysticism" in *The Other Half of My Soul: Bede Griffiths and the Hindu-Christian Dialogue*, edited by Beatrice Bruteau. Wheaton, Ill.: Quest Books, 1996, 198–222.

————. *Bede Griffiths: A Life in Dialogue.* Albany: State University of New York Press, 2001.

Index

Printed in the USA
CPSIA information can be obtained
at www.ICGtesting.com
JSHW022217140824
68134JS00018B/1098